INDONESIAN REVIVAL
Why Two Million Came To Christ

INDONESIAN REVIVAL
Why Two Million Came To Christ

by Avery T. Willis, Jr.

William Carey Library

533 HERMOSA STREET • SOUTH PASADENA, CALIF. 91030

Library of Congress Cataloging in Publication Data

Willis, Avery T
    Indonesian revival.

    Bibliography: p.
    1. Church growth--Java. 2. Sociology, Christian--
Java. I. Title.
BR1235.W54   275.98'2   77-12811
ISBN 0-87808-428-2

Second Printing 1978

In accord with some of the most recent thinking in the academic press, the William Carey Library is pleased to present this scholarly book which has been prepared from an author-edited camera-ready manuscript.

Published by the William Carey Library
533 Hermosa Street
South Pasadena, Calif. 91030

PRINTED IN THE UNITED STATES OF AMERICA

Dedicated to

SHIRLEY

who epitomizes the role of helpmeet

Contents

PART V: RETROSPECT AND PROSPECT

Figures

Tables

Foreword

Indonesian Revival: Why Two Million Came to Christ by Dr. Willis
is a remarkably perceptive account of an extraordinary instance of
great church growth. More than two million Javanese were baptized in the six years from 1965 to 1971, and growth is continuing.

Willis' book is the first adequate report of the event and is
both deeply spiritual and competently scientific. He maintains
that God has gathered these multitudes to Himself and has used a
glove - the religious, political, cultural and sociological
milieu in which Javanese live.

This eminently readable volume should be studied by Christians
in all six continents. It is both a fascinating description of
a huge and unexpected surge in church growth and a first class
analysis of what makes churches anywhere grow. Willis computer-
ized answers from more than 500 representative first-hand
witnesses of and participants in the massive turning to Christ.
He handles the data well. He tells us what really happened.
One reads with growing understanding of the complex processes by
which men come to Christian faith and of God's guiding hand
behind the machinery.

Writing ten years after the great ingathering began, Willis
makes good use of many sources. He tells us of what many others
have thought and written. He proves conclusively why some of

these were right and others were wrong. The Christian movement
is fortunate in having this considered assessment of the
Indonesian miracle. All future writings on the Great Turning
will have to consult this book.

August 4, 1977   Donald McGavran
                                  School of World Mission
                                  Fuller Theological Seminary
                                  Pasadena, California

Preface

God is doing something unique in Indonesia that has worldwide
implications. Many of the events I have experienced in Indonesia
can be explained only if one believes that they were shaped by
God's hand. But God wears gloves. His hand is often hidden
though his actions are evident in the events that affect us--
politics, culture, society, and of course, religion.

I believe my purpose in life is to be near God, to see where
he is moving, and to follow him. This book is my witness to his
acts--what he has done, is doing, and wants to do in Indonesia.
In it you will see how God penetrates a culture with the gospel.

What has been billed as "the Indonesian revival" is in reality
a Christward movement that has been gaining momentum since 1931.
For decades God wove the threads of revolution, independence, and
the building of a nation together with his redemptive acts to
create a receptivity to the gospel. This receptivity reached its
height with more than two million baptisms in six short years
(1965-1971). The possibility of another surge in the continuing
stream of new believers is immanent if the churches of Indonesia
regain their vision and seize the opportunity.

I hope this book will lead us to rediscover God's ways of working so that we can cooperate with him to help bring about another
harvest. Let us look beyond transitory events to eternal
principles God uses to bring nations to himself. Although the
events in Indonesia are unique, they have counterparts in other

countries. These counterparts are restrictive, as well as conducive, to the spread of Christianity.

Indonesia is not a monolith but a mosaic, as rich with
diversity as many whole continents. One must look at each part
to discover the best methodology for approaching its peculiar
blend of culture, society, politics, and religion. The Javanese
are a classic case study of a distinct people within a nation
made up of more than 250 ethnic groups.

What God is in the process of doing among the Javanese, he
wants to do among the peoples of the world. Hopefully this book
will give you some clues as to God's moving in your locale and
help you design a methodology that can be used of the Holy
Spirit to make Christ known.

The content of this book was originally a dissertation presented to the faculty of the School of Theology, Southwestern
Baptist Theological Seminary, Fort Worth, Texas, in partial
fulfillment of the requirements for the Doctor of Theology
degree. They have graciously given permission for wider distribution of the findings.

I am particularly indebted to Dr. Cal Guy, Bottoms Professor
of Missions at Southwestern Baptist Theological Seminary, under
whom I studied missions, for his pertinent suggestions and
counsel during the research and the writing of the original
material.

I am grateful to the Foreign Mission Board of the Southern
Baptist Convention for their cooperation in freeing me from many
furlough deputation duties in 1973-1974, so I would have time to
write. I am indebted also to the Indonesian Baptist Mission for
electing me chairman of the committee responsible for the Survey
of Baptist Work which was done in cooperation with the Indonesian
Council of Churches and for making me a member of both the Baptist
Board for Cooperative Work, which evaluated that survey, and the
Evangelism and Church Development Committee, which assisted Dr.
Ebbie C. Smith, Dr. Cal Guy, and Dr. Bryant Hicks in their surveys and evaluations of Baptist work.

Appreciation is likewise expressed to Dr. Frank Cooley,
Department of Study and Research of the Indonesian Council of
Churches, for his suggestions concerning the field research, his
aid in securing permission to conduct the field research in the
five denominations studied, his insights into the Javanese
Churches, and his files which were made available for the study.

I am especially obligated to the students in my missions
classes in 1972 and 1973 at the Indonesian Baptist Theological

Seminary who conducted many of the interviews with converts and provided a treasury of invaluable information on the worldview of the Javanese. Sutoyo Louis Sigar was particularly helpful.

A special debt of gratitude is acknowledged to the elected leaders of the Javanese Churches who cooperated in the research: The Rev. Ardi Suyatno, East Java Christian Church; the Rev. Probowinoto, Javanese Christian Churches; the Rev. Sujoko Paulus, North Central Java Christian Church; the Rev. Joyodiharjo, Java Evangelical Church; and the Rev. Eddy Wiriadinata and the Rev. Ishak Iskandar, Union of Indonesian Baptist Churches.

The directors of the evangelism departments of the following churches were also very helpful: the Rev. Sukrisno, East Java Christian Church; the Rev. Soesilo Darmowigoto, Java Christian Churches, and the late Rev. Mulus Budianto, Union of Indonesian Baptist Churches. The writers of the reports of the self-study surveys of the respective churches conducted in cooperation with the Indonesian Council of Churches provided voluminious raw material on their respective Churches: Mr. Iman Soegiri, Javanese Christian Churches; Mrs. Martati Kumaat, Java Evangelical Church; and the Rev. Eddy Wiriadinata, Union of Indonesian Baptist Churches.

Mr. Roger Hyde, International Business Machines, Fort Worth, Texas, made possible a detailed analysis of 500 interviews, by teaching me to code the material for the data cards and by using a IBM System 3 computer to answer the questions asked. Mr. Ernest Hamilton, Data Processing Department, Southwestern Baptist Theological Seminary, also aided in the preparation of the data cards.

Mr. Cecil White, Assistant Librarian, Southwestern Baptist Theological Seminary, provided inestimable assistance in securing books and dissertations from libraries throughout the United States.

I am also thankful to Mr. Eric Gustafson and First Baptist Church, Cleburne, Texas, for providing a furlough home for our family and an office where I could write undisturbed.

Miss Hilda The, my secretary in Indonesia, indebted me to her by typing the results of the library and field research done in Indonesia.

To my wife Shirley, who devoted much of her furlough to typing several drafts of the original dissertation, in addition to giving helpful suggestions concerning form and content, I can only say, *"Terima kasih"* (thank you, or literally, receive my love).

Although several people have urged the wider distribution of the research in book form, it was Dr. Tetsunao Yamamori, Dean of Northwest Christian College, Eugene, Oregon, who during a visit to Indonesia in 1976 provided the final impetus for putting it in book form. I am grateful for his continuing encouragement and help.

My deepest appreciation goes to my friend and missionary colleague, William N. McElrath, who extensively edited the material and is basically responsible for the present format of the book. The reader will benefit from the rearrangement of the presentation, the deletion of many Indonesian words and phrases, and the rectifying of many inconsistencies in style.

Although these and many others who shall remain unnamed have contributed to my understanding and the writing of this book, any inaccuracies or incorrect judgments are my responsibility.

Avery T. Willis, Jr.

PART I

Religio-Cultural Factors

1

God's Hand in
the Glove

Dramatic reports of revival, miracles, hundreds of thousands of
conversions, and unprecedented church growth in Indonesia since
1965 have attracted the attention of the Christian world. Prob-
ing questions concerning the validity of these events deserve an
answer(1). The reports have been at best, fragmentary, and at
worst, cursory descriptions by tourists(2).

   The only book on the subject by an Indonesian is a highly
imaginative account by an impressionable young man from the
remote island of Timor who overemphasizes the role of miracles
in the Indonesian revival(3). No books on the subject have been
written in the Indonesian language(4).

   Even more important than answering queries about miracles, is
the question of what caused approximately two million people to
embrace Christianity(5). This book seeks to answer that question for Indonesia's largest ethnic group: the Javanese.

   Church growth in Indonesia is not evenly distributed among
ethnic groups or geographical locations. A survey of the
churches in Indonesia reveals four outstanding church growth
areas since 1965: East and Central Java, Karo-Batak land in
North Sumatra, East and West Kalimantan (Borneo), and Timor.
Some church groups in other areas are larger, are growing, and
in some cases are experiencing revival; but those in the four
areas listed above have shown the greatest numerical increase
since 1965(6).

The growth of churches among the Javanese is the most significant of these, for several reasons:

1) Javanese compose approximately half the population of Indonesia. The other half is divided into more than 250 language groups(7).

2) Javanese command the highest posts of leadership in the government and are the most influential group in the political spectrum.

3) Javanese are among the most culturally advanced Indonesians: Java has been civilized longer than England has(8).

4) Members of the Javanese churches comprise the largest group of people ever to become Christians out of a Moslem background(9).

5) Responsiveness of the Javanese to the gospel presents one of the most promising evangelistic opportunities in the world. Fully 98 percent of them are still unevangelized.

THE PURPOSE

This book grew out of my own experience as a missionary in Java since 1964. My family and I have lived in all three provinces of Java, and we have seen and participated in the growth of churches among the Javanese. Out of this experience I became convinced that too simplistic reasons were being given for the unprecedented numbers of people becoming Christians. So I did detailed research to discover the factors involved in the numerical increase of Christians among the Javanese.

I believe that God prepares people and countries for response to the gospel. The glove of circumstances is worn by a purposeful God who desires to save the world. Inscribed on each successive finger of the glove are the words: culture, politics, society, economics, and religion. No one or two of these factors alone should be cited as the motivation for one's becoming a Christian; all of them need to be taken into account and evaluated.

I believe the hand of God moves in all the activities of men to produce a responsiveness to the gospel throughout the world. This book is not just an academic exercise or a theoretical excursion, but the result of a personal search fueled by an insatiable curiosity about the ways of God and men. I have been privileged to live through a bloody, abortive communist coup d'etat that changed the direction of the fifth most populous

nation in the world, to participate in a revival of religion
that resulted in unprecedented opportunities for evangelism in
Indonesia, and to experience a spiritual renewal that influenced dramatic changes in mission methods.

Through research involved in this study, I have observed
firsthand how churches grow in a Javanese context. Therefore,
the *purpose* of this book is to present a study of a specific
ethnic group, the Javanese, in an actual situation where
unprecedented numbers have become Christians; and then to draw
pertinent conclusions from that study.

Of necessity our study must have limitations. The first
limitation is that it involves a single ethnic group, although
similar studies could and should be done among other ethnic
groups. At times the Javanese are compared to other ethnic
groups, but the focus is on the Javanese.

We have focussed on a study of the numerical growth of
Christianity in the Javanese churches. Other aspects of church
growth will be considered in chapters 9 through 12, but only in
summary fashion.

We have chosen to concentrate on the years 1960-1971, because
of turbulent times, traumatic sociological convulsions, and
tempestuous political fluctuations during those eleven years.
The period is bracketed by political upheavals relating to the
end of parliamentary government in 1959, and the second general
election in 1971 which firmly established the Suharto government,
the New Order. In all of Indonesia's history of political
radicalism, social dislocation, and cultural adaptation to
modernization, no other period can compare with this one.

In addition to political demarcations, the period under consideration divides itself conveniently into three distinct
church-growth periods. From 1960 to 1965 the churches had to
withstand the pressure of the communist threat and the backlash
of a growing nationalism that expressed itself in anti-foreign
demonstrations. From 1965 through 1969 the churches experienced
unprecedented growth during instability caused by the attempted
communist coup, the establishment of the New Order, and the threat
from Islamic leaders who tried to curtail evangelistic outreach.
The third era, beginning in 1969 and continuing to the present,
has seen a growing stability in political and economic affairs
but a slowing of church growth.

Graphs of church growth show these fluctuations in all the
churches studied. (See representative Figure 4). By studying
all three periods, we can put into proper perspective the period
of greatest evangelistic response: from 1965 to 1969.

Factors already at work by the end of the period 1960–1971
continue to be essentially the same in 1977. The period of
1971–1977 is but an extension of 1969–1971. Some political and
religious trends have developed along the lines previously set,
but not enough to change the basic equation of church growth in
Indonesia.

Our study includes all five denominations which work primarily
among the Javanese. These denominations are:

East Java Christian Church (*Gereja Kristen Jawi Wetan*, or
GKJW).

Javanese Christian Churches (*Gereja-Gereja Kristen Jawi*, or
GKJ).

North Central Java Christian Church (*Gereja Kristen Jawa
Tengah Utara*, or GKJTU).

Java Evangelical Church (*Gereja Injili di Tanah Jawa*, or
GITJ).

Indonesian Baptist Churches (*Gabungan Gereja-Gereja Baptis
Indonesia*, or GGBI).

The membership of these denominations is entirely Javanese,
with the exception of the Baptist churches, whose membership is
81 percent Javanese. No other denominations working in Java
have a majority of Javanese Christians. (Both Pentecostal and
Catholic churches work among Javanese, but do not have a
majority of Javanese. Therefore, they were not included in this
study of why churches grew among the Javanese.) These denominations are all located in Central and East Java, except for
mission work among Javanese in other areas of Indonesia, and
some non-Javanese Baptist churches. Church membership in other
areas is included in the numerical totals, but is not large
enough to bias our conclusions.

The five denominations under study grew 232 percent from 1960
to 1971. This growth is portrayed in Figure 1.

THE SETTING

Java is the most important of three thousand inhabited
islands that constitute the world's largest archipelago--
Indonesia. Although Java has less than 7 percent of the total
land area of Indonesia(10), 64 percent of its population lives
there(11). The island, 650 miles long and 75 miles wide, has
the densest population in the world for an area of its size--
over 1,200 people per square mile(12).

FIGURE 1

JAVANESE CHURCH MEMBERSHIP
(TOTAL OF FIVE DENOMINATIONS)

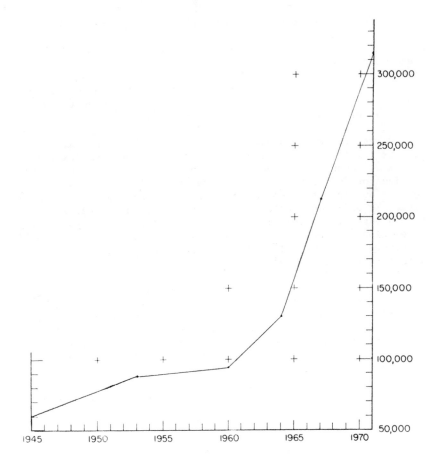

Waves of immigrants from Indo-China began to arrive in Java
around 3000 B.C., and succeeding waves have made it an anthropologist's wonderland. Four major ethnic groups, plus
scattered representatives from others, inhabit Java. Javanese
comprise 70 percent of the population, Sundanese about 15 percent, with the remainder being Madurese, Chinese, and immigrants
from other islands(13). Eighty-five percent of the Javanese
still live in traditional villages, barely subsisting on the wet-
rice cultivation system(14).

The twentieth century burst upon this idyllic land with the
force of nuclear weapons, sending a chain reaction of shock
waves through its traditional infrastructure. Java's soul has
been scarred by ravages of revolution, political confrontations,
international clashes, and bulldozers of modernization(15).
Rapidly shifting patterns of political and social change have
plowed the soil of the Javanese heart, leaving it open to the
gospel as preached in the Javanese churches.

The Western reader needs to realize that in Indonesia,
factors involved in decision-making are much more complex than
in his own country. Indonesians have lived in a revolutionary
boiling pot for 35 years. They have had to live with the fact
that at any moment it could overturn and plunge them into the
fire. In addition, Westerners are much more individualistic
than Javanese. Sociological factors relating to acceptance of
a religion may seem to be of minor importance, but the communal
structure of Javanese life demands that the individual comply
with strict sociological norms.

If we were to ask of Americans the same interview questions
that were asked of Javanese in this study, the Americans would
probably list only factors related directly to religion. The
Javanese, however, included the roles of government and society.
With this in mind, we need to examine the role of politics and
culture, as well as the religious situation, in decisions
related to the choice of a religion.

In the total evaluation of factors listed by Javanese who
were interviewed, spiritual factors accounted for 52.6 percent;
political factors, 25.2 percent; and social factors, 23.2 percent. Thus non-religious factors were almost as important (at
least statistically) as religious ones.

Here again we see "God's Hand in the Glove" . . . God working
in all areas of human activity to bring about responsiveness to
the gospel.

A Christward movement among the Javanese has been gaining
momentum for decades. Events of the turbulent 1960's stimulated

an unusual number of Javanese to opt for Christianity. The possibility of another surge in this movement is immanent, if the churches regain their vision and seize the opportunity.

NOTES

1. E. E. Plowman, "Demythologizing the Indonesian Revival," *Christianity Today*, 2 March 1973, pp. 49-50.

2. Kurt Koch, *The Revival in Indonesia* (Grand Rapids: Kregel Publications, 1970); G. T. Bustin, *Dead, Yet . . . Live* (Westfield, Inc.: Bustin's Books, Publishers, n.d.); Don Crawford, *Miracles in Indonesia* (Wheaton, Ill.: Tyndale House, Publishers, 1972).

3. Mel Tari, *Like a Mighty Wind* (Carol Stream, Ill.: Creation House, 1971).

4. The only in-depth study of the situation by an Indonesian is reported in a booklet in English by the Rev. Mr. Tasdik, who did research in four Javanese communities in 1968. See Tasdik, *Motives for Conversion in East Java Since September 1965* (Singapore: Foundation for Theological Education in Southeast Asia, 1970; hereafter cited as *Motives for Conversion*), and "New Congregations in Indonesia," *South East Asia Journal of Theology* 10 (April 1969): 1-9.

5. No accurate figure is available for the total number of baptisms since the coup. Justus M. van der Kroef, *Indonesia Since Sukarno* (Singapore: Asia Pacific Press, 1971), p. 53 (hereafter cited as *Since Sukarno*), reports 400,000 conversions in the first two years following the coup. The *Status of Christianity Country Profile: Indonesia* (Monrovia, Cal.: Missions Advanced Research and Communication Center, World Vision, 1973), p. 2 (hereafter cited as *Status of Christianity Profile*), estimates the number of baptisms, including Catholics, at two and one-half million. Frank Cooley, in an unpublished article, "The Church in Indonesia, 1945-1973," p. 5 (hereafter cited as "Church in Indonesia"), says that in a study of 22 denominations which have comparative figures, there was an increase of 967,903 members during the years 1964-1971. In a letter to the writer, dated 14 November 1973, Cooley projected the figure for member churches of the *Dewan Gereja Indonesia* (Indonesian Council of Churches) to be 1,160,512, and for non-Council members to be 710,000, making a total of 1,870,512 baptisms during the

period. He estimated Catholic baptisms to be 938,786, for a grand total of 2,809,298. He warns, and rightly so, that these figures are estimates, because statistics of the churches are incomplete and sometimes unreliable. Indonesian church leaders, in private interviews, have said that statistics given by the Ministry of Religion generally are higher than those of the Council. Before 1965 churches sometimes reported fewer baptisms to the Ministry of Religion than were actually recorded, in order to avoid attracting too much attention from their enemies. After 1965 the statistics were sometimes inflated in order to gain a larger voice in political affairs.

6. Cooley, "Church in Indonesia," p. 7, lists the first three. T. B. Simatupang, "The Situation and Challenge of the Christian Mission in Indonesia Today," *South East Asia Journal of Theology* 10 (April 1969): 22 (hereafter cited as "Situation and Challenge"), lists the following areas of church growth since 1965: Central and East Java, Karo-Batak land in North Sumatra, and Timor.

7. Ruth T. McVey, ed., *Indonesia* (New Haven: Human Relations Area Files, 1967), p. 24.

8. Clifford Geertz, *The Religion of Java* (Glencoe, Ill.: Free Press, 1960), p. 7.

9. Kenneth Scott Latourette, Foreword in David Bentley-Taylor, *The Weathercock's Reward* (London: Lutterworth Press, 1967).

10. Justus M. van der Kroef, *Indonesia in the Modern World*, 2 vols. (Bandung: Masa Baru, 1956), 2:92 (hereafter cited as *Modern World*).

11. *Status of Christianity Profile*, p. 24.

12. Benjamin Higgins and Jean Higgins, *Indonesia: The Crisis of the Millstones* (New York: D. van Nostrand Co., 1963), p. 20 (hereafter cited as *Millstones*).

13. *Status of Christianity Profile*, p. 25.

14. Frank L. Cooley, *Indonesia: Church and Society* (New York: Friendship Press, 1968), p. 125 (hereafter cited as *Church and Society*).

15. Jeanne S. Mintz, *Mohammed, Marx, and Marhaen: The Roots of Indonesian Socialism* (New York: Frederick A. Praeger, 1965), p. 218 (hereafter cited as *Mohammed, Marx, and Marhaen*), aptly characterizes twentieth-century Java: "The

foundations of Indonesian society, progressively undermined
since the turn of the century, were shattered in the years
of war and revolution.   Indonesian village and urban life
remain unsettled.   New patterns of society are emerging but
they are shallow and uneven; they fluctuate erratically, and
have not begun to take solid shape."

2

What is God Doing
in Indonesia?

A ruthless communist coup d'etat attempt on September 30, 1965 plunged Indonesia into a bloodbath of recrimination that brought death to approximately half a million people(1). These traumatic events sent a tremor throughout the nation that left millions scrambling for a new foothold in life. For approximately two million of them, Christianity offered the best alternative.

The attempted coup with its aftermath was undoubtedly the *occasion* of what is commonly known as "the Indonesian revival." But the key question is, "What was the *cause*?"

Common sense answers as to causes and motivations often focus on obvious current events, while scholarly assessments just as often explain all such events in terms of their roots in antiquity. While there are no easy or indisputable answers, we have tried to chart a course between the extremes of these two approaches by combining historical investigation with field research.

Five hundred representative firsthand witnesses were interviewed. (See the Appendix for details.) Results of these interviews were analyzed on a computer and provided the framework for our answer to the crucial question: "Why did so many Indonesians become Christians during the mid-1960's?" Figure 2 shows factors that were listed first by the interviewees.

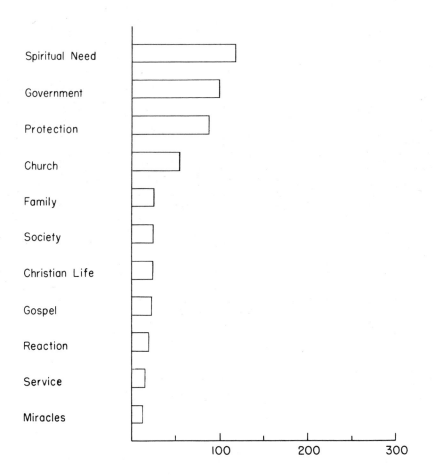

FIGURE 2

FACTORS INFLUENCING CONVERSIONS IN INDONESIA:
MOTIVATIONS MENTIONED FIRST

Spiritual Need

Government

Protection

Church

Family

Society

Christian Life

Gospel

Reaction

Service

Miracles

100   200   300

Although the sickle of political turbulence reaped a harvest of Indonesians for Christianity, the seeds of that harvest had been planted and nurtured in the soil of religio-cultural developments of preceding centuries. Variegated religious backgrounds had intertwined with the cultural life of the Javanese people, producing longings and hopes that were not met by those religions.

Let us examine spiritual needs that arose out of the failures of animism, mysticism, and Islam, and how the churches met those spiritual needs with the message of the gospel.

The failures of other religions to meet spiritual needs of the Javanese plowed furrows where the message of the gospel was planted and now thrives. The gospel itself was not lsited as the first cause in the conversion of most people; nevertheless, it played an important secondary role after other factors had made Javanese realize their need. If spiritual need is considered the negative aspect, and the promise of the gospel the positive aspect of the same condition, then these two spiritual reasons together outrank any other single motivation listed.

"Spiritual need," listed first by a majority of the Javanese interviewed, was most often identified by them with one or more of three characteristic expressions: *inner need, emptiness of soul*, or *not at peace*.

Concerning the Indonesian word (*batin*) usually translated "inner" in the term *inner need*, Clifford Geertz says that it "refers not to a separate seat of encapsulated spirituality detachable from the body but to the emotional life of the individual taken generally--what we call 'the inner life,' or 'the subjective'; it consists of the fuzzy, shifting shapes of private feeling perceived directly in all their phenomenological immediacy"(2).

In relation to *emptiness of soul*, Geertz states: "If one is upset, startled, or severly depressed, one becomes confused and disoriented, and one's soul is then empty and easily entered by the spirits"(3).

The third much-used expression, *not at peace*, is perhaps more easily understood. It signifies the lack of a feeling of safety, security, or calm. All three of these expressions describe a condition growing out of dissatisfaction with answers given by Javanese cultural and religious beliefs.

No man can be understood apart from his culture, and no culture can be understood apart from its religion. The contrariety of Javanese culture and religion is balanced by a

permissive tolerance which absorbs elements closely akin to
original Javanese beliefs, modifies alien elements into a conglomerate syncretism, and minimizes differences in elements
which cannot be modified. The tension and anxiety created by
such diverse elements in a single culture generate desire for
slamet, the state of well-being, free from defect or danger.

The spiritual need which brought many Javanese to Christianity resulted from failures of the three Javanese religious
traditions: *kejawen*, the primitive indigenous religion;
kebatinan, Javanese mysticism based on *kejawen* plus elements
from Hinduism and Buddhism; and Islam.

To learn which positive elements of the gospel appealed to
the Javanese, we asked this interview question: "What attracted
you to Christianity that was not in your former religion?"
Seven elements of the Christian message were listed by the 187
persons who answered the question:

the promise of eternal life	71
peace	40
forgiveness	23
fellowship	21
power	16
love	12
progress	4

The fact that 38 percent listed "the promise of eternal
life" as the most attractive element in the Christian message is
surprising, in light of voluminous literature proclaiming that
the Javanese are not much concerned about heaven and eternal
life. Given the social and cultural situation, one would have
expected "peace" to be ranked first; instead, it was second with
only 21 percent. The certainty of "forgiveness" attracted 12
percent, and "fellowship" among Christians attracted 11 percent.

"Power" (8.5 percent) and "love" (6.5 percent) did not
receive as much emphasis as was expected, in light of the quest
for power in mystical practices and the reaction to lack of love
shown by Moslems during the massacre. Evidently, "progress" was
not seen as an important part of the gospel message, since only
2.0 percent mentioned it.

An indication of the attraction of the gospel can be seen in
the distribution of Bibles and Scripture portions. The
Indonesian Bible Society reports that total distribution of
Bibles and Scripture portions grew from 182,539 in 1960 to
3,182,914 in 1971(4). The demand for Bibles after 1965 was so
great that by October 1967 the number distributed in *one month*
exceeded annual totals for the years 1961, 1962, 1964, or

1965(5). The demand for Bibles is still greater than the supply,
and the Society is concentrating more on printing New Testaments
and Gospel portions than on printing complete Bibles(6). More
than one informant told how a Scripture tract passed from hand to
hand had caused many to become Christians.

A youth in Ubalan, East Java, came into contact with the
Christian village of Sitiarjo. He procured a Bible and read it
to his family. A small group of secret disciples resulted, and
in 1968 they began to declare themselves for Christ. Now there
are approximately six hundred Christians in that village.
Another man near Pare loaned his Bible to a friend, who in turn
loaned it to another. This was repeated four times before it
was returned to the original owner. A group of believers sprang
up there following the events of 1965. One 65-year-old man said
that the message of the Bible was "what I have been longing and
hoping for all my life"(8).

SPIRITUAL NEEDS ANSWERED BY THE CHURCH

The gospel which answered the spiritual needs of Javanese
converts was proclaimed by the Church.

Gallaher, in his study of change, contends that accepters of
change must first be aware of their dissatisfaction with present
conditions. Only after that does change take place, when an
advocate of innovation interferes actively and purposefully with
the culture of this potential accepter. The accepter then
becomes the aggressor and accepts the innovation when his feelings, his wants, or his needs are more satisfied than frustrated
by the innovation. The amount of change depends on the prestige
of the initial donors, sanctions that may be imposed by
authortity, and how the innovation relates to the cultural
system and its values(9).

The Church as the community of love became the advocate of
change, and capitalized on the situation prevailing during the
1960's in Indonesia. It had attained a certain prestige; it
was sanctioned by the government; it had acculturated itself to
Javanese society enough to be acceptable.

Unintended Evangelism

Churches had been involved in a ministry of witness and service among the Javanese long before the cataclysmic events of
1965. They had contact with large numbers of Javanese through
their witness in day-to-day activities, at religious and community observances, in their schools, clinics, hospitals, and
other service ministries.

Ardi Suyatno, moderator of the East Java Christian Church, described their evangelism as "the self-proclamation of the Gospel, unintended evangelism"(10). After interviewing many individuals, Suyatno concluded that

> in practically all cases something happened in the lives of the individuals long ago, which left a lingering idea of Christianity in their minds: some got hold of a Bible or Bible portions, some attended Christian schools, some lived in villages where a Christian nurse was working for years, some had Christian families among their neighbors or friends. And then a new situation arose which constrained them to make a choice and say yes or no to Jesus Christ(11).

At another time Suyatno said,

> A prominent religious leader in Surabaya became a Christian after attending a Christian funeral; the remarks of a pastor at a wedding feast in Dampit led a religious leader to direct his children and grandchildren to attend catechism and follow Jesus. In the Tulungagung district some carpenters led all their clan to the Christian faith after observing the evening family worship of the Christian family whose house they were repairing. In the Dampit region an excommunicated Christian unintentionally became the cause of the developing of a new congregation, which event led to his own repentance(12).

Tasdik, in commenting on such events, said that he and Suyatno had agreed that in these cases, "even though it [Christianity] was a very small lamp, as long as it was still burning, it had a great influence"(13). Yet most of the leaders saw the rapid growth of their churches as an "unexpected event" and not the logical result of their methods of evangelism. Suyatno said that many of the converts were "Nicodemuses," secret disciples, who had not been bold enough to declare themselves before the events of 1965. Nevertheless, the churches' spiritual preparation and flexible response made possible the reception of large numbers of converts.

Spiritual Renewal in the Churches

Frequency and fervency of prayer increased during the difficult period prior to 1965. Leaders of three of the five Javanese denominations said that the acceleration of their denominations' growth rate actually began in 1964, prior to the attempted coup. Two of these credited it primarily to spiritual experiences.

The most dramatic revival occurred among congregations of the
Java Evangelical Church (Mennonite) in north Central Java.   In
1963 the head of the synod, the Rev. Mr. Joyodiharjo, became
dissatisfied with the progress of his traditional, slow-growing
denomination.   Renewed study of the Bible led him to recognize
the role of the Holy Spirit in New Testament church growth.   At
about this time the Rev. Mr. Edwin Stube, an Episcopal pastor
from Montana who was involved in the charismatic movement,
visited Indonesia and led a series of Bible studies at Pati.
Joyodiharjo reported these Bible studies as follows:

> We studied the Bible with other pastors for a week and we
> believed that it could happen now just like it did in
> Acts if the Spirit desired it.   We began to pray and
> strange things happened.   I began to speak in tongues and
> others followed.   We began to say, "It can happen again.
> It can happen again.   It can happen again."   I had to
> question what had happened, but we knew that God was pre-
> sent.   Before, we had been afraid to witness, but after
> this experience we became extraordinarily bold in our
> witness.   We became bold enough to pray for the sick and
> many were healed.   The preachers returned from the confer-
> ence to their churches and the young people were also
> caught up in the revival and began to witness.   There was
> a real breakthrough.   We didn't keep statistics, but much
> was happening.   Many were healed when we prayed for them.
> Some began to wait for me to come to pray for them and I
> said, "That is wrong; you can pray for them, too."   Even
> the new Christians began to pray for others and they were
> healed.
>
> Of course, this caused some problems, especially with the
> traditional preachers and members who said, "We have never
> heard of such a thing as this."   By the power of the Lord
> we were able to settle the problem and channel the power
> without a split in the denomination, except for one con-
> gregation where some Pentecostals had influenced them.
> God used this period of revival to prepare us for what
> was coming.   After 1965 we weren't looking for people,
> they were looking for us.   We cannot accept the credit.
> These people were a gift from God, but the church did
> have the power to witness and pray for the people and to
> accept them when they came(14).

Prior to the coup, Baptists were planning a Sunday school
enlargement campaign for 1966, to be followed by a simultaneous
revival campaign in 1967.   In spite of the fact that church
growth had slowed among Baptists in 1964 (probably due to
communist pressure and claims that Baptists were linked with
"American imperialists"), the decision was made to go on with

the plans, even though there seemed little hope that the political climate would allow them to be consummated.

At a precampaign conference of pastors and laymen in January of 1967, a spiritual revival prepared them for the reaping that was to come in the following two years. This revival was marked by confession of sin, prayer, and a renewed boldness in witnessing. One pastor returned from the conference saying, "Before I went to the conference, I did not expect much to happen this year. Now I believe God has really started a new movement"(15). His church experienced a 90 percent growth in membership and a 221 percent increase in baptisms in the 1967 church year(16).

The heavily increased responsibility of large numbers of responsive people caused Christians of all denominations to pray, read their Bibles, and depend on God more. This finally resulted in spiritual renewal in all five denominations studied.

The Church as the community of love holds particular significance for the Javanese, who seldom think of religion as an individual faith to be practiced in solitude. The communal nature of Indonesian society, and the Moslem emphasis on the oneness of believers, were spectacles through which the Javanese viewed Christianity as the community of love and faith.

Response of the Churches to the Coup

The Indonesian Council of Churches issued a statement only one week after the attempted coup in 1965, registering their reaction to atrocities inflicted by the communists, thanking God for deliverance, expressing prayer support for the leadership of the country, and calling for self-examination and repentance(17). The Rev. Mr. Probowinoto, moderator of the North Central Java Christian Church, wrote an editorial calling for due course of law for those involved in the conspiracy, and for the banning of the Indonesian Communist Party. To the Church he said, "The best preventive action that we can take is to fill the empty hearts of those who do not yet believe in God. . . . The Church must see the 30th of September Movement as a bill that has not yet been paid by the Church." He urged all churches to make sure their members really were Christians, and then to spread the gospel as far and as well as possible(18).

Other churches issued similar statements, calling for due process of law to be used in punishing the accused, rather than private or mob action. Churches refused to take part in the massacre, even though they were accused by Moslems of harboring "enemies of the state." Christians insisted that they must love sinners and must fill empty hearts with true belief in God(19).

Response to Calls for Spiritual Guidance

The seed that had been sown in previous years began to bear fruit. Calls for spiritual help usually came from one or two persons who had received some type of Christian witness; they usually invited a pastor from a nearby city to come to their village to conduct a service. In most cases, a number of people would then express an interest in becoming Christians or at least in studying Christianity. Worship services and catechism classes would be started in many new areas.

Pastors soon found that they could not possibly minister to all those requesting their counsel, so they turned to elders and other church leaders for assistance. Teams were organized by some churches to go into the surrounding countryside, teach the catechism or new members' classes, and conduct services. Groups usually gathered in the homes of interested parties or in nearby meeting places. In many cases local leaders took over the day-by-day ministry in their villages, with only occasional visits by representatives from the mother church.

Calls often came from surrounding villages, requesting these new groups of Christians to come tell about their new faith; thus some new churches were responsible for as many as nine or ten more new village congregations. The mother churches and their pastors sought to control the situation through occasional visits, administration of baptism and the Lord's Supper, and training classes for new leaders.

The head of the synod for the North Central Java Christian Church credits their growth to a new emphasis on evangelism as the responsibility of every member. When he became pastor of the Semarang church in 1965, that congregation was static, traditional, and pastor-centered. Members of the church board who did not agree with the new evangelism policy were replaced. The pastor used I Peter 2:2-5 to teach that every member was a "living stone." He said, "No matter where that stone falls, it is to live, and from it can be built another congregation." This staid city church began six other places of worship within the city of Semarang during the period of rapid growth. The emphasis spread through the entire synod until there were 77 places of worship served by fourteen pastors and numerous lay workers(20).

In Surabaya the East Java Christian Church divided the city into nine areas and established home worship services in each, led by local personnel. By the end of the rapid growth period, 450 groups had been started, 150 of which met weekly(21).

In Salatiga the North Central Java churches formed twelve teams of five volunteers each. After receiving training, these team members were sent out to proclaim the gospel, organize small groups, and teach them(22).

All the denominations began to emphasize training the laity-- through short courses taught in the churches, special short-term institutes, or other types of lay training designed for continuing study.

Response to Prisoners

The churches of Central Java acted quickly to extend pastoral care to prisoners detained for alleged implication in the communist coup. When individual church requests were not granted by the authorities, the Yogyakarta Council of Churches, representing all non-Catholic bodies in the region, requested that pastoral care for prisoners of all religious persuasions be permitted. The military agreed to a religious indoctrination program for the accused communists, which in practice amounted to pastoral care and evangelism.

In 1966 about 20,000 prisoners, of whom about 60 were already church members, received training in 25 places of detention. Each detention center was visited once or twice a week. Christian literature was distributed, indoctrination classes conducted, catechism classes taught, and some physical needs alleviated. The prisoners wrote home of this interest and concern, often thereby attracting their families to Christianity.

Some Christian prisoners felt that the Lord had allowed them to be detained so they could be witnesses in prison. They organized Bible study and prayer groups.

Those whose implication in the coup could not be proved, were eventually released and returned to their homes. One denominational report suggests that about 30 percent of those who attended Christian meetings while in detention made connections with a church after their release. Some were baptized while in prison and became witnesses to their families upon their return home(23). Similar stories could be told by the other denominations, all of whom participated in prison evangelism and pastoral care.

Planting Congregations

The heart of church growth among the Javanese lay even more in multiplying congregations than in adding members to existing ones. The churches expanded their base of operations by starting new congregations to provide spiritual support for the new

converts in their own communities, and by training new leaders
to guide these groups. This led to contacts with other people
who had never been associated with Christianity, and resulted in
even further expansion.

New congregations sprang up as the result of multifarious
contacts with villages.

+ In Nalen, Central Java, prior to the coup, a village leader
felt that he and his people were hypocritical in their profession
of Islam. Having been educated in a Christian school, he sug-
gested that they invite a local pastor to come to their community
and conduct catechism classes. After the coup, communist
villages surrounding Nalen began to ask for instruction. Within
a short time, nine other villages had congregations(24).

+ Near the Christian village of Peniwen, East Java, Javanese
had long been attracted by the calm, harmonious lives of Christians, although social contacts with Christians in Peniwen had
not produced much evangelistic response. Following the
attempted coup, six of the surrounding communities contacted the
Peniwen church and asked that congregations be established.

+ In Tempursari, East Java, only fifteen hundred out of
thirteen thousand people were Christians; but this number more
than doubled in the two years following 1965. One person would
ask for religious instruction and then bring a friend to the
next meeting, until "one would soon become twenty"(25).

+ In Segrumung, Central Java, two people who attended a
Christmas celebration in a nearby village then asked for a congregation to be started in their own village.

+ In Balun, East Java, the head of the village had a vision
the day before three Christians arrived from a nearby town asking if they could hold services. The vision had prepared the
way, and services were begun in his home. Many responded, even
though all other religions had been rejected there previously.

+ In several villages around Kediri, East Java, former
patients of the Baptist hospital requested services to be held
in their communities. An active program of follow-up evangelism
in the villages of patients enabled the hospital to take advantage of these opportunities and begin fifteen congregations
within one year(26).

In the majority of cases, congregations were started as
preaching points or missions of organized churches. Most of the
mother churches were slow in allowing these new congregations to

attain the status of independent congregations within their
denominations.

EVALUATING THE ROLE OF THE CHURCHES

In order to evaluate the over-all impact of each factor in
the wave of conversions during the Indonesian revival of the
1960's, note carefully Figure 3 on the following page. At a
glance it resembles Figure 2, but with a significant difference:
That earlier figure only showed which factors were named *first*
by the Javanese being interviewed; this figure also shows which
factors were named first, but in addition totals which factors
were named *most*. In order to see this graphically the reason
ranked first by interviewees was given an evaluation of 10, the
reason mentioned second an evaluation of 9, the third 8, and so
on. Thus this broader-based chart (Figure 3) shows that "Church"
ranked second to "Government" in over-all evaluation of factors
related to evangelistic response.

In studying Figure 3, note that the category "Church"
includes all activities of the institutional Church, such as
pastoral care, witnessing of members, evangelistic campaigns,
Sunday Schools, catechism classes, and special programs.

Thus we see that "Church" ranked second in the over-all
evaluation. However, it was cited as the primary cause by only
about 10 percent of the interviewees. Although the Church was
a secondary cause of conversions, the churches played a very
important role *after* other factors had aroused interest. It may
be inferred that most of the conversions would not have occurred
through the efforts of the churches alone; neither would they
have occurred if the churches had not become acclimated to the
Javanese context; nor would they have occurred had the churches
not had a receptive attitude toward those in trouble; nor would
they have occurred had there not been a flexible and active
response by the churches in an effort to minister to all those
in need.

For a complete evaluation of the role of the Church,
several other factors that are rated separately need to be
included, because these factors are intimately connected with
the Church. One motivating factor in the conversions was
"Christian life" as portrayed by church members, although it
ranked only eighth in over-all importance. In this context,
"Christian life" means the testimony of daily life in concrete
situations--the silent witness of "light" and "salt." Some
church leaders saw this as the most important single factor in
the growth of their denominations, but our research does not
substantiate their claim except in the case of the East Java
Christian Church. "Christian life" was listed as the

FIGURE 3

CONVERSIONS IN INDONESIA:
FACTORS NAMED FIRST AND FACTORS NAMED MOST

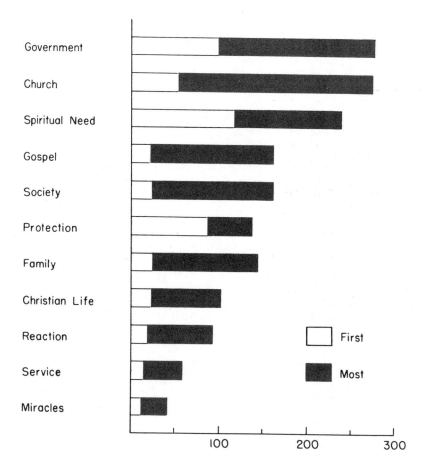

main cause for conversion by only 23 out of the five hundred interviewees.

Another motivating factor related to the Church is "Service," including all social acts of Christian institutions that appealed to the Javanese. Christian schools had planted seeds which lay dormant until the time of crisis. However, we should remember that attendance at Christian schools evidenced a proclivity toward Christianity, or at least a lack of fanatical opposition to the possibility of becoming a Christian. Medical care was also mentioned as a service ministry which aided the spread of the gospel. Yet, as Figure 3 shows, "Service" ranked tenth (3.0 percent) in the list of eleven factors, both as the primary cause for conversion and in the over-all evaluation.

One more spiritual factor should be mentioned: "Miracles." Leaders of only one of the five denominations named miracles as a significant factor in the Indonesian revival, and research bore this out, with only 2.4 percent attributing the primary cause of their conversion to miracles. It is interesting that miracles did not play a larger role, since the animistic background of the Javanese emphasizes the miraculous, and since other sections of Indonesia, such as Timor, reported miracles as one of the primary causes of conversions(27). In one Central Java area, congregations sprang up in nine villages as a result of miraculous manifestations. Yet, in the over-all evaluation of conversions, this factor ranked last in the list.

NOTES

1. Estimates of total deaths range all the way from the "official" count of 87,000 to over 1,000,000. Arnold C. Brackman, *The Communist Collapse in Indonesia* (Singapore: Asia Pacific Press, 1970), p. 114 (hereafter cited as *Communist Collapse*), estimates 150,000. John Hughes, *Indonesian Upheaval* (New York: David McKay Co., 1967), p. 188, says that possibly 250,000 were killed. J. B. Sterba, "Report from the Majority of the World," *New York Times Magazine*, 5 September 1971, p. 23, says 300,000. Gandasari Abdullah Win, "Political Socialization in Indonesia" (Ph.D. dissertation, Claremont Graduate School, 1968), p. 138 (hereafter cited as "Political Socialization"), says 500,000. A team of University of Indonesia graduates, specially commissioned by the army, reported that up to 1,000,000 had been killed, according to van der Kroef, *Since Sukarno*, p. 14. My own personal opinion is that from 400,000 to 500,000

    people lost their lives during the six months following
    September 30, 1965.

2. Geertz, *The Religion of Java*, p. 232.

3. Ibid., p. 97.

4. *Buku Programa Pekan Alkitab 1973* [Program Booklet for Bible
    Week 1973] (Jakarta: Lembaga Alkitab Indonesia, 1973),
    p. 21.

5. "Bible Society Launches Crash Program for Scripture Distri-
    bution," *Bible Society Record* 112 (April 1967):   57.

6. Ibid., p. 21.

7. Private interviews.

8. Private interview.

9. Art Gallaher, *Media and Educational Innovation* (Lincoln:
    University of Nebraska Press, 1965), pp. 17-34.

10. Tasdik, *Motives of Conversion*, p. 51.

11. Simatupang, "Situation and Challenge," p. 23.

12. Tasdik, *Motives of Conversion*, p. 5.

13. Tasdik, interview held at his home, Yogyakarta, 6 June 1973.

14. Joyodiharjo, interview held at the home of the rector of
    Akademi Kristen Wiyata Wacana, Pati, 13 April 1973.

15. "Minutes, Fifteenth Annual Session, Indonesian Baptist
    Mission," (Bandung, 1967), pp. 97-98.   (Mimeographed.)

16. Ibid., p. 99.

17. See "Pernyataan dan Seruan Dewan Gereja-Gereja di Indo-
    nesia" [Declaration and Call of the Indonesian Council of
    Churches], *Warta Gereja* (Salatiga: GKJ Church) 1 (November-
    December 1965):   5-7.

18. Ibid., pp. 3-4.

19. See Gainer Bryan, Jr., "The Pacific: Scene of Miracles
    Today," *Christian Life* 29 (April 1968):   55-56.

20. Interview with Sujoko Paulus.

21. Interview with Sukrisno, Director of Evangelism for GKJW, Surabaya, 16 May 1973.

22. Soesilo Darmowigoto, "P. I. Setjara Massal" [Mass Evangelism], *Warta Gareja* 6 (March 1966): 6-9.

23. Alan Thomson, "The Churches of Java in the Aftermath of the Thirtieth of September Movement," *South East Asia Journal of Theology* 9 (January 1968): 7-9.

24. This example and those that follow come from interviews conducted in these villages, March-June 1973.

25. Private interview with former pastor.

26. "Minutes, Fifteenth Annual Session," p. 80; also see pp. 81-87 for a description of the "Village Worship Program."

27. See Tari, *Like a Mighty Wind*, passim.

3

What God
Hath Wrought

Recent years have seen extraordinary response to the gospel
among the Javanese. But it was not always so. Had it not been
for acculturation of Christianity in the Javanese context long
before revival broke out, the gospel would have been as unpalat-
able to the Javanese as it was during the first two hundred
years of Dutch colonization. Although it had not been obvious,
God had been preparing the soil for over 100 years. By the
1960's, the Javanese churches had fortunately become rooted in
the culture, and therefore Javanese could become Christians without being separated from their race.

Javanese culture had been impervious to the gospel until
after the Java War began in 1825. The events that brought
responsiveness through the initial acculturation process were
very similar to the growth situation during the revival of the
1960's. It is important to see this connection, because it has
somehow escaped many Javanese church leaders. In general, they
have ignored factors that brought about the initial responsiveness among their own people. Only occasional catastrophic
events have caused the Javanese churches to employ the most
effective methods.

Hinduism, Buddhism, and Islam, introduced to Java through
traders and the use of force, were to some extent accepted by
the people of the island. By contrast, Christianity as introduced by the Dutch was rejected by the Javanese.

Nicholson says that the masses of the population in Sumatra and Java accepted the religious preferences of their rulers without question in the case of Buddhism, Hinduism, and Islam; but she raises the question, "Why did these same people not flock to Christianity when the Dutch assumed political control of the area"(1)?

Nicholson's explanation is that the attitude and expectations of the Dutch prevented Javanese from following their leadership. She cites Melink-Roelofsz' comparative assessment: the Protuguese felt the propagation of Christianity was more important than the prosecution of trade, while the Dutch made trade their primary concern and knew better than to endanger it by preaching their doctrines. "The Reformed Church was too dependent on the United Company to act contrary to their stipulations concerning missionary activity in the area"(3). Huyser, in 1878, said that Dutch leaders and missionaries encouraged the Moslem movement by their own ineptness and failure to provide enough missionaries (3).

Nicholson sums it up by saying:

Hence the Dutch attitude of tolerance toward Islam, the delay in sending for missionaries, the belief in predestination, and the emphasis on trade rather than conversion, all led to expectations on the part of the Dutch that differed from the donors of Islam, Portuguese Catholicism, or, as a matter of fact, the earlier Buddhist rulers. The Dutch attitude negated the traditional union of "state" and "church." Thus the situation in Sumatra and Java is [was] set(4).

As a result of the Napoleonic wars, England briefly ruled Java from 1811-1816. During this English interlude, missionaries to the Javanese were allowed to enter for the first time. Several were sent by the Baptist Missionary Society and the London Missionary Society, but the only one to make a lasting impression on the Javanese was Gottlob Brückner, who arrived in 1814(5). Although he labored until 1857, he was not able to reach the Javanese or to start a church; his only lasting contribution was a translation of the New Testament into Javanese and the publication of tracts which helped open Javanese hearts to the Gospel(6). The fact is that these first missionaries were not able to penetrate Javanese culture, although they provided the tools for others to do so(7).

Javanese or Dutch?

The gospel was effectively introduced to the Javanese through laymen and laywomen, particularly Eurasians who had

contact with both cultures. They were followed by Javanese who
presented the gospel in indigenous forms.

Most important of these was Coenraad Laurens Coolen, son of a
Dutch father and a Javanese mother from the Solo nobility. In
1829 he got permission to clear the jungle and establish a
village at Ngoro, East Java. This became the first place of
contact between the gospel and Javanese village life. It provided a laboratory for experimentation in penetrating Javanese
culture with the gospel.

Coolen was well suited for this task, because he was entirely
at home in the language, thoughts, habits, and feelings of the
Javanese. He was particularly well equipped to find points of
contact for spreading the gospel. He held Christian services
that resembled Javanese religious gatherings, sang Javanese
tunes, used the traditional shadow play and its heroes as types
of Christ, alluded to the Javanese messianic expectation of a
Just King (*Ratu Adil*), and put the Apostles' Creed and the Confession of Faith in the form of the Moslem confession.

Coolen was joined at Ngoro by other Javanese who wanted to
clear the jungle and establish a village. Under his leadership
they established a Christian community, even though Coolen would
not baptize them for fear they would think they had become Dutchmen and thus lose contact with their own people(8).

In contrast to Coolen, the "pious of Surabaya" led by J. Emde
sought to make the Javanese into *Kristen-Londo* ("Christian
Hollanders," or Dutch Christians)(9). Emde was a German watch-
maker in Surabaya who had been greatly influenced by Brückner's
friend, Joseph Kam, a missionary to the eastern isles of Indonesia who visited Surabaya in 1814. Emde's wife, who was
Javanese, and their daughter soon professed faith in Christ.
They distributed handwritten copies of the Javanese New Testament
that Brückner was translating and Emde was checking.

One of these fell into the hands of Dasimah, a Moslem priest
of a secondary order(10). Dasimah could not get away from the
statement, "The beginning of the Gospel of Jesus Christ, the Son
of God"(Mark 1:1). His friends at the village of Wiyung discussed this verse without comprehending its meaning. Later one
of them, Sadimah, heard a prayer at a wedding feast in the home
of Kiai Kunti which sounded as if it came from the same source;
Kunti said he had learned the prayer from Coolen. Ten members
of the Wiyung group then walked 25 hours through the jungle to
find Coolen and ask him about the "clear water," their symbol
for religion. They visited him every year for the next five
years, and followed what Coolen taught them(11).

Later, the son of Dasimah talked with Mrs. Emde, who was startled to learn that he knew something of Christianity. This contact led the group from Wiyung to contact Emde(12). Emde, who did not understand the role of culture, demanded that the Javanese cut their hair like Dutchmen, wear trousers instead of the traditional *sarong*, stop carrying the traditional sacred *kris* (dagger), and change their names. Only then could they be baptized. In addition, Emde used the Malay language, the forerunner of modern Indonesian, instead of Javanese. He also demanded that these Javanese converts abandon all practice of their cultural art forms, such as shadow plays and the *gamelan* orchestra(13). The Dutch Protestant church which baptized them did not realize that this implied the rejection of their Javanese culture and made them a laughing stock(14).

These beginnings of Christianity among the Javanese demonstrated a dichotomy in relation to culture that to some extent extends even to the present. Therefore,

two mutually independent groups of Javanese Christians sprang up, an unbaptized group at Ngoro, without organition or sacraments, thoroughly Javanese in character and in some danger of dissolving again into the Muslim world, and another group at Wiyung consisting of baptized persons but in danger of begetting Christians who were only imitation Westerners(15).

An exceptionally perceptive missionary, Jellesma, who came in 1849, was able to combine these two groups. He did so by working closely with Coolen's convert, Paulus Tosari, at Mojowarno, the Christian village that became a model for other Christian villages of East Java(16). "Paulus Tosari . . . combined in his leadership both Coolen's concern for indigenization and Emde's rootedness in the Bible"(17).

The Christians at Ngoro finally accepted baptism, but refused to give up their cultural heritage. In so doing, they firmly rooted the gospel in Javanese village society, and prevented its being isolated from the masses of Javanese. As van Akkeren says, "The gospel reaches the world most in those places where a maximum identification with the world takes place. This is exactly what we find at Ngoro"(18). In Chapter 9 we will show how the East Java Christian Church grew in this rural setting, and used its cultural ties to more than double its membership after 1965.

Pioneers With Old Testament Names

Three other ethnic Javanese denominations also owe their heritage and contact with the culture to pioneers who followed

Coolen's example(19). The example of these Christian pioneers
deserves full attention and interest, because

> in spite of all the questions raised, Christ is penetrat-
> ing into the old Javanese society through the method of
> evangelism used by those pioneers. This society, based on
> a specific socio-cosmic system of thinking and feeling, is
> humanly speaking impenetrable to the message of the
> Gospel(20).

Yet these pioneers so identified themselves with the culture
that they were able to penetrate it with the gospel.

The North Central Java Christian Church (GKJTU) and the Java
Evangelical Church (GITJ) owe a debt to Ibrahim Tunggul Wulung,
a follower of the mystic tradition of Java. He was a hermit on
Mount Kelud in East Java who sought, through meditation, power
to save the world from destruction. A copy of the Ten Commandments written by Coolen fell into his hands and brought him into
contact with Coolen, Jellesma, and Emde. After his baptism in
1857, he traveled throughout Java, convincing his people that
the gospel was the power of God unto salvation. He established
three Christian villages in the area of Jepara, Central Java.
By the time of his death in 1885, he had gathered 1058 followers
who called themselves "*Kristen-Java*" (Javanese Christians), in
contrast to the 49 "*Kristen-Londo*" (Dutch Christians) in nearby
villages established by Mennonite missionary P. Jantz.

The third Javanese pioneer, in addition to Coolen and Tunggul
Wulung, was Sadraeh Suropranoto who played a significant role in
the beginning of the Javanese Christian churches (GKJ). He had had
contact with Jellesma while attending a Moslem school in East Java,
but was not converted until after contact with Tunggul Wulung.
Sadrach was greatly helped by Dutch and Eurasian lay Christians;
he was trained by Anthing, assistant to the Dutch Attorney
General in Batavia (Jakarta).

In speaking of Anthing, Kraemer says:

> He was not blind to the fact that to Orientals religion,
> nation, social habits, etc., constitute an inseparable
> whole, so much so that leaving one's own religion and
> embracing another one purely as a *religion*, regardless
> of nation, social habit, etc. is to them an unthinkable
> absurdity and a denial of their proper identity as
> allotted to them by fate and the course of their lives.

> Not only did Anthing see all this, thus clarifying his
> thought, but--which is far more important--it came to
> be his working hypothesis. Hence he did not send out

his helpers as tools of a Dutch organization, nor as preachers of Christianity (the *agama* of the *Belandas* [Dutch]). They presented themselves as true Javanese, bearing a precious secret (an *ilmu*), yet unknown but which (oh unexpected opportunity!), they were willing to reveal. In this way the people could be approached with the gist of the Gospel, unhampered by the stigma of foreignness, and in its presentation it was attuned to one of the most sensitive strings of the indigenous heart; a craving for the saving mystery which renders man inperishable. To this I am inclined to ascribe, as Anthing did himself, his amazing "success" in those days of fruitless labor and spiritual stagnation"(20).

Sadrach Suropranoto now heard of Mrs. Johannes C. Philips, who had begun to spread the gospel in Purworejo, Central Java. He returned there to help her. Mrs. Philips was a Eurasian married to a Dutchman who had won her to Christ. She began to interpret gospel sermons for the Javanese; many became Christians.

Sadrach worked for Mrs. Philips and used Javanese *kebatinan* (mysticism) as a part of his witness to make contact with the Javanese. He debated *kebatinan* leaders and won many who also brought their followers with them. He followed Ibrahim Tunggul Wulung's and Coolen's examples and built a Christian village at Karangjoso. Twenty people were baptized by the pastor of the Dutch chruch in Purworejo during that first year of 1871, followed by 181 the next year, and 310 the following year.

These Javanese went back to their various villages, began witnessing, and started small groups. By 1886 they had baptized 1596 persons and had 23 groups of Christians who met in homes of local leaders. This movement grew to approximately three thousand Javanese believers by 1889, and nine thousand by the time of Sadrach's death in 1924(21).

Sadrach tried to Christianize the customs of his people. He used the *slametan*, a ceremonial meal with animistic origins, as an opportunity for Christian worship. He added Christian prayers to the ceremony to soften the insults of the Moslems who said that the Christians buried their dead like dogs without a *slametan*. He also added burial prayers in Arabic and Javanese. He composed a chant to keep spirits from molesting people. He gave them Javanese remedies for their illnesses. Infants were baptized with water from a spring with sacred flowers in it. He even kept the tradition of burning incense.

Like Coolen and Ibrahim Tunggul Wulung, Sadrach left himself open to the criticism that he incorporated too many original cultural patterns into Christian worship. On the other hand, he strictly prohibited certain Javanese dances, desecrating the Sabbath, adultery, and marrying a second wife after one became a Christian. He did allow men with more than one wife to become Christians, but not church leaders (23).

Sadrach also faced some of the same problems with Dutch mission groups as the other Javanese Christian pioneers faced. His relationship with the Protestant church of Purworejo began well, but later he came into conflict with the Dutch Reformed missionaries, who did not agree with his independent attitude or his churches' identification with Javanese culture. They tried at first to take over his work, but eventually broke with him and his congregations. After his death most of his members eventually followed the missionaries and formed the Javanese Christian Churches (GKJ)(24).

In each of the above cases, missionaries were not able to penetrate Javanese culture with the gospel, but Eurasians and their Javanese converts were. In each case the missionaries repudiated the practices of these pioneers and were eventually able to win the pioneers' converts over to the mission's position, thereby isolating the Javanese from their own people.

After missionaries took the leadership, a period of isolation threatened to short-circuit contacts with Javanese culture. Fortunately some missionaries such as Jellesma, who worked with Coolen, and Wilhelm, who worked with Sadrach, were able to keep the break with the culture from becoming irreparable. After several decades, these churches overcame many of the obstacles put in their way by mission boards that did not agree with their acculturation of Christianity. By the time Indonesia gained its freedom, all four of these denominations had become truly Javanese.

These churches today use many of the same methods that the Javanese Christian pioneers used to spread the gospel. In general, the shadow play, the *gamelan* orchestra, and in some cases, the *slametan* have become instruments for witness. Javanese ceremonies which take place at each change in the life cycle are used as points of contact to spread the gospel. Although foreign elements are still present, the Javanese churches at least have identified themselves enough with the Javanese people to be known as *"Kristen-Jawa."*

It is this identification with the culture that allowed Javanese who were seeking a religion after 1965 to associate with Christianity. (Indeed, without such acculturation the churches would even have had difficulty surviving the period of nationalism following independence.) The leaders of these

Javanese churches say that after 1965, such large numbers of
people came asking for services to be held in their villages,
that not all the invitations could be accepted. This happened
to the Baptist churches in a lesser degree, because they had not
yet become identified with Javanese culture as had the other
denominations(25).

The power of the gospel to revitalize a culture and to Christianize its forms is remarkable. But it can only do so after it
has once penetrated that culture. No doubt there were many
inadequacies in the ways those pioneer evangelists penetrated
Javanese culture . . . but the fact is, they did penetrate it.

As Coolen remarked to Medhurst after being upbraided for his
methods and his example, "How is it, then, that you and others
have been laboring, with all your good examples to boot, for
these twenty years and have obtained little or no success, while
my poor preaching and indifferent example have been crowned with
such a blessing that hundreds believe?"(26).

It is significant that

> with a few exceptions, . . . Christianity has had a differ-
> ent fate from other incoming religions. It has not become
> assimilated and unrecognizable; on the contrary, from the
> *desa* [village] it has moved into the central groups: the
> students, armed forces, and the lower civil servants(27).

Missionaries in general have feared the syncretistic attitude
of the Javanese. Yet Christianity has not just offered a new
ritual as clothes for old beliefs, but instead a new foundation
for life. It has brought with it the dynamic to change the
hearts of the Javanese, without having to clothe them in
Western forms.

NOTES

1. Clara K. Nicholson, "The Introduction of Islam into Sumatra
    and Java: A Study in Cultural Change" (Ph.D. dissertation,
    Syracuse University, 1966), p. 4 (hereafter cited as "Intro-
    duction of Islam").

2. Ibid.

3. Ibid., p. 42.

4. Ibid., p. 43.

5. See Bentley-Taylor, *The Weathercock's Reward*, pp. 16-28.

6. Ibid., pp. 39 and 82.

7. Ibid., p. 61.

8. See Philip van Akkeren, *Sri and Christ: A Study of the Indigenous Church in East Java* (London: Lutterworth Press, 1970), pp. 63-68, 71-73 (hereafter cited as *Sri and Christ.*

9. Ibid., pp. 72-72, 77.

10. Dasimah was a kind of Moslem priest whose duty it is to arrange services, solemnize marriages, and give religious instruction.

11. Bentley-Taylor, *The Weathercock's Reward*, pp. 57-60.

12. Ibid., p. 61.

13. Ibid., p. 77.

14. Van Akkeren, *Sri and Christ*, pp. 72-73.

15. Bentley-Taylor, *The Weathercock's Reward*, pp. 77-78. This is not to defend Coolen's group because, as Kraemer points out, they left much to be desired (although Kraemer's criticism seems too harsh). See Hendrik Kraemer, *From Missionfield to Independent Church* (London: SCM Press, 1958), pp. 76-77 (hereafter cited as *From Missionfield*).

16. For a full discussion of this conflict and its relation to the culture, see van Akkeren, *Sri and Christ*, pp, 51-91, and Bentley-Taylor, *The Weathercock's Reward*, pp. 56-85.

17. Hans-Ruedi Weber, *Asia and the Ecumenical Movement*, 1895-1961 (London: SCM Press, 1966), p. 171 (hereafter cited as *Ecumenical Movement*).

18. Van Akkeren, *Sri and Christ*, p. 59.

19. Baptists were represented in the introduction of the gospel to the Javanese by Brückner, but since he established no churches, his modern counterparts from America (who arrived in 1951) did not participate in this acculturation. Unfortunately they did not greatly benefit from lessons learned by the Javanese churches and were slow in adapting to the culture.

20. Van Akkeren, *Sri and Christ*, p. 154.

21. Kraemer, *From Missionfield*, p. 99.

22. See I. Sumanto, "Sedjarah Geredja Karangdjoso; Hidup
    Sadrach dan Kegiatan2nja" [The History of the Karangdjoso
    Church: The Life of Sadrach and His Activities], paper
    located in the files of the GKJ in the Department of Study
    and Research, Indonesian Council of Churches, Jakarta, 1971,
    pp. 1-19 (hereafter cited as "Hidup Sadrach"). See also Th.
    Müller-Krüger, *Sedjarah Geredja Di Indonesia* [A History of
    the Church in Indonesia] (Jakarta: Badan Penerbit Kristen,
    1959), p. 177 (hereafter cited as *Sedjarah Geredja*).

23. Sumanto, "Hidup Sadrach," pp. 20-21.

24. Müller-Krüger, *Sedjarah Geredja*, p. 180.

25. For an analysis of how each denomination met the culture,
    see Chapters 8, 9, and 10.

26. Bentley-Taylor, *The Weathercock's Reward*, p. 69.

27. Van Akkeren, *Sri and Christ*, p. 51.

4

Looking for
the Secret to Life

In studying causes for widespread conversions in Indonesia of
the 1960's, thus far we have looked at positive factors that
Christianity brought to the occasion. All too often Christians
stop here, pleased that believers have taken the initiative in
winning the lost. But an objective evaluation of all factors in
the Indonesian revival cannot and must not stop here. As was
stated earlier, the positive influences of Christianity were all
rated in a secondary position by a majority of Javanese interviewees. They ranked *spiritual need* first. It is to this matter
that we must now give our attention.

This spiritual need was produced by the failure of the three
Javanese religious traditions: *kejawen*, the animistic indigenous religion; *kebatinan*, Javanese mysticism; and Islam. An
understanding of these three traditions will reveal the spiritual need which made the Gospel attractive to the Javanese.

ANIMISM: DEVILS, DEMONS, *DUKUNS*

Kejawen, or Javanism, is not officially recognized as a
religion but is still practiced by the majority of Javanese. In
its present form it is a syncretic mixture of animism, Hinduism,
Buddhism, and Islam.

Kejawen is often confused with *kebatinan* (mysticism). Harun
Hadiwijono says that *kejawen* and *kebatinan* are much alike, but
that *kejawen* is the primitive religion which has become the soul
and spirit of the Javanese and is the underlying factor in most

of the religions found in Java. He says, for instance, that
although Hinduism in Central Java appears to be similar to
Hinduism in India, on closer examination one will find many
differences. Moreover, East Java Hinduism differs from Hinduism
in Central Java because it is closer to the original religion of
the Javanese.

The animistic background called *kejawen* is that original
religion. Over the centuries, this primitive religion has
come to the front through Hinduism, Buddhism, or Islam.
Although religions have been added like layers and have
become syncretic, the heart of the belief is still the
primitive religion(1).

Every religion that has been brought to Indonesia has con-
fronted this original religion. By comparative studies we could
possibly arrive at a formulation of *kejawen* in its original
form, but at present its separate identity is obscured by its
assimilation into Hinduism, Buddhism, Islam . . . and, at times,
into Christianity(2). To most Indonesians this part of their
religion is called *adat* (tradition). They have a common saying
that illustrates the indigenous character of *kejawen* in the
minds of the Javanese: "Religion comes in from the sea, but
tradition comes down from the mountains"(3).

The Javanese understanding of religion is pictured in the
Javanese-Malay word for religion, *agama*, which according to
Vlekke is used to "indicate the total of the beliefs, practices,
and customs which shows a concept of religion quite different
from that of Christianity"(4). Soesilo Darmowigoto calls this
"totalized thinking," indicating the Javanese feeling of oneness
with nature and with the life that pervades everything that
surrounds them(5). All manifestations of nature are the result
of the work of supernatural forces, mostly spirits who must be
appeased with offerings.

The two main elements of this primitive Javanese religion
are:

First, a pantheistic belief that everything and every living being has its "soul," its "life-energy," which is the
same for all but may be stronger in one than in another and
more concentrated in one part of the human body than in
another. . . . Second, the belief in the existence of a
personal soul that attends the human being through life.
The soul survives the body and after death is supposed to
remain in the neighborhood of the places where the body
lived. The soul was not withdrawn from the community of
the living but continues to take an interest in communal
life. Consequently, the souls of the deceased may be

angered when their descendants give up the old traditions
or fail to fulfill their duties toward the spirits(6).

Geertz categories the kinds of spirits as frightening spirits,
possessing spirits, familiar spirits, place spirits, and guardian
spirits. But he also warns that there is no consistent, syste-
matic, integrated scheme or doctrine, and that details about
spirits vary from individual to individual(7).

The activities of spirits provide ready-made answers for
inexplicable experiences. It is important to placate them so
that one may achieve *slamet* (the state of well-being, free from
defect or danger). Fear of these spirits produces a receptive
state of mind to the promises of the gospel.

The primary way Javanese people deal with the problem of
spirits is through observance of the *slametan*, a communal feast
symbolizing the domestic and social unity of those participating.
These rituals lie at the heart of Javanese belief, and serve
both a social and religious function. The incense and aroma of
the food at a *slametan* pacify the spirits so that they will not
disturb the living. A *slametan* neutralizes the power of spirits
to make one ill, unhappy, or confused; therefore, its purpose
is preventive rather than redemptive beneficence.

Every important event in a Javanese person's life is marked
by a *slametan*. *Slametans* fall into four main types: (1) those
centering around the crises of life--birth, circumcision,
marriage, death; (2) those associated with the Moslem ceremonial
calendar--the birth of the Prophet, the ending of the Fast, the
Day of Sacrifice, and the like; (3) that concerned with the
social integration of the village, the *bersih desa* (literally:
"the cleansing of the village"--i.e. of evil spirits); and
(4) those intermittent *slametans* held at irregular intervals and
depending upon unusual occurrences--departing for a long trip,
changing one's place of residence, taking a new personal name,
illness, sorcery, and so forth(8).

In addition to food that is offered both to spirits and one's
neighbors, there is a special offering for the spirits, the
sajen, which appears in nearly all Javanese ceremonies. Often
these offerings are placed in rice fields or at crossroads as a
gift to the spirits without a *slametan*(9). The presence of
spirits, and those continual reminders of their presence, the
slametan and the *sajen*, prey on the minds of Javanese.

Latourette, throughout his seven volumes of *The Expansion of
Christianity*(10), shows that Christianity has had its greatest
successes among animists, instead of among adherents of "higher"
religions. Although major religions are now claimed by the

Javanese, the heart of their belief is still animism, to which
Christianity has a definite appeal. In fact, Simatupang says,
"The majority of Christians in Indonesia, maybe more than 95%,
came to Christianity from an animistic pattern of life and
thinking"(11).

In addition to spirit beliefs and *slametans*, a third element
of Javanism is the complex of curing, sorcery, and magic centering around the role of a *dukun* (shaman)(12). Most Javanese,
reportedly even President Suharto(13), believe in some kind of
dukun--a diviner, a curer, or a sorcerer. The *dukun* possesses
ngelmu, a kind of esoteric knowledge, supernatural skill, or
magical power.

Even with this brief survey, it should be clear that elements
of *kejawen* are involved in the beliefs of most Javanese, no
matter what religion they profess, with Christianity being less
affected than other religions(14). These beliefs fill the
Javanese mind with fear, doubt, uneasiness, anxiety, and longings which are precursors of receptivity to the gospel.

Kejawen is the constant element that makes Javanese people
responsive to the gospel at any time. But in times of social
disorientation or political upheaval, they look for new ways to
achieve *slamet*. As Selosoemardjan points out, "Although the
underlying forces which have eventually built up the growing
desire for change may have been at work for a considerable
length of time, an immediate stimulus is needed to convert this
desire into a decision to change"(15).

The way in which each of the incoming religions has faced
kejawen forms one of the most important considerations in understanding Javanese acceptance of that religion. The way each
religion has dealt with these primitive beliefs, has largely
determined its degree of acceptance by the Javanese people.

MYSTICISM: WHEN I BECOME GOD

Kejawen is not exhausted by the above discussion, because in
present-day Javanese belief it includes mysticism. Javanism has
the locus of its power in the village, and its most common
adherents are peasants. *Kebatinan* (Javanese mysticism), on the
other hand, impinges on the beliefs of most Javanese, but its
locus is the court center and its adherents are usually aristocrats and intellectuals. Anderson says the "conception of the
entire cosmos being suffused by a formless constantly creative
energy provides the basic link between the 'animism' of the
Javanese villager, and the high metaphysical pantheism of the
urban centers"(16).

Geertz divides Indonesian society into three groups: *abangan* (peasants), *santri* (orthodox Moslems), and *priyayi* (gentry). The *abangan* basically follows the primitive religion with elements of mysticism which have filtered down to him. The *santri* has a basic antipathy for practices of the *abangan*, but in actuality, adopts some of them in a modified Islamic form. The *priyayi* observes *slametans* and other elements of *abangan* belief, but is more concerned with a mystical, pantheistic, speculative religious pattern than the *abangan*, whose pattern is ritualistic, polytheistic, and magical(17).

These divisions are helpful as categories of thought, but they are not distinct classes without overlapping beliefs and practices. The term *abangan*, though acceptable when Geertz did his research in the early 1950's, is no longer popular among the peasantry because it is associated with those who have no sanctioned religion. This group came under heavy fire following the coup of 1965, because the masses of communists were *abangan*.

Kebatinan, which is literally translated "inwardness," has various definitions depending upon the viewpoint of the definer. The Indonesian government will not recognize *kebatinan* as a religion(18), but its rapid growth in an organized form demands careful attention(19). Sayuti Melik says that *kebatinan* is "knowledge concerning the inward life of man, which is based upon the principle of Absolute Lordship, and the aim of which is to achieve a calm and peaceful life or the perfection of life by doing one's utmost to obtain noble character"(20). *Kebatinan* can be defined as the organized form of Javanese mysticism whose aim is to achieve oneness with God(21).

It has been debated whether mysticism was present in Java before the coming of Hinduism in the fourth and fifth centuries(22) or the coming of Buddhism in the eighty century; but Nicholson shows that the tenets of Hindu and Buddhist mysticism were assimilated at points where the Javanese system found them congenial(23). The amalgamation of these beliefs reached their apex in the Hindu Mojopahit kingdom in East Java, between the middle of the tenth century and the middle of the sixteenth century(24).

The essential principle of Javanese mysticism is that the inner self (microcosmos) and the external world (macrocosmos) are interdependent. Hinduistic and Buddhistic Javanese literature agree that the highest godhead is the Absolute. The Absolute is thought of as impersonal reality underlying all phenomena. Man, the microcosm, is the perfect manifestation of the Absolute, and man's soul is in reality the Absolute itself.

Man lives in misery on the wheel of suffering because of his
fascination with the phenomenal world, but he can obtain liberation through meditation and good conduct. The "liberated man"
possesses the positive being of the Absolute, and in fact, has
become inseparable from the Absolute(25). Although few Javanese
would claim to have reached this state, the desirability of it
and the means of attaining it affect the whole Javanese philosophy of religion.

The *summum bonum* for the Javanese is the achievement of inner
quietude, through a stilling of one's affective thoughts and
feelings. The Javanese go beyond this Hinduistic achievement
for its own sake by idealizing a state of inner stillness—a
fixity of spirit, which gives them power over worldly and cosmic
states of being(26). These beliefs are propagated and encouraged in that favorite entertainment of the Javanese, the shadow
play.

The importance of Javanese mysticism for this study is not
primarily in the organized mystic groups, which are rather
resistant to Christianity. The difficulty posed by followers of
kebatinan is that they claim their beliefs are unifying principles which can be found in every religion and can be practiced
alongside every religion. Some groups have consciously incorporated Christian beliefs into their system. Hadiwijono, in a
private interview, said, "Mysticism makes it harder to win them
to Christ, because they think religion is lower than they are.
Religion consists of outward ceremonies, but mysticism is
higher." According to Hadiwijono, those Christians who have
tried to use a philosophical mystic system in witnessing have
eventually failed. He believes that the simple proclamation of
the gospel is the best approach to mystics.

Our major concern, rather, is with the philosophical ideal of
kebatinan, which is accepted by the average Javanese although it
is beyond his ability to attain. The rigorous asceticism, the
difficulty of practicing meditation, and the long road to oneness with the Absolute discourage the majority of Javanese.
Yet it is this state of inner quietude and peace that they
seek.

Mystic movements have increased most rapidly when psychological stresses were most severe(27). The rapid growth of these
movements is but a symptom of underlying problems the Javanese
face(28).

Especially moral decay has disappointed many people. The
existing religions have not proved to be strongholds of
moral strength. And this just at the time when the
Indonesian people are searching for a new foundation upon

which the structure of human existence may be built, in
order to enable them to compete with the Western world(29).

These conditions point to Christianity as a viable alternative. Some leaders of *kebatinan* groups led their followers to
profess Christianity when the government declared that all
Indonesians must have a sanctioned religion.

In essence, desires created by mystic beliefs of the Javanese
have produced a vacuum which Christianity has been able to fill
when accepted. Their desire to be at one with God and nature
reaches out to God the Father; their search for peace reaches
out to God the Son; and their quest for power reaches out to God
the Holy Spirit.

MESSIANIC EXPECTATION: THE JUST KING

One other belief generally related to Javanese religious
thoughts has prepared the way for response to Christianity--the
Ratu Adil (Just King) expectation. This Javanese tradition was
probably influenced by cyclical Hindu philosophy, which divides
history into four world periods beginning with an ideal state
that deteriorates in succeeding periods until society is in
disarray by the end of the fourth period. Javanese expect the
Ratu Adil to lead them in restoration of the ideal state(30).
This idea was later reinforced by the Moslem tradition of a
coming *mahdi* (savior)(31).

These messianic expectations were once thought to be fulfilled by Indonesian leaders who led rebellions against the
Dutch, particularly Diponegoro I (1718-1723) and Diponegoro II
(1825-1830). But since both rebellions ultimately failed,
messianic hopes were transferred to a future liberator. Van
Akkeren shows that such expectations probably played a significant role in the introduction of Christianity to the Javanese
after 1825(32).

Much of the messianic and prophetic Javanese literature was
probably written around the time of Diponegoro II. This
literature contains the purported prophecies of King Joyoboyo,
who ruled between 1135 and 1157(33). In his two most famous
writings, the Moslem way of life comes under fire, particularly
the Arabic form of ritual and its lack of adaptation to Javanese
forms and ways of life.

These publications, which carry no date, have been confiscated several times. They were banned by Dutch colonial authorities in 1925, and by the Indonesian government in 1961, because
of injurious statements about Moslems and Chinese(34). Nevertheless, copies are circulated clandestinely, and the messianic

hopes they foster continue to be a very important element in Javanese thinking and feeling: There are bestsellers in contemporary bookshops that deal with the *Ratu Adil* expectations(35).

The prophecies of King Joyoboyo are common fare in daily conversation. Indonesians often point out that he prophesied a race of small yellow men from the North would come to Indonesia for the period of a corn crop (three and one-half months, which is interpreted as three and one-half years), after which the colonialists would be defeated. This event was to be followed by the rise of a leader from the common people who would usher in a period of prosperity and justice.

As one could imagine, each group finds something in the prophecy to support its religious or nationalistic viewpoint(36). The common interpretation is that the Japanese fulfilled the prophecy about a race from the North by their occupation of Indonesia during World War II, from early 1942 till mid-1945. Some groups have associated the *Ratu Adil* with President Sukarno in the past, and currently with President Suharto. The East Java Christian Church has virtually identified the *Ratu Adil* with Jesus Christ and the Second Coming; a hymn still sung by them calls Jesus Christ the *Ratu Adil*(37).

The most pertinent of these prophecies for Christians related to a section in which King Brawijaya of the Mojopahit kingdom asks his advisor, Sabdopalon, what he thinks about their accepting Islam. Sabdopalon replies that he does not want to become a Moslem as the king is determined to do, and therefore, will leave. He prophesies that after five hundred years of meditation he will return and exchange the Moslem religion with a religion of the spirit. This is interpreted by some to mean a return to the Hindu-Buddhist religion, and by others to mean the acceptance of Christianity by the people of Indonesia. Since the prophecy purportedly was given in the middle of the fifteenth century, it is to be fulfilled in the twentieth century(38).

The moderator of the Java Evangelical Church said that the book containing this prophecy is responsible for the existence of a large church near Pati, Central Java. The village clerk read the book and then came to the synod office asking for information about Christianity. He returned with his new knowledge and led approximately 75 percent of the village, about five hundred persons, to form a church.

The Director of Hindu-Buddhist Affairs for the Department of Religion in Central Java said that this prophecy had also caused many people to become Hindus. One informant said that the fact Mount Merapi had begun erupting again, just as the prophecy said

it would prior to the coming of the *Ratu Adil*, had influenced
him to become a Hindu. This had particular significance to him
since he lived on the side of the volcano, as did several
others in surrounding villages who also accepted Hinduism as
the fulfillment of the prophecy(39).

To the mystical Javanese this prophecy plays an important
role in the future of religion in Indonesia. It has had its
greatest influence in times of stress--during the colonial
period, the revolutionary period, and the tumultuous beginnings
of the New Order(40).

ISLAM: A POST-CHRISTIAN RELIGION GOT THERE FIRST

The process of Islamization, which has never been completed
in Java, was indicative of, and contributed to, the religio-
cultural situation in which churches grew. Today perhaps only
a third of the population follows orthodox practices(41),
although the majority of Javanese have absorbed many Moslem
beliefs into their Indic tradition(42).

The peasantry absorbed Islamic concepts and practices, so
far as it understood them, into the same general Southeast
Asian folk religion into which it had previously absorbed
Indian ones, locking ghosts, gods, jinns, and prophets
together into a strikingly contemplative, even philosophical, animism(43).

The process by which Islam entered Indonesia is instructive,
because it reveals an Islam very different from that practiced
in traditional Moslem countries. Islam first entered Indonesia
through traders, whose numbers increased in Southeast Asia
following the fall of Baghdad in 1258(44). They related well to
commercial elements in Indonesian society, particularly city-
states along the northern coast of Java.

Indonesian merchants found in Islam an egalitarian principle
which commended itself to them because of the dominance of the
competing Hindu-Mojopahit kingdom. Therefore, these *santri*
Moslems were basically limited to the merchant class, and have
never been able to induce the rest of the populace to embrace
Islam fully as a way of life(45). For several centuries it
remained an urban faith in Java(46).

When Islam was originally introduced to Java, its donors took
a gradualist position: first the Confession, then the Pillars,
later the Piety, and after that the Learning and the Law(47).
The original adherents of Islam in Indonesia intermarried with
the traders and accepted their religion. Islam was strengthened
by teachers and scholars who established schools, trained

disciples, and worked with the political hierarchy until the
rulers influenced the people to accept Islam as their religion
(48). "The history of Islam in Indonesia can be written as the
history of one protracted acculturation process of which the end
is not yet in sight"(49).

A second factor related to the introduction of Islam was the
type of Islam that was accepted in Indonesia: *Sufism*, of the
Sunni sect of the *Shafi'ite* school, which had already passed
through the mystical influence of India before it reached
Indonesia(50). Sufism had many points of contact with the Indic
tradition of Java and was, therefore, superficially accepted by
the masses of Javanese as simply a new framework for their
earlier traditional religious system. Clifford Geertz says,
"In Indonesia Islam did not construct a civilization, it
appropriated one"(51).

A third factor is that Islam was perceived as a political
force, to be used by part of the society to dominate the rest
of it. The princes of the city-states on the northern coast,
with the help of nine Moslem prophets, were able to overthrow
the Hindu Mojopahit kingdom(52).

During the short fifty-year reign of this new dynasty in
Demak, Central Java, it was in their interest to influence the
populace to accept the new religion.

This transitional government soon gave way to the interior
state of Mataram, located near the present center of Javanese
culture, Yogyakarta. Although the peasants followed the leadership of the rulers, their conversion to Islam was half-hearted
and did not penetrate their *batin* (inner life). Mataram court
scholars associated with the *priyayi* (aristocrats) developed a
Javanese Islam quite different from that propounded by the
Prophet(53).

It is significant that the aforementioned Moslem prophets
tried to use the cultural forms of the people to introduce their
religion, but they were never able to induce the majority to
accept more than its outward forms(54). Van Akkeren says,

> This "syncretistic," or as we prefer, Javanistic Islam,
> has a strong preference for the legendary saint Sunan
> Kalidjaga who was one of the first Moslem missionaries
> in Java, and who is supposed, after much meditation and
> asceticism, to have invented the *wajang*, the *gamelan*
> and the *slametan*, and introduced them into Java. In
> this manner the saint usurps the place of many older
> cultural heroes, such as Pandji of whom the same legend
> is told(55).

In this way the Javanese were able to hold onto their former beliefs and cultural forms, and still accept the religion of their rulers.

Clifford Geertz evaluates orthodox Islam by saying,

Sunni Islam did not, today still does not, represent the spiritual mainstream in Indonesia. Its main strongholds on the fringes of the archipelago, unIndicized enclaves in strategic pockets of Sumatra and the Celebes, and its main support in a marginal social class, itinerant market peddlers, it represented a challenge to that mainstream-- a challenge which grew stronger and more insistent as it took deeper root and firmer outline and as a truly national society slowly formed, but a challenge whose force was scattered, whose appeal was circumscribed, and whose triumphs were local(56).

The majority of converts to Christianity have come from this syncretic, Javanistic Islam rather than the orthodox *santri* variant. Of the 163 interviewees who were Moslem converts to Christianity after 1965, 63 percent specified that they were from the "statistical Islam" or animistic Javanese background. The percentage is probably higher than that, because the other 37 percent only cited "Islam" as their religious background, and this could mean either the syncretistic or the orthodox variety.

The reasons these interviewees gave for their dissatisfaction with Islam varied. Let's look at several of them.

Failure to Answer Heart-Hunger

A key reason that led many Javanese to become Christians was the fact that Islam did not answer their heart-hunger. It only emphasized the observance of prescribed rituals and external behavior. The Javanese submitted themselves to the authority of Islamic law, just as they submitted themselves to the tradition-al feudal structure of society. Thus they accepted a "secular-ized" Islam, which served to support existing social structures.

The man who felt the need of a more personal religious experience was obligated to turn to mysticism. But the individual had little independence in this field either. Here, too, he had to submit to the power and the author-ity of the religious teachers(57).

Many, therefore, investigated Christianity. According to the testimony of those interviewed, Christianity provided a dynamic experience that satisfied the deepest longings of their hearts.

Failure to Communicate Beliefs

Islam also failed to communicate its beliefs in the language
of the people. The fact that a Moslem was required to use Arabic
in prayer and memorization of the Koran gave Islam an alien
character, in addition to failing to satisfy the needs of those
who parroted words without understanding them(58).

One interviewee stated it this way:

Before the 30th of September Movement, my family did not
understand religion. Of course, we were statistical
Moslems, but we did not practice our religion. At that
time my family and I began to go to the mosque, and I
began to actively study the Koran and pray. For the
next five years I studied, but I did not understand.
Every afternoon I learned to read the Arabic and memorize
it, but I was never taught its meaning or purpose. I
was just like a parrot: he can speak, but doesn't know
what he says.

My family had begun to go to the church in the nearby
village. After some time, I went with them. From the
very first I was amazed because the Christians read the
Bible in a language I could understand. They taught us
clearly about life situations and our relationship with
with one another and God. This interested me. As time
went on, I became more interested in Christian teachings
and less interested in reciting the Koran which I could
not understand. Finally I stopped reciting the Koran,
and surrendered myself to the Lord Jesus(59).

Intolerance of Leaders

Another factor in the growth of Christianity during this
period was the attitude of Moslem leaders. In their attempts to
"purify"(60) Javanese Islam, they were intransigent and intoler-
ant--two non-Javanese attitudes(61).

Their problem centered in the incomplete Islamization of the
Javanese. During recent years Islamic leadership has grown
impatient with a gradualist approach, and the emphasis has been,
"MengIslamkan orang Islam" ("Islamize the Moslems"). Boland
says, "After 1965, Muslims have more and more realized that the
Islamization of Indonesia would in fact mean the Islamization of
Java, and that this was a question of now or never"(62).

Moslems used the government declaration that all Indonesians
must have a religion, to frighten statistical Moslems into
attending services at the mosque and trying to carry out obligations of the faith. But our interviewees frequently stated

that the Moslem religion was "too hard," or "had too many requirements." As Geertz states, "The otherness, awfulness, and majesty of God, the intense moralism, the rigorous concern with doctrine, and the intolerant exclusivism which are so much a part of Islam are very foreign to the traditional outlook of the Javanese"(63).

Many Javanese reacted by trying to find a religion that satisfied them, one which could be practiced without force. Although Javanese will follow their rulers, they have an aversion to force. During Dutch times they accepted the stronger power of the Dutch but delighted in circumventing it or scoffing at it in their shadow plays.

Participation in the Massacre

Many Javanese reacted against Islam's heavy-handed tactics by becoming Christians. Ninety-three of the five hundred persons interviewed stated that their reaction to the Islamic religion was a factor in their coming to Christ.

One element in this reaction was Moslem cruelty in the massacre of communists following the abortive coup. Javanese were horrified at the thought of worshipping with murderers of their families and acquaintances. They could not accept the fact that one could be religious and still participate in such slayings. On the other hand, Christians refused to take part in these clandestine affairs, demonstrated love, and imparted a faith which could bring forgiveness and newness of life.

Use of Ridicule

Many Javanese also reacted against ridicule by the *santri* (orthodox Moslems), who even made fun of them when they attended prayer times at the mosque. Those who had formerly been related to the communist party were often called "dogs"(64).

One informant stated that he went to the mosque every afternoon to pray, but it was no use:

The situation did not allow me to worship, because every day I heard slander, felt pressures, and heard threats to those of us who had been communists. One day they called together all of us who had been involved with the communists, and then, one by one, they left us standing alone. Then from a far distance they said things that really offended us. After about two years I began to be very unhappy with the actions of the Moslems, and so when I heard there were Christians in a nearby village, I decided to go and see what they believed. I was very impressed by Jesus' teachings on love. The Christians

were very different from the Moslems, who were cruel and
showed hate toward their fellowmen(65).

Moslem Polemic

The reaction to Islam also involved tactics used by certain
Moslems in the Indonesian government's Ministry of Religion(66).
All religions are represented in the Ministry of Religion, but
the majority of its employees are *santri* Moslems. In addition
to the primary task of providing religious instruction for students in the public schools(67), local Ministry of Religion
offices attempted to indoctrinate the populace.

The Central Java Ministry of Religion established a semi-
official *Pilot Proyek Pembinaan Mental Agama* (Pilot Project for
Fostering a Religious Mentality), popularly dubbed P$_3$A(68).
Local Moslem leaders used this project as a means of calling
together statistical Moslems and lecturing them about the
deficiencies of Christianity and the glories of Islam(69).
These attacks offended the sensibilities of the tolerant Javanese and caused some of them to investigate Christianity, which
was evidencing a spirit of love and tolerance even in the face
of unfair accusations. It was the unanimous opinion of
Javanese church leaders that the Christian faith was helped
more than hindered by P$_3$A.

The book *Missi Kristen dan Pendjadjahan* is an example of the
Moslem polemic. Its thesis is that the exclusive purpose of
missions is to serve the interests of Western colonists(70).
A final chapter on Indonesia states that mission efforts are
proof that Christians are attempting to "Christianize" Indonesia
while neutralizing Islam by claiming Moslems are intolerant(71).
Due to their own political orientation, Moslems feel that
Christians would like to use politics to make all Indonesians
Christians, and on occasion they cite "evidence" of the Chris-
tians' plans to "Christianize" the nation(72).

Much of the polemic of these *santri* Moslems borders on the
paranoid, and quotes indiscriminately from any Christian
"source" to prove that Christians contradict themselves and
cannot be trusted(73). It is this type of fanaticism against
which the average Javanese reacts(74).

A long-standing antipathy to Islam on the part of many
Javanese is illustrated in one of the old Javanese chronicles.
This book rejects Islam as a foreign religion and scoffs at the
institutions and daily practices of Islam. According to this
chronicle, the conversion of the Javanese to the faith of the
Arabs changed them into a half-hearted people. It says that the
Javanese will not recover their strength of purpose until they
have reinstated their ancestral religion.

Indonesia's present Minister of Religion, Mukti Ali, is leading Moslems to develop a modernized form of Islam and to
cooperate in the development program of the nation(75).

In summary, orthodox Islam was never accepted by the majority
of Javanese, and they continue to resist efforts by the *santri*
to complete the process of Islamization(76). In the process of
acculturation, Islam did not change the concepts of the
Javanese; they only appropriated its forms. Anderson says that
the *abangan* (animistic peasant) religious culture "has been
engaged in an ill-concealed competition [with Islam] for
centuries"(77).

CONCLUSIONS

One might sum up the Javanese view toward religion in general,
as a way of life and conduct that will bring about harmony
between himself and a system of beliefs--including a distant
god, an aristocratic ruler, a ceremonial Islam, and ever-
present spirits that must be placated. He lives one day at a
time, but his life orientation is to the past, with occasional
glimpses of the future through the coming of the *Ratu Adil* who
will reestablish the harmonious system idealized in the shadow-
play classics. Although he seeks this static state of *slamet*,
he continually faces encroaching modernization evidenced in
education, technology, and progress. His identity is bound up
with the solidarity of the community; thus his sense of tranquility is disturbed by incongruous forces in society.

Therefore, we see the opportunity for Christianity to come to
terms with Javanese religious beliefs. But there is also the
threat that Christianity might suffer a similar fate to Islam--
that is, to be accepted in name and form, but not in heart. The
future of Christianity among the Javanese lies in accomplishing
both types of acceptance.

If all the religious factors in conversion that were listed
by our Javanese interviewees (spiritual need, gospel, Church,
service, Christian life, and miracles) are added together, they
more than double the total points amassed by political factors
(governmental decree, and protection). Yet, except for the
category of "Spiritual Need," all of the religious factors were
ranked in a secondary position.

This means that the religio-cultural-political situation has
produced a responsiveness in the hearts of the Javanese which
can be capitalized on by Christianity. The religio-cultural
factors remain fairly constant and, therefore, the Javanese
continue to be responsive. The political factors between 1965
and 1971 represented a crisis in the life of the nation and its

people, and brought to fruition the salvation of large numbers of Javanese. Political factors receded into the background after 1971, and church growth slowed.

If the Javanese churches are to experience massive growth again, there must be a greater emphasis on spiritual factors and a better use of the culture. Those who follow the traditional religion of Java will continue to face a crisis of belief as education and modernization encroach upon them; they will continue to be disorientated and alienated by the modern world which seems to be closing in on them, and will continue to look for answers to these problems.

If the churches can effectively witness to the power of the gospel through the community of faith and love, using every means available to proclaim salvation, there is hope for a great harvest in the future. If the churches fail to meet the culture on its own terms and to give its forms and ceremonies new meaning, they will suffer the same fate that Islam suffered in its attempt to capture the hearts of the people(78).

NOTES

1. Private interview with Harun Hadiwijono, author of *Javanese Mysticism* and *Agama Hindu dan Agama Budha* [The Hindu Religion and the Buddhist Religion] (Jakarta: Badan Penerbit Kristen, 1971), Yogyakarta, 6 June 1973.

2. Nicholson, "Introduction of Islam," p. 7, lists some animistic practices that originated in the Paleolithic and Neolithic periods.

3. Higgins, *Millstones*, p. 38.

4. Bernard H. M. Vlekke, *Nusantara: A History of Indonesia* ('sGravenhage: van Hoeve, 1959), p. 15 (hereafter cited as *Nusantara*).

5. Soesilo Darmowigoto, "Pemashuran Indjil Keradjaan Allah" [Spreading the Gospel of the Kingdom of God] (Salatiga: Synod of the Javanese Christian Churches, n.d.--mimeographed), p. 6 (hereafter cited as "Pemashuran Indjil").

6. Vlekke, *Nusantara*, pp. 14-15.

7. Geertz, *The Religion of Java*, pp. 16-29.

8.   Ibid., p. 30.

9.   For the contents of such offerings, see Geertz, *The Religion of Java*, p. 42.

10. Kenneth Scott Latourette, *The Expansion of Christianity*, 7 vols. (New York: Harper and Row, 1962).

11. Simatupang, "Situation and Challenge," p. 17.

12. For a listing of kinds of *dukuns*, see Geertz, *The Religion of Java*, p. 86.

13. Peter Polomka, *Since Sukarno* (Middlesex, England: Penguin Books, Harmondsworth, 1971), p. 156 (hereafter cited as *Since Sukarno*).

14. See van Akkeren, *Sri and Christ*, who structures his history of the East Java Christian Church around the motif of Sri, the rice goddess, the gospel of Christ, and the resulting battle between the two over the minds of Javanese Christians.

15. Selosoemardjan, *Social Change in Jogjakarta* (Ithaca: Cornell University Press, 1962), p. 385 (hereafter cited as *Social Change*).

16. Benedict R. O'G. Anderson, "The Idea of Power in Javanese Culture" in *Culture and Politics in Indonesia*, ed. Claire Holt (Ithaca, N.Y.: Cornell University Press, 1972), p. 7 (hereafter cited as "Idea of Power").

17. Geertz, *The Religion of Java*, pp. 5-6.

18. See Mukti Ali, "Aliran Kebatinan Bukan Agama" [Mystic Sects Are Not Religions] in *Almanek 1973: Dewi Sri*, ed. Kamadjaja (Yogya: U. P. Indonesia, 1972), pp. 107-11 (hereafter cited as "Aliran Kebatinan").

19. The first Congress of Mystical Schools in Indonesia held in 1955 was attended by representatives from 67 *kebatinan* groups. The fifth Congress of this body, meeting in 1963, had representatives from 86 groups, excluding Sumatra. See Hadiwijono, *Javanese Mysticism*, p. 1. Darmowigoto, *"Pemashuran Indjil,"* p. 12, written at least five years later, said there were 48 mystic groups in Yogyakarta alone. Rahmat Subagyo, *Kepercayaan Kebatinan Kerohanian Kejiwaan dan Agama* [Mystic Beliefs and Religion] (n.p.: Spectrum 3, 1973), pp. 242-50 (hereafter cited as *Kebatinan dan Agama*), lists 285 sects.

20. Hadiwijono, *Javanese Mysticism*, p. 2.

21. For a summary of the beliefs of mysticism, see Geertz, *The Religion of Java*, pp. 310-12. For a more detailed analysis of Hindu and Buddhist beliefs in *kebatinan*, see Hadiwijono, *Javanese Mysticism*, pp. 21-140.

22. See B. Schrieke, *Indonesian Sociological Studies*, vol. 2: *Ruler and Realm in Early Java* (The Hague: W. van Hoeve, Ltd., 1957), pp. 308-9 (hereafter cited as *Ruler and Realm*).

23. See Nicholson, "Introduction of Islam," pp. 12-17.

24. See Schrieke, *Ruler and Realm*, for a discussion of this kingdom.

25. See Hadiwijono, *Javanese Mysticism*, pp. 63-67.

26. See Win, "Political Socialization," p. 148.

27. Selosoemardjan, *Social Change*, p. 404.

28. See Subagyo, *Kebatinan dan Agama*, p. 121.

29. Hadiwijono, *Javanese Mysticism*, p. 3.

30. Moertono, *State and Statecraft*, p. 81.

31. Van der Kroef, *Modern World*, p. 120.

32. See van Akkeren, *Sri and Christ*, p. 45.

33. Vlekke, *Nusantara*, pp. 49-50.

34. Van Akkeren, *Sri and Christ*, p. 45.

35. Ibid., p. 40.

36. See Tjantrik Mataram, *Peranan Ramalan Djojobojo dalam Revolusi Kita* [The Role of the Prophecy of Joyoboyo in Our Revolution] (Bandung: Masa Baru, 1966), pp. 47-57 (hereafter cited as *Ramalan Djojobojo*), for various interpretations.

37. Van Akkeren, *Sri and Christ*, pp. 151 and 161.

38. Mataram, *Ramalan Djojobojo*, pp. 85-86.

39. Private interviews.

40. See van Akkeren, *Sri and Christ*, pp. 40-48, for a further discussion of these messianic beliefs.

41. Hildred Geertz, "Indonesian Cultures and Communities," in
     Indonesia, ed. Ruth McVey (New Haven: Southeast Asia
     Studies, Yale University, HRAF Press, 1967), p. 43. Also
     see B. J. Boland, *The Struggle of Islam in Modern Indonesia*
     (The Hague: Martinus Highoff, 1971), pp. 186-188 (here-
     after cited as *Struggle of Islam*), for a discussion of how
     many Moslems are true adherents of Islam.

42. For a description of contrasting views between Hinduism and
     Islam and social changes that resulted from their amalga-
     mation, see James L. Peacock, *Indonesia: An Anthropological
     Perspective* (Pacific Palisades: Goodyear Publishing
     Company, 1973), pp. 31-34 (hereafter cited as *Anthropo-
     logical Perspective*).

43. Clifford Geertz, *Islam Observed: Religious Development in
     Morocco and Indonesia* (New Haven: Yale University Press,
     1968), p. 13 (hereafter cited as *Islam Observed*).

44. Nicholson, "Introduction of Islam," p. 19, cites evidence
     of an Arab Settlement in Sumatra as early as A.D. 654. See
     pp. 1-153 for a thorough study of the acculturation of
     Islam. An analysis of its form and content is found on
     pp. 78-127. Peacock, *Anthropological Perspective*, p. 23,
     says the fall of Baghdad marked the beginning of the spread
     of the Sufi branch of Islam.

45. Anderson, "Idea of Power," pp. 58-59, says, "Yet this
     overt Islamization of the rulers does not seem to have
     caused major alterations in their way of life or outlook.
     The penetration of Islam scarcely changed the composition
     and the recruitment of the Javanese political elite or
     affected the basic intellectual framework of traditional
     political thought. . . . The self-consciousness of pious
     Moslems remained strictly 'corporate.'"

46. Nicholson, "Introduction of Islam," p. 29.

47. C. Geertz, *The Religion of Java*, p. 123.

48. For the role of these donors, see Nicholson, "Introduction
     of Islam," pp. 1-67. "Political conversion did not occur
     everywhere at the same time, but until the ruler accepted
     Islam, or a Moslem seized control of the political struc-
     ture, the mass of the indigenous population did not
     convert" (ibid., p. 31).

49. Van Nieuwenhuijze, *Aspects of Islam*, p. 29.

50. Nicholson, "Introduction of Islam, pp. 83-85, and C.
     Geertz, *The Religion of Java*, p. 123.

51. C. Geertz, *Islam Observed*, p. 11.

52. Schrieke, *Ruler and Realm*, pp. 230-32, propounds the theory that the coming of the Portuguese caused Indonesians to adopt Islam as an ally in their fight against the encroaching Christian Portuguese.

53. See Higgins, *Millstones*, p. 41, for differences between Islam in Pakistan and Islam in Indonesia.

54. See C. Geertz, *Islam Observed*, pp. 25-41, for a description of how one of the Moslem prophets, Kalijaga, became a symbol connecting Indic Java with Moslem Java. He is "the bridge between two high civilizations, two historical epochs and two great religions" (ibid., p. 27).

55. Van Akkeren, *Sri and Christ*, p. 30

56. C. Geertz, *Islam Observed*, p. 42.

57. W. F. Wertheim, *Indonesian Society in Transition* (The Hague: W. van Hoeve, 1959), p. 196 (hereafter cited as *Society in Transition*).

58. See G. W. J. Drewes, "The Struggle between Javanism and Islam as illustrated by the *Serat Dermangandul*," *Bija-dragen tot de Taal-, Land-, en volkenkunde*, 122 (1966): 309-65 (hereafter cited as "Struggle between Javanism and Islam").

59. Private interview.

60. The approach of the reformers is illustrated by Al-Amier Sjakieb Arsalan in the book *Mengapa Kaum Muslimin Mundur, dan Mengapa Kaum Selain Mereka Madju?* [Why Is Islam Retreating, and Why Are Other Religions Advancing?], trans. H. Moenawar Chalil (Jakarta: Bulan Bintang, 1967). This book by a Moslem scholar answers the question in its title (asked by one of the faithful) by saying that Moslems have retrogressed because they are not willing to become martyrs, obey the Koran, and work. He accuses them of betraying the faith to modernization by being lazy, by not living up to moral standards, and by not studying. He calls on Moslems to sacrifice and to separate from the world.

61. See Benedict R. O'G. Anderson, *Mythology and the Tolerance of the Javanese* (Ithaca: Modern Indonesia Project, Monograph Series, Cornell University, 1965), pp. 1-6 (hereafter cited as *Mythology and Tolerance*).

62. Boland, *Struggle of Islam*, p. 191.

63. C. Geertz, *The Religion of Java*, p. 160.

64. Boland, *Struggle of Islam*, p. 233, reports that one Moslem informant said, "You Christians can have them; we don't want to get a fifth column in Islam."

65. Private interview.

66. See Boland, *Struggle of Islam*, pp. 9-10, for the beginnings of the Ministry of Religion, and pp. 188-190, for an up-to-date appraisal.

67. See van der Kroef, *Modern World*, p. 216, for the decision on 1 February 1951 that each student would receive two hours of religious instruction per week, beginning in the fourth grade. Religion teachers are hired and paid by the government, and the kind of religious instruction received is determined by the government. If as many as ten of any one religion are in a school, they may be taught by leaders from their religion. C. Geertz, *The Religion of Java*, pp. 197-98, says that there was a great deal of resentment on the part of the non-*santri* community at this religious "invasion" of the secular schools.

68. Decision #102/DI/EI/1/67, issued 15 November 1967 (Darmowigoto, *Pemashuran Indjil*, p. 13). This effort had three objectives: "(1) to step up the role of religion among the masses and to put into effect the first pillar of *Pancasila*, the state idealogy; (2) to create a religious mentality among the masses and produce a spiritual climate where they will be content physically and spiritually; (3) to rebuild the religious foundation which has been undermined by the 30th of September Movement and other atheists, as is evident in the daily lives of the people." The word "Pilot" was later dropped, and the project was thereafter called P$_2$A.

69. See booklet distributed to Moslems describing the tactics to be used to prevent the "Christianization" of Indonesia. Abdullah Wasi'an, "Benteng Islam" [Fortress of Islam], Surabaya, December 1967, pp. 1-29. (Mimeographed.)

70. Mustafa Khalidy and Omar A. Farrukh, *Missi Kristen dan Pendjadjahan* [The Christian Mission and Colonialism] (Surabaya: Penerbit C. V. Faizah, 1969), p. 3.

71. Ibid., pp. 253-60.

72. See M. Natsir, *Islam dan Kristen di Indonesia* [Islam and Christianity in Indonesia] (Bandung: Penerbit Pelajar dan Bulan Sabit, 1969), pp. 1-3, 188-216.

73. For a discussion of Moslem polemical writings during this period, see Boland, *Struggle of Islam*, pp. 224-42.

74. See Drewes, "Struggle between Javanism and Islam," pp. 309-65, for a discussion of the chronicle, *Serat Dermangandul*.

75. See "Langkah Mukti Kepedesaan" [Multi's Step Toward Rural Areas], *Tempo*, 6 November 1971, pp. 16-17, and "Tubuh Islam jang Purba" [The Ancient Body of Islam], *Tempo*, 23 October 1971, pp. 38-39.

76. Anderson, *Mythology and Tolerance*, p. 2, says, "since a majority of Javanese do not feel themselves to be Islamic in any profound sense, their tolerance of non-Islamic religious beliefs is scarcely a matter of high principle. In many cases it is simply a useful defense against the political and moral claims of an aggressive and orthodox Islamic minority. . . . 'Tolerance' is basically a weapon to deny ascendency to the *santri* and assure the continued legitimacy of traditional *abangan* domination."

77. Ibid., p. 4.

78. Methodology which the churches should use will be discussed in Chapters 12 and 13.

PART II

Political Factors

5

Three Become One . . .
or Do They?

The political situation in Indonesia profoundly affected the
rapid growth of Javanese churches. It provided the crises that
triggered the decisions of a majority of those deciding for
Christ during the decade of the 1960's.

At one point in my research, it even appeared that most of
the conversions could be traced to political motivations. It
was only after in-depth study that I could put all the factors
into proper perspective.

Let us examine the political climate that brought the
religious factors to a climax in the Indonesian revival. Without understanding something of Indonesia's historical and
political background, it is impossible to evaluate accurately
the religious situation.

In the wake of a communist putsch against leading generals of
the army on 30 September 1965, the government decreed that all
Indonesians "*must* believe in God and *must* have a religion"(1).

Without question, this new stance of the government influenced
many to become Christians. Twenty percent of the 500 persons
interviewed for this study pinpointed the government as the most
important reason for conversions to Christianity after 1965. An
additional 17 percent said that the initial cause of their
response was a desire for protection in the wake of the vendetta
against communists. That makes a total of 37 percent who listed
a political reason as the first motivation for the conversions.

Of the 500 persons interviewed, a total of 275 (55%) mentioned the government, and an additional 137 (27.4%) listed protection, as one of several factors in their decisions. So in all, 82.4 percent of those interviewed said that the political situation had some influence on those who became Christians after the abortive coup.

To validate the results of these interviews, we also asked specifically on a questionnaire: "Did the government's decree have any effect on those who became Christians after 1965?" An affirmative answer was given by 83 percent of the 306 who answered the question. The remaining 17 percent said it had no effect. The abovementioned interviewees also included those who became Christians before 1965 and were asked to give their opinions about post-1965 conversions. One would expect people who had themselves made decisions after 1965 not to rank a non-religious reason as high as those merely evaluating their motives, and this was indeed the case. Yet, fully 72 percent of these post-1965 converts also stated that the government did affect their decisions in some way.

Note again the over-all evaluation of factors, as shown on the chart on page 24. Using the scale of 10 for the reason ranked first, 9 for the reason mentioned second, and so on, we see that "Government" outranked each of the other ten factors in overall importance.

We must be cautious when assessing the motivations of others. Yet we can unequivocably say that political events after 1965, and the resulting political climate in Indonesia, played a significant role in the decisions of many people to become Christians. It not only affected those who became Christians, but also many statistical Moslems who began to practice their religion, as well as others who became adherents of Hinduism and Buddhism(2).

The uniqueness of the role of government in influencing these citizens to embrace a religion cannot be understood outside the context of Indonesian political life and history. Five decades of intensive indoctrination, flaming rhetoric, scathing polemic, and revolutionary upheaval have produced such a high political awareness that it is difficult for an Indonesian to make any decision apart from the political implications of that decision.

The crushing of the communists and establishment of the New Order climaxed decades of mounting conflicts and pressures. A survey of these events will give us a deeper understanding and a better evaluation of the role of the political climate in Indonesia from 1960 to 1971.

We may summarize political factors relating to church growth in Indonesia under three major headings:

1) *The role of instability and insecurity resulting from political conflict.* We will discuss this factor in the rest of Chapter 5, and also the first part of Chapter 6.

2) *The role of fear in the search for a protector.* We will discuss this factor in the latter part of Chapter 6.

3) *The role of the government's stance concerning religion.* We will discuss this factor in Chapter 7.

Colonial Period

Conflicts among the forces of nationalism, communism, and Islam were rooted in the legacy of Dutch colonialism lasting from 1596 to 1942. During their last eighty years of colonial rule, the Dutch changed traditional patterns of the Indonesian people and artificially determined the boundaries of modern Indonesia(3).

The Dutch ruled by the policy of "divide and conquer." They encouraged and instigated divisions among various ethnic groups. Thus they were able to conquer and rule a far-flung island empire with only a small army(4). They subjugated the masses by exploiting traditional rulers. In Java the Dutch collaborated with the *priyayi* (court aristocrats). This enabled them to maintain their positions, so long as they would give the Dutch the material gains these European adventurors had sailed to the Indies to seek. The Dutch also used alien minorities, such as the Chinese, to control the economy, thereby exacerbating racial divisions.

The Culture System of cultivation(5), instituted by the colonial government after the Java War of 1824-1829, bankrupted Indonesian sectors of the economy and doomed the masses of Javanese to subsistence agriculture(6). The Dutch educated only those Indonesians who would sustain their system, leaving 93 percent of the population illiterate at the time of independence(7).

The exploitation of Indonesia, particularly the Javanese, produced personality traits of inferiority and dependence(8). But in contrast to the acquiescence of the majority, a militant minority began to demand the right to govern their own country. Eventually the oppression of the Dutch resulted in overthrow of the system they had so carefully constructed.

Java, the center of colonial government and area most domin-
ated by the colonial system, was also the seedbed for nationalism. The tree of nationalism flowered in the twentieth
century, but its roots reached deep into older strata of history.
The Java War ended effective Javanese resistance during the
nineteenth century, but the roots of nationalism grew deeper and
stronger until it could bloom again in the more fertile soil of
the twentieth century.

With the advent of the Ethical Policy of 1901 and improved
educational opportunities for brilliant youths, the shoot of
nationalism began to break through the ground of colonialism.
Its first expression came through the *Budi Utomo* (Noble
Endeavor) Study Club, organized in 1908. The purpose of this
club was essentially non-political and encouraged the establishment of educational institutions for agriculture, industry,
commerce, and finally, "everything . . . that will guarantee the
life of a dignified people." Indonesia observes the *Budi Utomo*
birthdate as the "Birthdate of the Awakening of the Nation"(9).

Dutch colonialists sought to offset the influence of the
Pan-Islamic Movement in Indonesia by educating the elite. Ironically, they undermined their colonial empire by doing so. Once
endowed with Western and Reform Islam's social and political
ideals, Indonesians could no longer live in the colonial strait-
jacket.

Islamic nationalism first expressed itself in the establishment of the *Sarekat Islam* Party in 1912. Although the immediate
cause for the emergence of this party was a desire to compete
with Chinese entrepreneurs, it soon became the political voice
of Moslem aspirations for independence. Four years after its
founding it had a membership of 360,000. By 1919 its membership
had grown to two and one-half million patriots demanding self-
government(10).

The wedding between Islam and nationalism formed the basis
for Islam's claim to power in the political system. At the same
time it laid the foundation for division and conflict of later
years, when orthodox Islamic leaders sought to establish an
Islamic nation.

Communists immediately saw the implications of the Islamic
mass movement. They engaged in a power struggle with the Moslems
that was finally to culminate in the massacre of approximately
500,000 people in 1965-1966.

Communist activity began early in Indonesia. By 1917 they
had already infiltrated the *Sarekat Islam* Party. In their
attempt to take over leadership of its branches, they alienated

Moslem leaders and peasant followers by violating religious
sensitivities and making religion an issue(11). Finally they
were forced to form the *Partai Komunis Indonesia* (PKI) in 1921.

The *Sarekat Islam* lost a large part of its huge following
about 1922, when it opposed radical socialist trends. It was
their mania for orthodoxy that isolated Moslems from the center
of political power. They built *Sarekat Islam* into a fortress,
shutting out other groups which might otherwise have been com-
patriots. They did not allow aliens, Christians, or the *priyayi*
to be a part of their party (although they did make some exceptions in the latter case). They set themselves against
Christians, whom they considered lackeys of the colonial power.
Schools, hospitals, and other service organizations were viewed
as proofs that colonialists were using religion for their own
ends.

The crux of the problem was summed up well by Slametmuljana:

> A religious man desires to spread his religion to others,
> especially his own race, but a nationalist will use
> religion to obtain political power. . . . What is said
> to be a tool for one is the goal of the other, and vice
> versa(12).

He goes on to say that the desire of both the religionist and
the nationalist is power, and that power is found only in
politics.

It is this attitude that has set orthodox Moslems over
against nationalists, communists, Christians, and other political groups. Robert R. Jay says,

> It was the naive belief of the orthodox Moslem leaders
> that all Indonesians, other than those under the deep
> influence of the *kaum feodal* or of the West, were as a
> matter of course basically loyal to Islam and needed
> only sound instruction, for which they would be duly
> grateful, to become good orthodox Moslems. They viewed
> the syncretism of the traditional court circles and the
> secularism of the modern urban communities as veneers,
> beneath which lay the body of villagers, the "true"
> Indonesians, who were theirs(13).

This attitude continues to the present day.

The Moslem party in Indonesia tried to follow the conservative lines of the international Pan-Islamic movement, and was
therefore shunted to the sidelines by the masses. An attempted
communist coup d'etat in 1926 alienated still another segment of

the nationalist camp. The *Partai Komunis Indonesia* (PKI) receded
into the background after this abortive coup, and did not again
emerge as a serious political factor until after World War II
(14).

Into this vacuum of alienated peasantry, the nationalists
moved with verve. The remaining groups helped form a purely
nationalistic party, Sukarno's *Partai Nasional Indonesia* (PNI).

The dilemmas created by choices--Islam versus communism,
traditional versus modern ways of life, urban versus rural
environments, the aristocracy versus the peasantry--set the
stage for an integrative symbol. Sukarno with his revolutionary
nationalism embodied Indonesian ideals. His image became the
integrative rallying point for the next 35 years. He prided
himself in so echoing his fellow countrymen's beliefs that he
became known as the "Voice of the Indonesian People." He
remained so until those tragic days in the 1960's when he became
so enamored of his own oratory that he mistook his feelings for
theirs, and claimed that what he said was what they felt.

Dutch colonialism ended abruptly, in the early days of World
War II. The Japanese occupation of 1942-1945 strengthened the
hand of Moslems and nationalists, and helped create the
Indonesian army(15). In three short years the Japanese became
catalysts for revolutionary forces that led the fight for
independence.

Revolutionary and Parliamentary Government

The fight for independence which began with Sukarno's and
Hatta's Declaration of Independence on 17 August 1945 is well
told in many places. Here, we will only call attention to
various events which relate to conflicts that erupted in the
abortive 1965 coup.

At the outset of the revolutionary period, the forces of
nationalism, communism, religion, and the army united to overthrow the Dutch colonialists. Confrontations, skirmishes, and
battles raged across the land and the negotiation tables for the
next four years, as the Dutch fought to reinstate their rule
over Indonesia.

Among forces that fought the Dutch were private armies of
political parties, such as the *Masyumi* (all-Islamic) Party(16).
It is significant that Christians fought shoulder-to-shoulder
with other patriots, and thereby erased forever the suspicion
that they were lackeys of the colonial government. The revolutionary zeal of Indonesians was so great that they thought
nothing of going into battle against machine guns with only

sharpened bamboo poles, or even without weapons, if they had
amulets or other mystical powers which they thought would protect
them.

Communists also climbed on the revolutionary bandwagon, tried
to take the lead, and eventually were pushed aside until after
independence was won(17). During the Japanese occupation, the
communists had no choice but to oppose the "fascist" Japanese
regime. This put them in opposition to Indonesian collaborators,
including Sukarno, and to that extent further separated them
from the nationalist camp.

The process of polarization continued until 1947, placing the
PKI (Indonesian Communist Party) against virtually all sections
of the Moslem political movement, middle-class segments of the
nationalist movement, anti-Stalinists, socialists, nationally-
oriented communists, and Christian confessional groups. This
polarization led inexorably to another attempted coup d'etat in
1948, and the PKI's temporary eclipse(18).

Results of that 1948 coup are important to this study,
because the seeds of conflict were sown, and a situation
developed that was almost identical to the situation following
the 1965 coup attempt. Jay describes results of the 1948 coup:

> The revolt triggered a bloodbath between leftwingers and
> orthodox Moslem elements in the population. In towns and
> villages under rebel control the irregulars used their
> power to exterminate not only the central government
> officials but also those ordinary citizens against whom
> they bore ill will. They especially singled out ortho-
> dox Moslem teachers, students, and others known for
> their Islamic piety; these were shot, burned to death,
> or hacked to pieces, sometimes all three. Mosques and
> religious schools were burned and their adherents' houses
> sacked and destroyed. As these areas were reoccupied by
> loyalist Republican troops, those suspected of leftwing
> or anti-Moslem sentiments as well as the actual rebels
> were shot out of hand and otherwise subjected to mob
> wrath. . . .

> Reactions elsewhere in Javanese society were severe.
> Orthodox Moslems everywhere were inflamed against those
> whom they identified with the leftwing, which included
> many of the syncretist elements locally critical of
> orthodoxy. Cultural and political tensions were greatly
> sharpened between syncretist and orthodox communities in
> the countryside(19).

Strangely enough, the Indonesian Republic took a lenient position toward the Communist Party (PKI). Its leadership had been decimated, and it no longer posed a serious political challenge. Nevertheless, the coup left scars which constantly reminded the army and the Moslems that while they were fighting their common enemy, the Dutch, they had been "stabbed in the back by the PKI"(20).

It was felt that the PKI would be easier to control if it were not underground. This opened the door to its almost unbelievable renaissance under the leadership of D. N. Aidit, who took advantage of the many problems the new Republic faced. He outlined guidelines of the new strategy: the uniting of a national front which included the national bourgeois; the liquidation of the fanatical Moslem movement *Darul Islam*; and the development of a communist mass movement(21).

Aidit's policy succeeded so well that by the first national election in 1955 the PKI was able to secure a position as one of the "Big Four." It received a total of 6,176,914 votes, or 16.4 percent of the total cast(22). Its strength was in East and Central Java, as was that of the *Partai Nasional Indonesia* (PNI) which finished first. These areas formed

the ancient heartland of traditional pre-Islamic Javanese culture, and the PKI strength here showed to some extent how successful the party had been in appealing to traditional and nativistic Javanese currents of thought and expectations and to the radical nationalistic mystiques with which this nativism is frequently blended these days. Here . . . the party found support among the rural uprooted, among estate and peasant laborers and the landless, among the urban poor, and organized labor and among the youth, both in city and countryside(23).

By the time of provincial elections in 1957, the PKI ranked first, not fourth, in Central Java(24).

Shortly after the 1957 elections, President Sukarno, taking his cue from the communists, proposed a national-front government composed of the Nationalist Party (PNI), two Moslem parties (*Masyumi* and *Nahdatul Ulama*), and the Communist Party (PKI)(25). He justified the presence of the communists by asking the simplistic question, "Whoever heard of a three-legged horse?"(26).

An impressive PKI campaign in support of President Sukarno's proposal fell on deaf ears, because the other parties feared communist power with the masses. The Moslems and the army also faced added frustrations: *Darul Islam*, which had proclaimed a

Moslem state in 1949, stepped up guerrilla activity(27), and
rebellions involving dissident army elements posed the most
serious threat to the government up to that time(28). At every
opportunity the army, the Moslems, and the communists attempted
to sabotage one another.

"Guided Democracy"

The genius of Sukarno was his ability to play off the power
of the army, the Moslems, and the communists against one another,
thereby maintaining his own position as the integrative factor.
In 1957 he moved to unite these three powerful factions into one
ideology: Guided Democracy.

By that time parliamentary democracy and the party system had
been discredited by scandal and mutual suspicion. Sukarno presented his new concept to save the nation: In effect he would
become his own Prime Minister and form a government not answer-
able to the political parties. Vice-President Hatta resigned in
protest(29), and the outer provinces rebelled against Sukarno's
rule, resulting in the fall of the second Ali Sastroamidjojo
cabinet.

Sastroamidjojo, in his final act as Prime Minister, signed a
decree declaring the country in a state of emergency under
martial law. With this mandate the army crushed the rebellion
of dissident factions in the outer islands, and openly entered
the political arena. When no compromise could be reached by the
political parties, the army supported Sukarno in a return to the
1945 constitution which gave strong powers to the President(30).

On 5 July 1959, the President published a decree which
instituted the era of Guided Democracy. With this decree
Sukarno accomplished several things: He became the *Bapak*, or
father-figure, who proclaimed himself as the only "savior" of
the nation. He appealed to the deepest cultural instincts of
his people, particularly the Javanese, by saying that the
government would be based on the principles of village life:
gotong royong (mutual assistance), *musyawarah* (mutual deliberations), and *mufakat* (consensus), in which the people talk over
a problem and the leader draws conclusions(31).

Sukarno fused dissident elements into a single body, thus
forcing warring factions to tolerate one another. But in effect
he was bringing together the elements of a bomb which would
later explode and bring his government down to defeat.

In reality, Sukarno's action resulted in the collapse of
parliamentary democracy, the establishment of himself as the
autocratic ruler of Indonesia, and the strengthening of two

bitter enemies: the Army and the PKI. He suppressed the influence of the Moslem sector in the triumvirate by banning the
Masyumi and the *Partai Sosialis Indonesia* (PSI) for their part
in the recent rebellion. He was no longer riding a "three-
legged horse" but a two-legged one--the army and the Communist
Party!

Sukarno visualized himself as the embodiment of the Indonesian revolution and, paradoxically, as the historical heir of
the Indic tradition in which the whole state emanated from the
center of power, with the king as its integrative symbol. He
mesmerized the populace, especially the Javanese, with his
oratory and mystique. Many of them believed him to be supernatural, perhaps related to the Goddess of the South Sea.

He was the single most important factor in this period of
unrest. He maintained his position until 1965 by playing off
one force against another like a shadow-play puppeteer. Mintz
said of him in 1963,

He allows one faction to gain ground at the expense of
another, and then, just when he seems to be preoccupied
elsewhere, he swiftly moves in and throws his weight
behind the underdog of the moment, thereby redressing
the balance. In all these abrupt reversals of position,
he has never lost his balance(32).

The army backed Sukarno in his establishment of Guided
Democracy. It consolidated and expanded its political position
following successful suppression of the rebellion. It used its
special powers to expand its influence over economic affairs of
the country by taking supervisory control of former Dutch
properties during the confrontation over West Irian. It
installed military officers in strategic positions whenever the
opportunity arose(33).

The Indonesian Communist Party, archenemy of the army, also
found Guided Democracy advantageous. In Java provincial
elections of 1957, the PKI had cut into the strength of the
other three large parties. In fact, it had gained so much
power that both political and military leaders feared the
communists would gain control of the government. Such fears
were not without foundation, because Sukarno determined that
they should have a larger role than ever before.

The PKI advanced on all fronts by a combination of strategies:
It enthusiastically endorsed the President's popular slogans of
radical nationalism. It attacked other parties as authors of
corruption and instability. It advocated social change with
pledges of material prosperity. Communists were able to back

the government enough to gain popular support, and at the same
time to criticize actions of the government which did not fit
their program. The phenomenal gains of the PKI catapulated it
from 8000 members at the time of independence to 3,000,000
card-carrying members, with 18,000,000 members in its associated
organizations, by 1965(34).

President Sukarno aided the communists in their march to the
front. Beginning in 1960, it became more evident that he
thought himself a Marxist. His speeches championed the theories
of Marx and Lenin(35). To the end Sukarno maintained that he
was not a communist(36). If this were true (and most people
agree that it was, because nationalism and Sukarno's own
megalomaniac self-image precluded surrender to any other
ideology), then why did he advocate the inclusion of communists
in his government?

He did so because he agreed in principle with many of their
tenets(37), and because he appreciated the fact that the PKI was
the best organized party of the masses(38). But more than anything else, he saw the communists as a counterbalance to the army
and its growing power(39). Sukarno did not want to be the ser-
vant of the army (as he so clearly proved after 1965), but he
reacted so forcefully that he overbalanced the equation and led
to his own downfall.

NASAKOM and Confrontation

Indonesia's struggles of the early 1960's can be summed up in
President Sukarno's ideology called NASAKOM, a word he coined
using the first letters of *NASionalisme* (nationalism), *Agama*
(religion), and *KOMunisme* (communism). Sukarno introduced the
concept with one of his first articles, published in 1926(40).

His conviction that a coalition of nationalism, religion, and
communism could be formed caused Sukarno to force his brand of
cooperation upon the three incompatible groups, after he gained
the power to do so under Guided Democracy. NASAKOM became his
battle cry, up to the very night of the attempted coup d'etat
on 30 September 1965.

Communists took up the cry for NASAKOM, because they saw it
as a wedge to power. By 1965 Sukarno was strengthening the
communists' hand by saying not only that nationalism, religion,
and communism must work together, but also that in the spirit of
NASAKOM each part of the body politic, including the army, must
be at least one-third communist(41).

The period 1960-1965 in Indonesian foreign policy was
divided equally between two international events: the question
of autonomy in West Irian, and Confrontation with Malaysia.

At the end of 1962, President Sukarno's popularity and
effectiveness were probably at their peak. He had established
internal security and had liberated West Irian (Western New
Guinea) from the Dutch. In doing so he had managed to calm the
simmering hostility between the army and the communists(42).
Having gained victory in West Irian over the NEKOLIM imperial-
ists(43), Sukarno turned to the next shadowy manifestation of
neocolonialism: the new Federation of Malaysia.

The two reasons most often given for Confrontation are
political ascendancy of the communists, and a rapidly deter-
iorating economic situation that demanded some outside event to
take people's minds off their plight(44). The army was not
opposed to Confrontation, because it gave them an opportunity to
expand their power and demonstrate their revolutionary spirit.
But the Confrontation policy was most advantageous to the
communists: They used it as a shield for their preparations to
take over the government. And, at the same time, it kept their
old foe, the army, preoccupied with international affairs.

Amid vociferous shouts of encouragement by the communists,
Sukarno increased the tempo of his rhetoric. During this
period Sukarno used up his options with foreign powers, such as
the United States and Russia (whom he had played off against
each other), and was forced to turn to Communist China for
support. This Jakarta-Peking axis further strengthened the
Indonesian Communist Party(45).

In 1963 PKI chairman Aidit gave official sanction to (and
probably instigated) unilateral action by peasants in East Java
to put into effect a land reform law voted in 1960. Since the
army controlled most of these areas, the communists' action was
directed against its authority. With this action, the PKI put
itself on collision course with the army(46).

But the PKI lacked one essential: an armed force. They
began to agitate for a "Fifth Force" in addition to the army,
navy, air force, and police. They said peasants must be armed
to protect the country against the NEKOLIM.

The communists got President Sukarno's approval of their plan
in his 17 August 1965 speech(47). This was the result of a
well-organized PKI scenario to increase psychological pressure
through warning of invasions by foreign paratroopers, berating
Western powers, heightening the militancy of the peasants, and
proclaiming a material utopia under communism. Every organ of

the mass media was attuned to the Indonesian news service, which followed the communist line against the NEKOLIM.

Sukarno kicked off this campaign during the final year before the attempted coup, with his 17 August 1964 speech, "A Year of Living Dangerously"(48). The country was near hysteria by the next 17 August, when Sukarno gave another Independence Day speech in which he proposed "A Radical Turn"--meaning, of course, a turn to the left.

Church Growth Before 1965

Before moving on to the catastrophic events of 1965 and the resulting evangelistic harvest, let us draw some conclusions about church growth among the Javanese prior to 1965. Note once again Figure 1, page 7.

During the eight-year period from 1945 to 1953, the Javanese churches added 28,376 members, for an increase of 47.7 percent. The general instability of the period, plus the traumatic communist coup attempt in 1948, evidently played significant roles in this growth. No doubt the new leadership role of the Javanese also fostered Javanese church growth during this period of nationalistic fervor. Thus many of the same factors that affected church growth after 1965 were also operative during this period.

Following this rapid growth from 1945 to 1953, the figure shows an obvious slowdown in the growth process for the rest of the parliamentary democracy period. The Javanese churches added only 8,995 members, or 10.2 percent, during this seven-year period, in contrast with the next seven-year period from 1960 to 1967 when 115,241 members, or 119 percent, were added. During these three periods the annual growth rate was 5 percent, 1.2 percent, and 11.8 percent respectively.

Obviously some factors were present during the second period that slowed church growth. We can only speculate as to what they were. One factor is that the churches were intent on consolidating gains of the previous period and organizing themselves for action. In the political realm, the struggle for power during the parliamentary period was carried on principally in urban centers, particularly Jakarta--far removed from East and Central Java villages where the majority of Javanese lived. So, although the peasants were politically conscious, the struggle did not impinge upon their daily lives (as did events during the other two periods) and cause them to turn to religion.

The third, seven-year period needs to be divided, in order to
get a clearer understanding of church growth during the period
of Guided Democracy. From 1960 to 1964 the Javanese churches
added 33,420 members, or 7.7 percent per year, showing that
growth during this period was almost five times greater than
growth during the parliamentary democracy period, but only one-
third as great as during the period following the attempted
communist coup of 1965. It is obvious that the greatest growth
came after 1965, but that the churches had already begun to grow
by 1960.

Political factors involved in this growth during Guided
Democracy are worthy of note. For one thing, Sukarno involved
his people in the political situation during Guided Democracy by
appealing directly to them and by using the village principle of
musyawarah (mutual deliberations) as the basis for the central
government. This meant that he had closer contact with the
masses, and that their response to the political situation in
the capital city was more active than it had been during the
previous period.

The early 1960's were also years of war: first with the
Dutch over West Irian, and then with Malaysia during Confrontation. War psychology evidently affected many Javanese. Confrontation also had another effect on the religious situation,
as one leader of his denomination stated:

> Although Confrontation was not helpful to the country,
> politically or economically, it was helpful to Christian-
> ity. During this period our Church could grow. Moslem
> leaders were afraid to oppose Christianity, because their
> relationships with the strong Moslem leaders of Malaysia
> were cut off(49).

Another factor was the pressure of the communists. They
agitated in the villages, cajoled some leaders, deposed others,
and in general brought all their power to bear on the masses to
enlist them in the communist cause. This pressure caused some
to seek answers in Christianity. But on the other hand, it
slowed the growth in Baptist churches which were identified with
American missionaries(50).

These were the primary political factors in church growth
prior to 1965. (Economic, social, and religious factors were,
of course, also important during this time.) In summary,
political factors did influence Javanese church growth from 1960
to 1964, but were not as important as they were to be in the
period following 1965.

NOTES

1. "Harus ber-Tuhan dan harus ber-agama." See Decision No. XXVII/1966 MPRS (*Majelis Permusyawaratan Rakyat Indonesia*, Provisional People's Consultative Congress).

2. Boland, *Struggle of Islam*, p. 225, reports that Hinduism has added 250,000 adherents a year since 1965, and Darmowigoto, "Pemashuran Injil," p. 13, reports a larger increase in the number of Buddhist adherents attending religious ceremonies at the world's largest Buddhist shrine, Borobudur, in Central Java.

3. J. D. Legge, *Indonesia* (Englewood Cliffs, N. J.: Prentice-Hall, 1964), p. 20.

4. George M. Kahin, *Nationalism and Revolution in Indonesia* (Ithaca, N. Y.: Cornell University Press, 1952), pp. 1-44 (hereafter cited as *Nationalism and Revolution*).

5. Wertheim, *Society in Transition*, pp. 61-62.

6. See Clifford Geertz, *Agricultural Involution: The Process of Ecological Change in Indonesia* (Berkeley: University of California Press, 1966), pp. 130-31 (hereafter cited as *Agricultural Involution*), for a theory of why the Javanese economy stagnated while the Japanese economy grew. He says that at the beginning of this Culture System of cultivation, Japan and Java had approximately the same number of people, but over the years Japanese moved out of the agricultural setting into an industrial, urban economy and continued to grow, while Javanese involuted and stagnated on the same plots of ground with an ever-increasing population.

7. McVey, *Indonesia*, p. 256.

8. Kraemer, *From Missionfield*, pp. 84-85.

9. See Kahin, *Nationalism and Revolution*, p. 65.

10. Ibid.

11. Ibid., p. 76.

12. Slametmuljana, *Nasionalisme Sebagai Modal Perdjuangan Bangsa Indonesia* [Nationalism as the Resource for the Struggle of the Indonesian People] (Jakarta: Balai Pustaka, 1968), p. 124 (hereafter cited as *Nasionalisme*).

13. Robert R. Jay, *Religion and Politics in Rural Central Java*
     ([New Haven]: Yale University; Southeast Asia Studies,
     1963), p. 22 (hereafter cited as *Religion and Politics*).

14. See Arnold C. Brackman, *Indonesian Communism: A History*
     (New York: Frederick A. Praeger, 1963; hereafter cited as
     Indonesian Communism), for the most definitive study of
     this period.

15. Harry Benda, *The Crescent and the Rising Star* (The Hague:
     W. van Hoeve, 1958; hereafter cited as *The Crescent*),
     details the benefits to Moslems. See Boland, *Struggle of
     Islam*, pp. 7-15, for a summary of Benda's conclusions.

16. Kahin, *Nationalism and Revolution*, p. 163.

17. See Brackman, *Indonesian Communism*, pp. 13-43.

18. See Kahin, *Nationalism and Revolution*, pp. 301-3, for
     reasons why the coup failed.

19. Jay, *Religion and Politics*, pp. 28-29.

20. See Arnold C. Brackman, *The Communist Collapse in Indonesia*
     (Singapore: Asia Pacific Press, 1970), pp. 116-17
     (hereafter cited as *Communist Collapse*).

21. See Brackman, *Indonesian Communism*, pp. 171-214, and
     Justus M. van der Kroef, *The Communist Party of Indonesia:
     Its History, Program, and Tactics* (Vancouver: University
     of British Columbia, 1965), pp. 44-81 (hereafter cited as
     Communist Party). Also see Rex Mortimer, "Class, Social
     Cleavage, and Indonesian Communism," *Indonesia* 8 (October
     1969): 1-13, for a discussion of how the PKI changed basic
     communist strategy to meet the Indonesian situation.

22. Van der Kroef, *Communist Party*, p. 80.

23. Ibid., p. 81.

24. Bernhard Dahm, *History of Indonesia in the Twentieth
     Century*, trans. P. S. Falla (New York: Praeger Publishers,
     1971), p. 181.

25. Nono Anwar Makarim, "Student Activism in Indonesia" in
     Kejakinan dan Perdjuangan [Conviction and Struggle], ed.
     P. D. Latuihamallo et al. (Jakarta: BPK Gunung Mulia,
     1972), p. 275 (hereafter cited as "Student Activism"), says,

"The 1955 general election produced four massive political forces. Respectively according to their strength in the legislature, they are the PNI (Indonesian Nationalist Party comprising mostly the *'abangan'* elements in the Javanese cultural pattern or the statistical Moslems, or the Javanese syncretists), the *Masjumi* (comprising modernist coastal Moslems), the *Nahdatul Ulama* (a more orthodox rural Javanese Moslem Party), and the PKI (the Indonesian Communist Party)."

26. Brackman, *Indonesian Communism*, p. 223.

27. See Boland, *Struggle of Islam*, pp. 54-75, for an updated analysis of the *Darul Islam* movement.

28. See Alisa Zainu'ddin, *A Short History of Indonesia* (New York: Praeger Publishers, 1970), pp. 254-63.

29. See Mohammed Hatta's evaluation of what Sukarno had done in an article, "A Dictatorship Supported by Certain Groups," quoted in *Indonesian Political Thinking*, ed. Herbert Feith and Louis Castles (Ithaca: Cornell University Press, 1969), pp. 138-41 (hereafter cited as *Political Thinking*). He says,

"If we examine the groups within the *Gotong Royong* Parliament which are to support Sukarno's system, it is clear that they are not homogeneous. . . . They are able to co-operate with each other on the basis of *musyawarah*, because Sukarno is the one who makes the decisions and because they do what he says" (ibid., p. 140).

30. See Jon McEwen Reinhardt, "Nationalism and Confrontation in the Southeast Asian Islands: The Sources of Indonesian Foreign Policy" (Ph.D. dissertation, Tulane University, 1967), p. 86 (hereafter cited as "Nationalism and Confrontation"); and Donald Hindley, *The Communist Party of Indonesia, 1951-1963* (Berkeley: University of California Press, 1964), pp. 255-63 (hereafter cited as *Communist Party*).

31. See Modestus Widojoko Notoatmodjo, "*Gotong Royong* in Indonesian Administration: A Concept of Human Affairs" (Ph.D. dissertation, Indiana University, 1962; hereafter cited as "*Gotong Royong*"), for an analysis of the concept as it is applied to Guided Democracy.

32. Mintz, *Mohammed, Marx, and Marhaen*, p. 208.

33. See David Ransom, "The Berkeley Mafia and the Indonesia
     Massacre," *Ramparts*, October 1970, pp. 27-29, 40-49 (here-
     after cited as "Berkeley Mafia"), for an anti-army, pro-
     communist evaluation of the rise to power of the army. See
     Herbert Feith, *The Decline of Constitutional Democracy in
     Indonesia* (Ithaca, N. Y.: Cornell University Press, 1962),
     pp. 246-73, for a more objective account.

34. Brackman, *Communist Collapse*, p. 29.

35. The first clear declaration was made in Sukarno's speech
     of 17 August 1959 at the inauguration of Guided Democracy.
     Soeripto, *Surat Perintah 11 Maret: Muntjulnja Orde Baru,
     Runtuhnja Orde Lama* [The 11th of March Order: The
     Emergence of the New Order and the Fall of the Old Order]
     (Surabaya: Penerbit P. T. GRIP, 1969), p. 25 (hereafter
     cited as *Surat 11 Maret*).

36. See Sukarno, *An Autobiography*, as told to Cindy Adams
     (New York: Bobbs-Merrill Co., 1965), pp. 294-95.

37. Soeripto, *Surat 11 Maret*, p. 19.

38. Brackman, *Communist Collapse*, p. 13.

39. John Hughes, *Indonesian Upheaval*, p. 10.

40. See Sukarno, "Nationalism, Islam, and Marxism," in *Indo-
     nesian Political Thinking*, ed. Herbert Feith and Louis
     Castles (Ithaca, N. Y.: Cornell University Press, 1969),
     pp. 357-61. In it he posed a question:

     "Can Islam, a religion, work together in facing the
     colonial authorities with Nationalism, which attaches
     prime importance to the Nation, and with Marxism which
     is based on teachings of materialism? . . . We say
     with conviction: 'Yes, it can be done!'" (ibid.,
     p. 359).

41. See Jerry Mark Silverman, "Indonesian Marxism-Leninism:
     The Development and Consequences of Communist Policentrism"
     (Ph.D. Dissertation, Claremont Graduate School, 1967), p.
     215 (hereafter cited as "Marxism-Leninism"), for an explan-
     ation of the PKI's aims in gaining power through NASAKOM.

42. Reinhardt, "Nationalism and Confrontation," p. 118.

43. See Eduard Quiko, "The Role of Foreign Minister Subandrio
     in Indonesian Politics: An Analysis of Selected Indonesian
     Foreign Policies, 1957-1965" (Ph.D. dissertation, Southern

Illinois University, 1970), pp. 60-61, for the development of this idea.

44. See Reinhardt, "Nationalism and Confrontation," p. 153.

45. For a development of this axis, see Sheldon W. Simon, *The Broken Triangle: Peking, Djakarta and the PKI* (Baltimore: John Hopkins Press, 1969), pp. 13-110 (hereafter cited as *The Broken Triangle*).

46. Ransom, "Berkeley Mafia," p. 43.

47. "In army eyes, the fifth force would be a communist one" (Hughes, *Indonesian Upheaval*, p. 12).

48. See Willard A. Hanna, "The Indonesia Crisis--Mid-1964 Phase," *AUFS Reports: Southeast Asia Series* 12 (August 1964): 1-11, for a report of events leading to this speech.

49. From private interview. Also see Soeripto, *Surat 11 Maret*, p. 26, for a political viewpoint of the situation.

50. Ebbie C. Smith, *God's Miracles: Indonesian Church Growth* (South Pasadena, Cal.: William Carey Library, 1970), p. 153 (hereafter cited as *God's Miracles*).

6

Midnight Massacre

Traumatic events from 1965 to 1968 changed the face of Indonesia
--politically, socially, and religiously--and produced instability that aided the growth of Christianity. Once again,
President Sukarno's Independence Day speech in 1965 lends itself
to an apt analogy of the political changes, and the "turn of the
steering wheel" of the Indonesian revolution sharply to the
left.

The long-predicted communist "wave of the future" reached
tidal proportions. At the beginning of 1965, Sukarno--enraged
by the seating of Malaysia on the Security Council--withdrew
Indonesia from the United Nations. The World Health Organization, a U. N. subsidiary, and American organizations, such as the
Ford Foundation and the Peace Corps, withdrew from Indonesia:
USIS libraries were closed. Communists led in confiscating some
foreign companies and threatened a takeover of others. The
propaganda campaign against America was stepped up; Uncle Sam
was hung in effigy with a dollar sign around his neck.

The forty-fifth anniversary of the Indonesian Communist Party
was extravagantly celebrated in May 1965, with financial aid
from Peking and with President Sukarno's blessing. "It was on
this occasion, as the stadium shook with approval, that Sukarno
embraced Aidit and the PKI, lauding the party as Indonesia's
'most revolutionary, progressive group' and describing Aidit
himself as 'a fortress' of the Republic"(1).

Missionaries, particularly Americans, found it more and more difficult to work. An American missionary in West Irian was arrested and accused of aiding rebels, primarily because he owned a shortwave radio which was like those the Dutch had used, and because he had been friendly with some rebel troops(2). Dr. Bob Lambright, a Baptist missionary in East Java, was given an ultimatum to leave the country because he removed the "KOM" (for *komunisme*) from a NASAKOM sign placed on the Baptist Hospital in Kediri by a communist labor union. Members of a church which met in the Baptist Student Center in Yogyakarta reported that they had confiscated the buildings to prevent communists from seizing these "American-owned" properties. Missionaries were asked to sign a statement that they would not do anything to "disturb the situation or to prevent the government from functioning"(3).

Three comments given shortly before the coup illustrate the atmosphere that pervaded the land:

+ Justus van der Kroef, expert on Indonesian communism, wrote: "Thus the centre of political gravity had, for the time being, notably shifted in the PKI's direction, and no forces or factors were in sight that might be able to reverse the process"(4).

+ Henry Pitney van Dusen reported in May of 1965: "One discovers everywhere a sort of fatalistic, wave-of-the future, anticipation that the day of Communist takeover cannot be far distant"(5).

+ At that same time van Dusen asked one of the nation's influential Christians what the outlook for Indonesia was in the immediate future.

"Bad, very bad," he replied gloomily. But he offered no explanation and made no specific forecast. Neither he nor his comrades express such pessimism publicly, probably because they feel it would serve no useful purpose. The churches remain silent as well(6).

Less than a week before the coup, President Sukarno turned the wheel even farther to the left. He said, "We are now about to enter the second stage of the Indonesian Revolution, namely implementation of socialism"(7). He also pointed out that certain generals who were resisting the revolution might have to be eliminated. Speaking at a reception on the very night of 30 September 1965, the President emphasized that one should not be afraid to take action against his friend, his neighbor, or even his family if it were for the cause of the revolution. He gave

an illustration from a Javanese shadow-play in which Arjuna
destroyed his brothers from Kurawa(8).

With this much encouragement, Indonesian communists grasped
the steering wheel with both hands and wrenched it violently to
the left.

30th of September Movement

On the last night of September 1965, armed soldiers killed six
top Indonesian generals, including Achmad Yani, army chief of
staff. Calling themselves the "30th of September Movement," the
plotters intended to complete the attempted communist coup of
1948, which had been defeated on 30 September of that year.

Ironically, the man most feared by coup leaders, General
A. H. Nasution, escaped with only a broken ankle when the men
assigned to storm his house bungled the job. Later Nasution was
to become the leader of Indonesia's congress and help doom hopes
of a communist comeback.

Major General Suharto, commander of the army's strategic
reserve, was next in line of command. Some say that Suharto was
not marked for execution at that time, because 18 months earlier
he had attended the wedding of Lt. Col. Untung, a leading
communist conspirator(9). Other sources say he merely happened
to be at the hospital with his little daughter who had suffered
burns; still others say he was fishing where the river runs into
the sea (upon the recommendation of his *guru*)(10).

In all likelihood General Suharto was not thought important
enough at that time to be eliminated. If such is indeed the
case, then the communists seriously miscalculated. Suharto
moved quickly and decisively to crush the 30th of September
Movement--within 24 hours in Jakarta, and throughout the nation
within six weeks.

Suharto enlisted public support by exhuming the bodies of the
murdered generals from *Lubang Buaya* (Crocodile Hole), an
abandoned well south of Jakarta, where they had been stuffed
after being tortured by members of communist youth and women's
groups. Pictures were taken; descriptions of grisly events
surrounding the murders were told in macabre detail by the mass
media(11).

As much as any other one thing, this bombarding of the sensitivities of gentle Indonesians with vivid accounts of such
grotesque murders provoked them to take action against the PKI.
They had been duped into believing that communism in Indonesia
was different from communism in other lands. Even Christians

had often said, "You can be a Christian *and* a communist, because
Indonesian communism believes in God." The heartless murders of
the generals convinced Indonesians that communists really were
atheists, who could no longer be trusted to be true to the
Pancasila (the five pillars of Indonesia's state ideology, of
which the first is "Belief in the One and Only God")(12).

The Armed Forces Day Parade scheduled for 5 October was
cancelled. Instead, state funerals were held for the slain
generals. Before the nation could recover from this tragedy,
the five-year-old daughter of General Nasution died--victim of
a bullet fired by men who had come to kill her father. It was
at her funeral that Navy Chief Admiral Eddy Martadinata brushed
close to anti-communist Moslem student leaders and spat a single
word from the corner of his mouth: *"Sikat!"* ("Sweep!")(13). To
Indonesians (who pride themselves on being able to interpret
enigmatic sayings), this word meant the time had come for the
Moslems to loose their pent-up fury on their atheistic enemies,
the communists.

The next morning they started their "sweep" by demolishing
the new PKI headquarters building. The purge had begun.

Who's Steering?

For the next six months there was a continual fight between
Sukarno and Suharto over control of the steering wheel.
Sukarno had stated that Suharto had been given authority to
restore order, but each time Suharto moved against the communists
who had tried to wreck the country, Sukarno countermanded his
actions. Sukarno accused the army of trying to turn the revolution radically to the right, and dismissed the coup attempt as
just a "ripple on the ocean of the Indonesian Revolution"(14).
Sukarno seemed determined to rehabilitate the Communist Party
and re-establish his control over the two main forces, the army
and the PKI, in order to maintain his own control.

Sukarno's blatant intransigence was the last straw for the
army, who decided there must be a change of leadership. The
President probably could have remained in office had he been
willing to ban the Communist Party, but his adamant refusal to
do so guaranteed his downfall. While Sukarno and Suharto
struggled for control of the steering wheel, the people began
to demand that this *"dualisme"* be resolved(15).

The dualism was clear in speeches of the two men: Suharto
condemned the 30th of September Movement and its attempted coup
as counter-revolutionary, but Sukarno did not mention the coup
attempt. Suharto said that three of the four armed services
were resolved to crush the Movement, while Sukarno ordered the

armed forces to return to their respective posts and remain
there. Suharto invited the support of the people to annihilate
the Movement, and Sukarno urged the people to remain calm.
Suharto announced that he had temporarily been given the leadership of the army, but Sukarno announced that he himself was
leader of the army.

By 11 November 1965 the insurrection could be declared
defeated, but the war over the steering wheel was in no way
over. Sukarno refused to ban the PKI, but the army insisted,
reminding Sukarno (and the public) how the communists had
stabbed them in the back in 1948. Mass killings of communists
took place in the countryside (particularly in Central and East
Java) through December 1965, and small-scale killings continued
through the first quarter of 1966. When Sukarno implored the
army to help stop the killing of communists, they replied that
the people could not be controlled because Sukarno had refused
to ban the PKI(16).

During this time the army still gave lip-service to all the
revolutionary slogans of Sukarno, proclaiming that they were
continuing Confrontation against the NEKOLIM. They knew the
almost magical hold Sukarno had on his people, particularly the
Javanese. General Suharto and the army strove desperately to
avert a civil war between communists and other elements. Such
a war had been predicted for whenever Sukarno died. To dump
the first President of the country unceremoniously could have
precipitated such a clash. The army was careful not to use its
arms to gain victory at the sacrifice of national unity.

The contrast between the two forces began to be characterized as *Orde Lama*, or *Orla* (the Old Order), led by Sukarno and
Orde Baru, or *Orba* (the New Order), led by Suharto.

It was at this point that the students, calling themselves
"the '66 Generation," came to the aid of *Orde Baru*. They
organized the Action Committee of Indonesian Students, and
began to demonstrate for lowered taxes and prices, the "re-
tooling" of the cabinet, and a ban of the PKI and all its
affiliates. Members of this Action Committee were in almost
every case affiliated with student religious organizations--
precisely those groups that had suffered most from political
trends of the past several years(17). Hindley states that they
were largely non-*santri* (non-Islamic)(18). They were later
joined by the High School Pupils Action Front(19).

Orde Baru, lacking a mass organization, used the students to
gain authenticity and popular leadership. They used the
communists' own tactics to overthrow the PKI: scapegoating,
which the PKI had employed against them with great effect in
the pre-coup period; and student demonstrations, which the PKI

had used so cleverly against American interests(20). The army
refused to be precipitated into taking action ahead of public
opinion. Patiently they allowed such sentiment to be generated
by the students. Thus they acted only when pushed from behind
by a wave of popular indignation.

This tactic is best illustrated by the crucial events leading
to Sukarno's surrender of power to Suharto. On 21 February 1966
Sukarno said he had reached his "political solution." He named
a new cabinet, including communists and ousting General
Nasution. But he had greviously miscalculated the mood of the
nation. The populace expected Nasution or Suharto to react
immediately, but it appeared they were retreating to the sidelines and allowing Sukarno once again to grasp the steering
wheel.

Meanwhile students demonstrated in the streets and sacked the
Foreign Ministry office; they claimed to find evidence that the
Indonesian Communist Party had masterminded the 30th of
September Movement in an attempt to overthrow the government(21).
In retaliation, Sukarno banned the student action fronts and
forbade any meetings of over five persons. Instead of slowing
the students, this action inflamed them, and they were soon
joined by their brothers and sisters from the elementary schools.
One informant said, "When the little children began to march, I
knew we would win, because no soldier is going to shoot a little
boy who is the age of his son or brother"(22).

Fifty thousand demonstrators brought the city of Jakarta to a
standstill on 24 February, the day the new cabinet was to be
installed at the Presidential palace. One student, Arif Rachman
Hakim, was shot and became the martyr around whom other students
rallied(23).

Sukarno talked with military leaders on 10 March and called a
cabinet meeting for the following day. It appeared he was still
going to try to come out on top of this very difficult situation,
just as he had done so many times in the past. As he sat in the
meeting on 11 March, someone whispered to him that unidentified
armed troups were marching on the palace. Sukarno quickly
boarded his helicopter and flew to Bogor, near Jakarta.

That afternoon three army officers, after consulting with
Suharto (who was sick and had not attended the meeting), proceeded to Bogor and finally succeeded in getting Sukarno to sign
a document which in effect legalized the *Orde Baru* and turned
the steering wheel over to Suharto(24). The next day an order
went out under Suharto's signature to ban the PKI.

One week later Prime Minister Subandrio and many other
cabinet members were arrested. It was only at this time, 18
March 1966, that Suharto issued a command to stop the killing of
communists, and, in a companion command, ordered the students
back to school(25).

With these edicts the first phase of the toppling of the Old
Order had come to a close. Of the students' role in bringing
these changes about, Makarim said:

In 60 days they managed to topple two cabinets, bring tens
of thousands of students and secondary school youth into
the streets, voice their demands, rule Djakarta for one
full month, arrest Ministers of cabinet, search the Central
Bank and establish "the Children's Revolution"(26).

Deposing a Dictator

General Suharto was now steersman of the ship of state,
although the title was still held by Sukarno. Suharto immediately began establishing the New Order. The cabinet was
reshuffled, and new Foreign Minister Adam Malik began talks with
Malaysia to end Confrontation. Plans were announced for
Indonesia to return to the United Nations. Reparations were
promised for confiscated property of foreign countries.
Political prisoners of the Sukarno regime were released. And
Sultan Hamengkubuwono, new Minister of Economics, Finance, and
Development, began efforts to slow down soaring inflation and
restore economic stability(27).

Sukarno did not take these actions lightly; he balked at
every announcement by Suharto(28). He ranted and raved, even
claiming he had not surrendered his power in the document he had
signed on 11 March 1966. Suharto, on the other hand, calmly
insisted that Sukarno be treated courteously but firmly.

Suharto waited a full year before he officially replaced
Sukarno as acting President(29). The students did not always
agree with Suharto's tortuously slow pace, and sometimes this
strained relationships between them and the army. But Suharto
showed he was in control of that situation also, when he
forcibly stopped their demonstrations.

During that year, the trials of Lt. Col. Untung, leader of
the 30th of September Movement; Nyoto, second in command of the
PKI; Air Force Marshal Omar Dhani, who had been implicated in
the coup attempt; and Subandrio, Prime Minister during the Old
Order, proceeded before a military tribunal. These trials not
only implicated the men involved, but also seemed to be shadow-
plays pointing to the old puppeteer, Sukarno, as mastermind of

the Old Order (if not an actual accomplice in the coup attempt) (30).

The public demanded that Sukarno give congress an account of his actions related to the coup. His statement on 10 January 1967, dismissing any suggestion that he was in any way responsible for any of the country's ills, infuriated the New Order and the '66 Generation. Further demonstrations would possibly have forced Sukarno to go on trial, had it not been that Suharto appealed to congress to act authoritatively but tactfully toward Sukarno. On 12 March 1967 they stripped Sukarno of his powers and left his trial up to Acting President Suharto, who quietly let the matter drop. After another year, congress made Suharto full President of Indonesia.

Sukarno, a lonely and discredited individual, died two years later. The last vestiges of the Old Order were buried with him.

Crisis and Christ

Tension created by the instability of the government probably had more effect on Indonesians' becoming Christians than the decree that everyone must profess a religion. When congress and parliament proposed that President Sukarno be relieved of his office in 1967, his millions of Javanese followers were shocked. Their whole mind-set was toward the stable "king," who produced security and peace throughout the realm(31). Soeripto says, "The resolution and memorandum of the Congress and Parliament really shook the people, because they had not counted on or expected a proposal that was so strict and hard(32).

Bidney proposes a theory of change based on crisis situations. He says people are willing to accept new behavior patterns during times of stress which arise as members of a given society become aware that their present condition is intolerable and decide to accept innovation.

Bidney divides such times of stress into *practical* and *theoretical* crises: A *practical* crisis arises when some form of resistance causes suspension of normative behavior, and human interaction becomes incompatible with the existing framework of institutions, customs, or behavior. A *theoretical* crisis occurs when accepted theories, ideals, or beliefs lose their validity because new facts or evidence have altered the normative belief system. A practical crisis may lead to a theoretical one(33). Both of these crisis situations occurred in Indonesia, particularly to those who found their animistic beliefs challenged and no longer acceptable.

Traumatic events occurred in Indonesia of the 1960's: the
fall of Sukarno; dissolution of the Communist Party; the death
of friends and family; worsening economic conditions; conflicts
among the army, the Moslems, and the communists; and uncertainty
of the future political system. As these traumatic events con-
verged on the average Javanese, they produced disorientation(34).
Disintegration of the order he had known caused him to seek a
new foothold.

The government contributed to this crisis syndrome by continually warning of a communist comeback(35). Communists did
continue sporadic efforts to sabotage the New Order throughout
the 1960's. No doubt the government found it to their advantage
to continue warning people of such attempts, but this also
helped keep the situation unstable.

In regard to the role of conflict, Tasdik says, "Marxist
Communism has always been a militant rival to the Christian
faith, as a matter of principle. So disappointment towards
communism might be considered as one of the serious reasons for
them to enter the Church." He goes on to say that the aim and
purpose of the converts involved:

(1) Looking for a refuge in the Church in a time of great
tribulation. The Church is recognized as a place for
security and peace. (2) Hoping to achieve a better and
orderly way of living in peace and harmony, as is testified by Christian people(36).

Christianity was one of the beneficiaries of these political
events that plowed up traditional foundations. The Javanese
churches took advantage of the situation by dropping in the seed
of the gospel.

The greatest church growth occurred during the years 1965-
1968. Taking into account that many of those baptized in 1968
had begun catechism classes in 1967, the most productive years
were from 1965 to 1967. Our evaluation of this period will be
withheld until the end of Chapter 7 because other factors were
also involved.

In Chapter 5, and in Chapter 6 to this point, we have
focussed our attention on the first of three major political
factors relating to church growth in Indonesia, namely: *The
role of instability and insecurity resulting from political
conflict.* But for some 21 million Indonesians (including
families) previously associated with the Communist Party, there
was a more difficult problem than general instability and
insecurity: They faced the prospect of violent death.

This leads us to the second of the three major political factors, *the role of fear in the search for a protector*, which will be discussed in the remainder of the chapter.

FEAR AND THE SEARCH FOR A PROTECTOR

The massacre that followed the fall of the 30th of September Movement provoked thousands of people to seek a protector. The ransacking of PKI headquarters in Jakarta was only the beginning. Pent-up fury and frustration of decades of conflict was turned loose.

Word passed throughout Indonesia via an incredibly fast grapevine to members of Moslem youth groups that the *kafir* (infidels) must be eliminated(37). Simultaneously, the army, with emergency powers given it during Confrontation with Malaysia, arrested thousands of communists in Jakarta. Fifty-seven members of Parliament and more than a hundred members of congress were suspended for suspected complicity in GESTAPU (a clever catchword with an obvious double meaning, coined from *"Gerakan September Tigapuluh,"* or 30th of September Movement(38).

Communist mayors of the important Central and East Java cities of Cirebon, Solo, Magelang, Salatiga, and Surabaya were either dismissed or imprisoned. A purge began of government departments, including the armed forces.

Aidit, leader of the PKI, fled to Central Java and attempted to rally communist forces. Members of the army's Diponegoro division in Central Java who were loyal to the government fought against these communist bands. Para-commandos of General Suharto's Strategic Command helped bring the situation in Jakarta under control during the first two weeks of October, and then set out on a "parade" through Central Java. Communists distributed leaflets declaring that these red-bereted troops were really Malaysian troops invading Indonesia and must be resisted.

General Sarwo Edhy, commander of the para-commandos, convinced the populace with the crisp efficiency of a machine gun that he represented the legal Indonesian government and would brook no rebellion in the area. He found the bodies of the Yogyakarta regimental commander and his chief of staff, who had been murdered by communists, and used them as examples of communist brutality. Just as the army was preparing for a massive show of force at their funerals in Yogyakarta, word came that communists had launched a wholesale liquidation of their enemies in the nearby Klaten-Boyolali area. Two hundred and fifty political leaders were killed and about fifteen thousand people fled the region(39). Para-commandos quickly smashed the

revolt and ended effective resistance to the government in
Central Java.

Mass defections from the Communist Party had already begun in
West Java. But this was not to deter the Moslems, who had
declared a *jihad* (holy war) on the *kafir* (heathen)(40). Sarwo
Edhy said,

> We decided to encourage the anti-Communist civilians to
> help with the job. In Solo we gathered together the
> youth, the nationalist groups, the religious (Moslem)
> organizations. We gave them two or three days training,
> then sent them out to kill the Communists(41).

Red is Dead

Persons who had been listed as members of the Communist
Party or its affiliated organizations were rounded up by the
army or sought out by anti-communists. Usually they were led to
a lonely area, their throats cut, and their bodies buried in
shallow graves or thrown in a river. The Central Java executions were more orderly than those in East Java, where the
Islamic *Nahdatul Ulama* party was strongest(42). In East Java
mass killings took place because the army did not exercise as
close control over the people as in Central Java. On occasion
members of the armed forces participated. One officer informant
bragged, "Day after day I did nothing else from morning till
night but kill, kill, kill the communists"(43).

Mass executions continued unabated through December of 1965;
smaller scale executions continued for the first three months of
1966. So many people were killed that the disposal of bodies
became a serious problem: The Brantas River near Kediri was
choked with bodies. Countless shallow graves were dug on
lonely rubber planations in East Java. Other parts of Indonesia
experienced much the same thing, but the Central and East Java
provinces were probably the hardest hit(44).

A spokesman for a Moslem youth organization said, "So from
October to January, we took revenge. We knew who were communists, and we would go to the villages and *kampongs* and kill
them. The people just went wild against the communists"(45).
Doubtless many innocent people died, as some seized the opportunity to participate in these clandestine affairs and settle
longstanding business, personal, political, and ethnic debts.

No one knows how many people lost their lives in this pogrom:
estimates vary widely. The most common figures range between
300,000 and 500,000(46).

Why?

The oft-asked question, "Why did Indonesians turn on their own countrymen with such ferocity?" has many answers.

+ The most immediate reason is expressed in the statements often heard, "It was them or us," or "We killed them before they could kill us"(47). Win makes the point that if the coup had succeeded, killings would still have been carried out, but this time either against the army or against the religious groups(48).

+ A second reason was the constant pressure that communists had brought to bear upon the people. Often the PKI would turn village heads out of office, pressure others to submit to their demands or move, and force landlords to give up their land. Religious groups especially felt this pressure(49). Two statements will illustrate: "To understand, you must appreciate the bullying tactics of the Communists," and "Westerners do not understand the mental terror they [Communists] inflicted on us"(50).

+ A third reason was the desire of Moslems to eliminate those who had blocked their path to power in politics. In addition, some Moslems believed that they would ensure their salvation by killing the *kafir*.

+ A fourth reason, as mentioned above, was the settling of old scores in personal, business, or ethnic conflicts.

+ A fifth reason has been stated in the form of a psychological reaction inherent in the Indonesian personality. Van der Kroef says that Indonesians' inadequate super-ego formation incites a commensurately unbearable effort to repress hostile drives. Unless these hostile drives are constructively channeled, they must vent themselves on hate objects. "The need for hate objects and for repetitive ritualization in personal and collective behavior, is the response to the profound feelings of anxiety engendered by the rebellion against the traditional, dominant authoritarian culture traits so deeply embedded in Indonesian life"(51).

Van Niel adds that violent village outbursts are endemic to Indonesian life, when a combination of fears and frustrations are combined with a leader who fulfills some of their aspirations for the *"Ratu Adil"* (the proverbial "Just King," whose coming will herald a better life for all)(52). The average Indonesian will patiently forbear social, political, and religious pressure far longer than one would expect, but when

he reaches the breaking point or gets an opportunity that
promises some possibility of success, he may react violently.

Some authors have tried to say that the Malay stock (from
which many Indonesians are descended) has a tendency to "run
amok." *Amok* is indeed a Malay derivative, but this seems too
broad a generalization to be accepted for a whole race of
people. The killings were not done in a state of amok, but
carefully, individually, and quietly.

All the above factors were operative during the time of the
massacre. One other should also be mentioned. There is a
fatalism inherent in Indonesian life which easily accepts whatever happens as the will of God. The majority of communists who
were killed died without resistance and often without even a
murmur(53). One Indonesian teenager said quietly to her tor-
mentors, "Go ahead and kill me; I would have killed you had we
won"(54). This same fatalism caused others to accept the events
as being the will of God. After all, the highest authorities of
the land appeared to condone the massacre and allowed their sub-
ordinates to participate in it.

The Massacre and Church Growth

It should not be difficult to see why multitudes of Indonesians sought for a protector during and after the reign of
terror. Soeripto reflects the general opinion of the populace
when he says, "The majority of the people of Indonesia are
religious; therefore, it is self-evident that they reject
communism and the PKI. Only a very small group of Indonesians
do not yet have a religion; it is clear this includes (among
others) the communists"(55). This means that any person who was
not officially registered in one of the recognized religions was
suspect. When coupled with the government's decree that all
Indonesians must believe in God and accept one of the recognized
religions, one can see the strong incentive to make a decision.

Tasdik's conclusion is:

The aftermath of the G-30-S PKI Movement created severe
tensions and culminated in murder and assassination,
especially in East Java. Murder and killing were directed
toward the adherents of religions (Islam, as well as
Christians [*sic*] and this evoked repercussions of the
same kind. This created chaos and disorder, fear, dis-
tress, suspicion, and so on. Those who felt their life
[*sic*] to be threatened took their refuge in religion, and
others who were not directly in danger followed in a mass
movement(56).

In another article, Tasdik included a table which showed that reasons most often given for the decisions were "fear of other people" and "being threatened"(57). No doubt the fear of being associated with the communists, and thereby losing one's job, position, influence, possessions, or even life, was the initial reason for many turning to religion. The search for protection, linked with the decree of the government, continued to play a significant role on through the year 1971(58).

An important question for consideration is, "Why did so many turn to Christianity, a minority religion?" No more than 8 percent of the Indonesian population professes to be Christian, and the percentage was even smaller in 1965.

Our discussion of religio-cultural factors has already given a broad base for answering this question. Later chapters dealing with social and religious reasons for conversions will further broaden that base. Here, it is sufficient to establish the fact that recriminations following the communist coup attempt in 1965, and the government's emphasis on religion as a deterrent to communism's staging a comeback, played significant roles in the large number of Indonesians who embraced Christianity.

NOTES

1. Brackman, *Communist Collapse*, p. 38.

2. Harold Lovestrand, *Hostage in Jakarta* (Chicago: Moody Press, 1969).

3. Personal experience.

4. Van der Kroef, *Communist Party*, p. 294.

5. H. P. van Dusen, "Indonesia Today," *Christian Century* 82 (5 May 1965): 586.

6. H. P. van Dusen, "Indonesia Today," *Christian Century* 82 (12 May 1965): 617.

7. Simon, *The Broken Triangle*, p. 109.

8. See Soeripto, *Surat 11 Maret*, p. 191, and Brackman, *Communist Collapse*, p. 71. Also see Arthur J. Dommen, "The

Attempted Coup in Indonesia," *China Quarterly* 25 (January–
March 1966): 160–64.

9.   Roger K. Paget, "Indonesian Politics: The New Order
     Emerges," *The Bulletin of the Atomic Scientists*, February
     1968, p. 30 (hereafter cited as "New Order Emerges").

10. See van der Kroef, *Since Sukarno*, p. 13.

11. Paget, "New Order Emerges," p. 31.

12. See Boland, *Struggle of Islam*, p. 38.

13. Hughes, *Indonesian Upheaval*, p. 132.

14. Ibid., p. 198.

15. See Donald Hindley, "*Aliran* and the Fall of the Old Order,"
     Indonesia 9 (April 1970): 46–65 (hereafter cited as "Fall
     of the Old Order"), for a description of this struggle for
     control.

16. Hughes, *Indonesian Upheaval*, pp. 197–99.

17. Paget, "New Order Emerges," p. 32.

18. Hindley, "Fall of the Old Order," p. 58.

19. For an analysis of the student movement, see Stephen A.
     Douglas, *Political Socialization and Student Activism in
     Indonesia* (Chicago: University of Illinois Press, 1970),
     pp. 153–74 (hereafter cited as *Student Activism*).

20. Simon, *The Broken Triangle*, p. 112.

21. For evidence that the PKI was implicated in the coup as the
     government claimed, see van der Kroef, *Since Sukarno*, pp.
     8–9, and Peter Polomka, *Since Sukarno*, pp. 72–78. Polomka
     does not commit himself to either position, but states that
     the army's explanation makes the most sense. See Silverman,
     "Marxism-Leninism," pp. 212–50, for arguments that the
     evidence is inconclusive.

22. Private interview.

23. Hughes, *Indonesian Upheaval*, p. 213.

24. See Lt. Gen. M. Jusuf, "Pengalaman Saya Dgn: Super Semar"
     [My Experience with Super Semar], *Suara Merdeka*, 17 March
     1973, for a first-person account of the meeting.

25. See Soeripto, *Surat 11 Maret*, pp. 92-93, for the text of these announcements.

26. Makarim, "Student Activism," p. 275.

27. For brief descriptions of Adam Malik and Sultan Hamengku Buwono, see Polomka, *Since Sukarno*, pp. 101-2.

28. See L. G. M. Jaquet, "From Sukarno to Suharto," *Round Table* 243 (July 1971): 240-48.

29. The first reason for Suharto's delay was his own genuine insistence on upholding the constitution and doing everything legally. Second, he was a Javanese and preferred to accomplish the changeover in the indirect Javanese manner. Third, he knew the sway Sukarno held over his people, particularly in Central and East Java. Fourth, his own patriotism and national pride at what Sukarno had accomplished in welding three thousand inhabited islands into one nation deterred him. Fifth, he perhaps realized that he needed Sukarno to help deflect criticism from himself and the army during the interim period while the New Order was being planned and set up. See Hughes, *Indonesian Upheaval*, pp. 252-54, for his reasons.

30. See Nugroho Notosusanto and Ismail Saleh, *The Coup: Attempt of the September 30 Movement in Indonesia* (Jakarta: P. T. Pembimbling Masa-Jakarta, 1968), pp. 107-51 (hereafter cited as *September 30 Movement*).

31. Soemarsaid Moertono, *State and Statecraft in Old Java: A Study of the Later Mataram Period, 16th to 19th Century* (Ithaca, N. Y.: Modern Indonesia Project, Cornell University Press, 1968), p. 37 (hereafter cited as *State and Statecraft*).

32. Soeripto, *Surat 11 Maret*, p. 169.

33. David Bidney, *Theoretical Anthropology* (New York: Columbia University Press, 1953), pp. 131-34.

34. Simatupang, "Situation and Challenge" p. 20, says: "The ever-present danger of the state being turned into an Islamic state, the latent threat of communism, the possibility of Militarism always preoccupy the mind of the people."

35. Seven years after the coup, a cover story, "30 September, 7 Tahun Kemudian" [Seven Years After the 30th of September Movement], *Tempo*, September 1972, pp. 5-10, warned of new

attempts by the banned PKI to sabotage the government. For
an extended analysis of PKI efforts, see Polomka, *Since
Sukarno*, pp. 157-76.

36. Tasdik, *Motives for Conversion*, p. 12.

37. See Donald Kirk, "Anti-Communist Crusade of Indonesia's
Moslems," *Illustrated Reporter* 34 (January 1966): 41-42.

38. Hughes, *Indonesian Upheaval*, pp. 137-38.

39. Brackman, *Communist Collapse*, p. 109. Also see Notosusanto
and Saleh, "September 30 Movement," pp. 41-65, 75-76, for
actions taken by local commanders in Central Java.

40. The order was first given by individual Islamic leaders,
and later given the backing of the Muhammadiyah movement,
9-11 November 1965. See Boland, *Struggle of Islam*, pp.
145-47, for the text of the announcement, which said in
part:

"The extermination of the GESTAPU/PKI and the Nekolim
is a religious duty. . . . This religious duty is not
(only) recommended . . . but obligatory . . . , even an
individual obligation. . . . And because this action
and this struggle must be carried out by consolidating
all our strength--mental, physical, and material--there-
fore, this action and this struggle are nothing less
than a holy war (*jihad*). This holy war, according to
religious law, is not (only) recommended, but obligatory, even an individual obligation" (p. 146).

Boland quotes one of his informants as claiming that the
destruction of the GESTAPU/PKI was "*the* greatest victory of
Islam in Indonesia" (p. 147).

41. Hughes, *Indonesian Upheaval*, p. 151.

42. See Jacob Walkin, "Moslem-Communist Confrontation in East
Java, 1964-1965," *Orbis* 13 (Fall 1969): 822-47.

43. Private interview.

44. Hughes, *Indonesian Upheaval*, p. 188.

45. Ibid., p. 159.

46. See Chapter 2, Note 1.

47. Brackman, *Communist Collapse*, p. 116.

48. Win, "Political Socialization," p. 139.

49. See Walkin, "Moslem-Communist Confrontation," pp. 822-47.

50. Brackman, *Communist Collapse*, p. 116.

51. Justus M. van der Kroef, *Indonesian Social Evolution: Some Psychological Considerations* (Amsterdam: N. V. Boekhandel Antiquariaat en Uitgeverij, C. P. J. van der Peet, 1958), pp. 93-95 (hereafter cited as *Social Evolution*).

52. Robert van Niel, *The Emergence of the Modern Indonesian Elite* (The Hague: W. van Hoeve, 1960), p. 20 (hereafter cited as *Modern Indonesian Elite*).

53. Hughes, *Indonesian Upheaval*, p. 60.

54. Private interview.

55. Soeripto, *Surat 11 Maret*, p. 3.

56. Tasdik, *Motives for Conversion*, p. 11.

57. Tasdik, "New Congregations in Indonesia," p. 4.

58. The Director of Hindu-Buddhist Affairs for the province of Central Java said in a private interview that Hinduism's resurgence began in 1968 and has continued unabated. It appears that the Hindu religion got a later start and is continuing to grow, while the Christian movement began to slow down toward the end of the period.

7

A Government Opens the Door

Pancasila is the statement of five principles upon which the Indonesian nation was established: divine omnipotence, humanity, national consciousness, democracy, and social justice. The interpretation of the first principle, *Ke-Tuhanan Yang Maha Esa*(1), relates to this study.

The foundation of state ideology upon *Pancasila* established religious freedom which made church growth possible. Suharto's actions of 1965 and thereafter, in crushing the attempted communist coup and setting up the New Order, were all based on the Indonesian constitution and *Pancasila*.

This brings us, then, to a consideration of the third of three major political factors relating to recent church growth in Indonesia (the other two having been discussed in Chapters 5 and 6).

THE GOVERNMENT'S STANCE CONCERNING RELIGION

Sukarno's exposition of the five principles called *Pancasila* reveals that he had tried to synthesize all the divergent thought he found in Indonesian life. He enunciated some of these principles as early as 1927, clarified them while in exile in 1933, and promulgated them as the basis for the new nation on 1 June 1945(2).

Later enunciations by Sukarno, such as the ill-fated NASAKOM, were really elucidations of his basic beliefs expounded in

Pancasila, which is a synthesis of Western Democratic, modern Islamic, Marxist, and indigenous-village democratic and communal ideas. It is the embodiment of the Indonesian motto, "Unity in Diversity," and herein lies both its strength and its weakness. Diversity of thought and belief in Indonesian culture constantly threatens to disrupt the basic unity that Sukarno devoted his life to inspiring(3).

The Moslem, the Marxist, and the nationalist each has found in *Pancasila* his own belief. Struggles since independence can be viewed as a series of attempts by each of these groups to gain a dominant position(4).

Moslems challenged the vagueness of the first principle as Sukarno had stated it. They were demanding "one religion," while Sukarno and Hatta were emphasizing "one God"(5). Sukarno's answer to them, in his *Pancasila* speech before independence was declared, revealed his perceptive evaluation that orthodox Moslems did not form a majority in the Indonesian nation:

> If we really are a Muslim people, let us work as hard as possible so that most of the seats in the people's representative body which we will create, are occupied by Muslim delegates. . . . Then, automatically, laws issuing from this people's representative body will be Islamic, also.

> I am even convinced that only if this has actually happened may it be said that the religion of Islam truly lives in the souls of the people, so that 60 percent, 70 percent, 80 percent, 90 percent of the delegates are Muslims, prominent Muslims, learned Muslims. Therefore, I say that only when that has happened, will Islam be alive in Indonesia, and not merely lip service to Islam. We assert that 90 percent of us profess the religion Islam, but see in this gathering how many percent give their votes to Islam? Forgive me for raising this question. For me, this is proof that Islam is not yet truly alive among the people(6).

Between the time Sukarno made that speech in June 1945 and the time independence was declared in August 1945, Moslems issued their own declaration of independence, the Jakarta Charter. It stated that the Republic "shall be based on Belief in God, with the obligation of practicing the laws of Islam for the adherents of that religion"(7). But it was the nationalists' Declaration of Independence that won the day, not the one proposed by Moslem leaders.

The resulting guarantee of religious freedom cannot be over-emphasized as the factor that opened the door to church growth

in Indonesia. Had Moslems been able to form a government on the
basis of the Jakarta Charter, Christian missionary and evangelistic efforts would have been permitted among less than 10 percent of the population as is the case in neighboring Malaysia.
Once again we can see God's hand in the glove, using political
events to prepare the way for future spread of the gospel and
growth of churches.

Although Moslems accepted the Declaration of Independence by
the nationalists, attempts to get the Jakarta Charter instated
as the law of the land have never ceased. When peaceful means
failed, an armed attempt was made beginning 7 August 1949, which
was not completely defeated until 1965(8).

When Sukarno proclaimed "Guided Democracy," he gave credit to
the Jakarta Charter as one of the inspirations for independence.
Moslems felt this gave them legal acknowledgment of the validity
of the Charter.

When in 1968 the Indonesian congress sought a new ideology to
replace the deposed Sukarno's ideology, orthodox Moslems proposed the Jakarta Charter, citing Sukarno's previous acknowledgment as tacit approval(9). Opposition from Christians, the
Partai Sosialis Indonesia independent group, and army leaders
resulted in a deadlock. The Jakarta Charter was again rejected
as state ideology, much to the disappointment of Moslem leaders.

One reason why Christianity was favored (or at least protected) following the coup was the fact that the government did
not want orthodox Moslems to try once again to attack *Pancasila*
and institute Moslem law as the law of the state for its adherents. The Moslems protested that they were not asking for an
Islamic state, but that they only wanted to require those who
professed Islam to practice it(10). In effect this would be
almost the same thing, since any Indonesian not claiming another
religion is considered a Moslem. It would mean that 85 to 90
percent of the population would be forced to follow Islamic law.

Since the New Order had come to power by defending *Pancasila*
(11), its leaders were under obligation to continue to defend
it. (In September 1964 D. N. Aidit, Indonesian Communist Party
chief, had allowed himself to stray away from the agreed-upon
strategy of collaboration with the nationalists when he said
that once unity had been achieved, *Pancasila* would no longer be
needed because it was only a unifying instrument. Nationalists
remembered his words and used them against the PKI following the
attempted coup.)(12).

Christians had also defended *pancasila*; in fact, a large
number of the student demonstrators were from Christian

political groups(13). We cannot say that the army purposely
gave any advantage to Christianity, but rather than both groups
found it advantageous to be on the same side.

Religion by Decree

It was on the basis of *Pancasila* that the New Order (President
Suharto's administration) decreed that all Indonesians must
believe in God and must profess a sanctioned religion. Religions
recognized by the Indonesian government are Islam, Balinese
Hinduism, Buddhism, Catholicism, and Christianity. A sixth,
Confucianism, was finally granted the status of a religion after
the initial decree was made.

It has already been established that this decree was perhaps
the single most important political factor in conversions to
Christianity--and to other religions as well. (See pp. 63-64.)
Tasdik says,

> Due to the State propaganda and encouragements [*sic*] to
> adhere to some (established) religion (based on the idea
> of the *pancasila*), most people who were living in this
> situation did not hesitate to enter and join the existing
> established religions according to their choice, Christian-
> ity, Buddhism, Hinduism, or, of course, Islam(14).

The decree excluded animistic religions and mystic groups,
thereby leaving their adherents groping for a religion that was
authorized by the government. In some cases entire mystic cults
followed their leaders into Christianity or another religion.
Many Javanese testified that the decree caused them to rethink
the whole matter of religion and to seek the best one.

The Director of Hindu-Buddhist Affairs for Central Java
stated that thousands of animists became Hindus, especially
after 1968. He said one factor was that they had examined other
religions and had not found them satisfactory; but when he had
explained that their animistic practices were in reality Hindu,
entire communities in Central Java (particularly near Klaten,
Boyolali, Solo, Yogyakarta, Wonosari, Pekalongan, and Tegal)
accepted Hinduism(15). This gave them an easy way to meet the
government's demand and still maintain the status quo.

It was reported that one village posted a sign saying, "This
is a Christian village." A government official asked the
villagers when they had become Christians. They replied, "Well,
we haven't yet, but we've already decided to become Christians
and are just waiting for somebody to come tell us how"(16).

The effect of the decree was that some Indonesians immediately accepted an authorized religion; others began to seek for a religion that they could truly believe and follow; and a third group began to rethink their religious situation, thus opening the door to Christian witness.

Government Resistance to Moslam Pressure

After the Sukarno-Suharto struggle was settled, the nation did not have to wait long for the next political crisis--this one with religious overtones. The Moslems believed it was time they were paid their due. Their archenemy, the Indonesian Communist Party, had been banned; Sukarno, who had kept them from establishing a Moslem state, was out of power; and the army, which they had supported throughout the critical political struggle, was in control. They felt that surely at this time they would be able to reap the benefits of half a century of struggle, and institute Islamic law as the law of the land. The urgency of their situation was made more pressing by the fact that while they were busy eradicating communists, thousands of their own adherents had become Christians.

Moslems staged an offensive against Christianity in several areas, beginning in April 1967 after congress had settled the issue of who was president. Religious liberty became a political issue for the rest of the year, and intermittently, up to the present. The Moslems mounted a well-planned (if sporadic) offensive to recoup their losses to Christianity. They aimed to consolidate their position against Christians by a legalization of the Jakarta Charter or, at the very least, by a law which prohibited both missionary activity among adherents of another religion and one's changing his own religion.

A series of demonstrations, burnings of churches, and ransackings of church buildings and schools by Moslems were used in a kind of reverse logic as "evidence" that Christian missionary aggressiveness had incited the Moslems to react. Articles in Moslem publications alleged that Christian missionaries were exploiting the needs of the people by giving interest-free loans, food, and the like, to win converts from Islam. In July 1967 a bill was introduced in congress to restrict foreign funds or personnel from entering Indonesia to aid the churches. It failed to pass(17).

Continued incidents between Moslems and Christians caused the government to call for tolerance and peace, lest "communist elements" be allowed to divide the Indonesian people again. (Communists were blamed for almost any disorder that threatened the uneasy peace.) The Department of Religious Affairs in each province sought to settle the issue by getting groups of

Christians and Moslems to agree not to proselyte. But the
Christians, and often the Buddhists and Hindus as well, would
not agree to be limited to working only with their present constituencies.

In an effort to prevent major conflict, the administration
sponsored a national *Musyawarah Antar Agama* (Inter-Religion
Consultation). President Suharto in his opening speech
reaffirmed basic guarantees of religious freedom under the constitution and *Pancasila*. But he also opened the way for a
compromise that would in effect freeze the existing balance
between the various faiths, by stating that "the government
should be cautious of religious activities aimed merely at
increasing the numbers of followers, especially when it seemed
to one religion that these efforts were merely aimed at attracting its own followers"(18).

The Christians, much to Suharto's dismay, adamantly rejected
the Moslem proposal that missionary activities be banned among
people already professing a religion. They protested that one
of the tenets of the Christian religion was witnessing to all
people. They secured Suharto's support by pointing out that to
accept this proposal would mean the Jakarta Charter would be put
into effect in spirit, if not in law(19). All the groups that
were non-*santri* (not consciously and exclusively Moslem) were
opposed to this *de facto* Islamic state. Therefore, the consultation ended without any decision being made.

> Christians alone could never have prevented the establish-
> ment of an Islamic state in Indonesia--and this is the
> crucial point of the political issue. At no time have
> Christians ever numbered more than six or seven percent
> of the population(20).

Christians see this as the hand of God holding the door open for
them.

Moslems also tried to use the governmental decree that all
Indonesians must embrace a religion, to force those who professed Islam to practice it. This led temporarily to a larger
attendance at the mosques, but in the long run it backfired on
them. Many of these nominal Moslems decided to find a religion
that answered their needs better than Islam--a religion that did
not force them to obey rules or to pray in a language they did
not understand. (See Chapters 2, 3, and 4 on religio-cultural
factors.)

A government interpretation of religious freedom was distributed to leaders in Central Java stating, "The Indonesian
people as a whole, and each Indonesian as an individual who

lives with others, professes a belief in God." In regard to
freedom of religion, it stated, "Every Indonesian has a moral
obligation to have a religion, but he is free to choose and to
practice his religion according to his individual convictions"
(21).

One might expect that accessions to Christianity would slow
down in 1967-68, during this period of persecution and intimida-
tion. But the almost unanimous appraisal of church leaders is
that church growth which had begun to slow down in 1968 was
actually quickened in response to the Moslem offensive, and
that the spurt of growth in 1969 was largely in reaction to
Moslem pressure.

After 1969 additions "from the world" slowed, although some
churches continued to show increased "biological growth"
(McGavran's term for baptism of children of Christians, as
opposed to baptism of persons with a non-Christian background)
(22). The stability that was being achieved by the New Order
and the build-up for the 1971 election related to this slowdown
in church growth.

Political Structure and Religious Freedom

When Suharto became Acting President in March 1967, the major
political parties, except for the Moslem *Nahdatul Ulama* party,
were weaker than they had been ten years earlier. From 1957
onward the political parties had survived solely when they were
of use to one of the major contenders in the power struggle.
The *Masyumi* party and the *Partai Sosialis Indonesia* (PSI) had
been banned in 1960, the *Murba* Party in 1964, and the PKI in
1966. That left only the *Partai Nasional Indonesia* (PNI) and
the *Nahdatul Ulama* (NU) from the "Big Four" of the 1955 elections. By 1966 the PNI organization was in a state of chaos.

Only the NU emerged stronger, as an organization, from
the previous decade. It had bowed before the Sukarno
wind, risen again with the New Order, benefited from the
dissolution of the *Masjumi*, and throughout, retained
control of the patronage-dispensing department of
religious affairs(23).

The vacuum left by the fall of the Communist Party was filled
by other political parties that asserted themselves in the in-
fighting leading up to the proposed election of 1968(24). This
struggle proceeded along lines already drawn: Moslem-Christian,
Moslem-nationalist, *abangan-santri*, civilian-army, and tradi-
tionalist-modernist. The period was characterized by an
attempted resurgence of the Moslems, restoration of the PNI, and
the New Order's forming an alliance both with modern technocrats

and intellectuals on the one hand and with traditional *abangan* and *priyayi* Javanese on the other.

The Moslems were the first to take the initiative. As early as December of 1965, the Moslem Co-ordinating Body representing sixteen former *Masyumi*-affiliated groups began to spearhead a drive to rehabilitate the *Masyumi* Party. These leaders were from the Reform Moslem community, sympathetic to modernism, somewhat socialistic, and generally anti-communist. After their banning in 1960 they had been isolated from the center of political power until they supported the army in disposing of the communists and Sukarno. Nevertheless, army officers were reluctant to allow the *Masyumi* Party to be resurrected because many of its leaders had taken part in rebellions of the late 1950's(25).

The election proposed for 1968 was postponed until 1971, due to a deadlock over a new elections bill proposed by the administration in 1967. This bill would have made local districts the electoral and constituency units. Orthodox Moslems felt this plan would allow thinly populated districts outside Java, including some Christian areas, to have a disproportionate influence in the new legislative body(26).

The New Order moved carefully but decisively to consolidate its position before the 1971 election. The PNI was allowed to come back into favor, after its leftwing group had been purged from leadership. A new party was authorized, *Partai Muslimin Indonesia* (PMI or PARMUSI), composed of sixteen Moslem organizations. With these two actions, the New Order had gained two allies: the PNI gave them influence among traditional Javanese masses, and the PMI gave them influence among modern Moslem intellectuals.

To consolidate its position further, the administration restructured congress to represent functional groups: peasants, farmers, women, and youth. These functional groups were later incorporated in the General Elections Law of 1969 as the Joint Secretariat of Functional Groups (GOLKAR)(27).

In effect this meant that while the parties were debating about a new political structure, the administration had taken the initiative by proposing a new "political party" (although protesting that it was not a party)(28) composed of several functional power blocks. The Moslems' refusal to accept districts as units in the election process had "boomeranged, and now was coming back to hit them"(29).

The Indonesian newsmagazine *Expres* pointed out that while the parties fought to retain the old political system, the

administration had formed a new political structure, GOLKAR,
oriented toward the executive branch and the technocrats. The
political parties had already built their platforms on the constitution, *Pancasila*, and the government's own five-year
development plan. Therefore they had no distinctive issues to
use in their campaigns(30). With these steps the New Order was
assured, even before the election was held. At least 50 percent
of the congress and the parliament would support the Suharto
administration.

With GOLKAR, the New Order had forged an alliance between
the army, the *priyayi* who held administrative positions, the
abangan who were usually members of functional groups, and
modern technocrats and intellectuals who had devised and implemented the government's program.

The Indonesian ruling faction's appeal to the Javanese
masses was quite different from the one presented to elite
builders of the New Order. From personal observation it is my
opinion that propaganda for GOLKAR was designed by a Javanese
who appealed to their deepest ethnic traditions. The symbol for
GOLKAR on posters and ballots was the banyan tree, signifying
kingly rule which produces regularity and tranquility (rather
than progress)(31). Ancient beliefs of most Indonesians include
a banyan tree shading the abode of their ancestors.

The election scenario also seemed designed to appeal to
Javanese belief in numerology. There were nine (sacred number
related to the grouping of Javanese villages) parties, not
counting GOLKAR which maintained it was not a party(32). On
the ballot GOLKAR was number five, which for the Javanese is an
even more sacred number than nine. The date of the election was
also moved from 3 July to 5 July. The number five represents
the center of the compass, the kingly profession, the compound
metal, and the central market(33).

It was no surprise that the election of 5 July 1971 gave
GOLKAR its expected victory at the polls. GOLKAR got 34,348,673
votes, or 63 percent of the total, thus guaranteeing it 227
seats in congress. Add to this 100 seats appointed by the army,
and the New Order received a total of 327 seats out of the 451
finally allotted.

The *Nahdatul Ulama* party garnered 19 percent of the votes;
PNI, 7 percent, PMU, 5 percent; and all others, including the
Catholic party, the Protestant party, and *Murba*, received a
total of 6 percent. The NU party actually gained slightly over
their percentage of 1955, but they were no match for the coalition put together by the New Order.

In an Indonesian magazine article, Ali Wartopo listed factors in GOLKAR's spectacular victory of 1971:

1) A strong, efficient organization, all the way down to minor village officials.

2) The most intellectuals and technocrats of any party.

3) Cooperation with Moslem teachers, who are influential with the masses.

4) Use of the arts and culture of each area to present GOLKAR's claims in a way no other party attempted to.

5) Traditional leaders' (*priyayi*), such as Hamengku-buwono IX, Sultan of Yogyakarta, actively campaigning for GOLKAR.

6) The psychological factor of GOLKAR's offering a new alternative to failures already experienced by other political parties.

7) The development by GOLKAR leaders of a five-year development plan, which all parties felt compelled to incorporate into their platforms(34).

Despite some disclaimers, the 1971 election gave a mandate to the Suharto regime to proceed with the modernization and development of Indonesia. It also brought more political stability than the nation had ever before experienced in its quarter-century of independence(35).

The elections of 1955 and 1971 both showed that Moslems lacked the majority of votes needed to claim supremacy. In 1955 all Moslem parties got a total of 43 percent of the vote, according to Polomka(36). In 1971 they received only 24 percent of the vote, according to Denoon(37) (although other sources place the figure at 27 percent). It is interesting to note that the 1977 general election, held as this book was being prepared for publication, seemed strangely like a rerun of 1971: GOLKAR's percentage sagged less than one point, while the Moslems were able to increase their total by less than two percent(38).

Political events leading up to the election of 1971 greatly influenced church growth. During the time Moslems were struggling for a bigger role in the government, Javanese who were interested in becoming Christians often felt intimidated or ostracized.

The GOLKAR victory in 1971 gave fresh guarantees of religious liberty for the foreseeable future. No doubt there will be challenges again, but President Suharto and the New Order firmly positioned themselves in favor of complete religious freedom.

Conclusions

   In light of all that has gone before--as set forth both in this chapter and also in Chapters 5 and 6--let us now evaluate the role of political factors in church growth among the Javanese from 1960 to 1971. Church membership of the five denominations grew from 96,871 to 311,778, or 221.9 percent, during these eleven years(39). This means that the churches averaged an 11.5 percent increase in membership per year.

   If the total number of members at the conclusion of each of these periods is used as the base for figuring the percentage for the following period, the actual average increase per year for each period is as follows:

1960-1964	7.7%
1965-1967	27.6%
1968-1971	13.7%

It is obvious that growth from 1965 to 1967 far exceeded growth during the years preceding and following.

   The figure of baptisms on the following page pictures growth of the East Java Christian Church, but it is also representative of baptismal trends in all five Javanese denominations. Following a very slow period of growth prior to 1960 and a gradual increase from then to 1965, there was phenomenal growth in 1966 and 1967 before dropping off again in 1968. This figure illustrates the importance of political factors relating to the number of baptisms. All three of the major political factors cited--the governmental decrees on religion, the search for protection during the massacre, and general instability and insecurity--had their greatest influence during the 1966-1969 period of greatest growth.

   The drop-off in 1968 was partly caused by the fact that (1) many of those looking for an immediate protector and those merely meeting the government's requirements on religion had already made their decisions; (2) the political situation was much more stable after March 1967 when Suharto was named Acting President; (3) the beginning of the Moslem offensive against those becoming Christians.

   The East Java Christian Church recorded an increase in baptisms in 1969, probably as a backlash against Moslem pressure. Initial reactions had been to wait for a more opportune time, but continued harassment caused many Javanese to rebel and

FIGURE 4

BAPTISMS IN THE EAST JAVA CHRISTIAN CHURCH

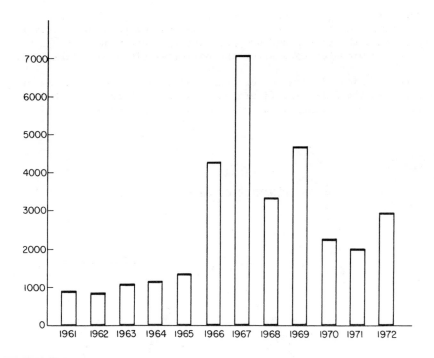

become Christians. Another factor involved (which we have
already considered in Chapter 4) was the fact that many who had
begun to practice the Moslem religion in 1966 and 1967 became
disenchanted and began to look for a religion that could satisfy
their spiritual needs.

In 1970 and 1971 church growth again slowed. This time one
of the important factors was pressure brought to bear by the
coming election. Informants often commented, "After the election
(and GOLKAR wins, guaranteeing religious freedom), many people
will become Christians; but right now they are afraid"(40).
They were afraid to join any party that might fall out of favor
later, thus bringing recrimination upon themselves. Therefore,
they postponed their decisions to declare for Christ until they
could see who would win. Those who had embraced religion for
protection felt that the pressure was off during and after the
election, and perhaps as many as 10 percent of those who earlier
had joined the church now dropped out(41). Attendance at many
church services dropped after the political situation stabilized.

Eugene Nida diagrams major characteristics of the dynamics of
change in the following figure(42). A study of this will help
explain the relationship of politics to the growth of Christianity in Indonesia.

FIGURE 5

DYNAMICS OF CHANGE

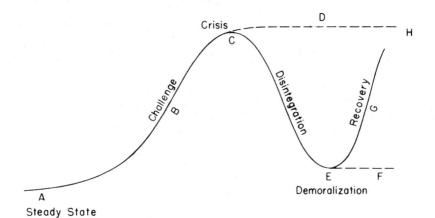

"A movement toward change normally begins with what may be called a steady state, at least with regard to the type of change under consideration"(43). The Indonesian political situation moved from a relatively steady state (A) in the early 1950's to a time of challenge (B) in the early 1960's, coming to a crisis (C) in 1965. The churches grew during the time of challenge from 1960 to 1964, but the greatest growth came during the period of disintegration (D) following the coup.

The period of demoralization (E) was short for the government, but it was quite extended for the communists (F). The government began its strong movement toward recovery (G) in 1967, when Suharto was named Acting President, and the upward trend still continues. It is possible that the slower growth following 1968 is in part related to demoralization of the communists (E and F). Most of the churches showed a slight increase beginning in 1971, perhaps related to the recovery of the government and fresh guarantees of freedom of religion.

The village of Cuntel will serve as an apt illustration of the effect of political factors on acceptance of Christianity. Cuntel is a truck-farming village located near the top of Mount Merbabu, not far from the city of Salatiga in Central Java. This area was known as the "Merbabu-Merapi complex," a hiding place for guerrillas who did not agree with the government during the revolutionary years of 1945-1949(44). It became a stronghold of communists, who exerted political and economic pressures on villages in the area and prevented their being open to Christianity.

After the abortive coup of 1965, communists were discredited, and the government demanded that everyone profess a religion. Leaders of Cuntel asked a Christian male nurse, who had served in the area faithfully for many years, which religion they should follow. He replied, "Christianity." Because his Christian example had interested them, they asked him to tell them more.

They then contacted leaders of the North Central Java Christian Church. The village head and his assistant became Christians early in 1966. Soldiers accompanied these leaders to prevent any problems and to give sanction to Christianity. (Soldiers also did the same thing for adherents of other religions.) Following a year's study of the catechism, there were mass baptisms in 1967 and 1968. Church membership soon reached 240 persons, which was a majority of the village population. But there has been very little growth since that time, because most of the villagers accepted a religion during those years. A majority of the members of the church have some kinship relation.

In the Merbabu area 24 places of worship have been begun
since 1965, with a membership total of approximately seven thousand. People in the area faced some pressures from Moslems in
1968. A few returned their baptismal cards when one of the
Christian village heads was said to be a former communist. During the period leading up to the 1971 election, there was some
confusion when village people were told, by the Christian Workers
Union from the city of Semarang, that they should become members
of GOLKAR, the government's political group. The church maintains a steady witness, using cultural art forms of the people.
Church members go to Salatiga periodically for leadership train-
ing(45).

From my own research I have drawn several conclusions concerning the influence of political factors relating to church growth
among the Javanese from 1960 through 1971:

(1) The guarantees of religious freedom inherent in the
state ideology, *Pancasila*, allowed Christianity to become a
viable alternative in the Indonesian situation. The New Order's
clarification of *Pancasila*, thus continuing to guarantee
religious freedom, opened the door even wider for Indonesians to
become Christians.

(2) The decree of the government that all Indonesians must
embrace a religion was the primary political factor in church
growth, and was operative throughout the entire period.

(3) The massacre of approximately 500,000 persons caused
others to look for both a physical and a spiritual protector.

(4) The government did not allow Moslems to prohibit Christian missionary activity.

(5) The identification of Christians with the government
enhanced their image and gave them influence. During the fight
for independence, Christians had vindicated themselves on the
battlefield. During the struggle of the mid-1960's, Christian
students in the streets and Christian intellectuals in pivotal
positions helped defeat the Old Order and establish the New(46).

(6) Nationalists, including leaders of the New Order, sought
allies in the political struggle, and so looked with favor on
members of their groups becoming Christian(47).

(7) The churches grew rapidly during times of political
instability, 1945-1953 and 1965-1969. The conflict of ideologies and power groups produced pressures on people which aided
or slowed growth. When pressures were extreme, many waited until
a more advantageous time to make their decisions.

(8) The rate of growth in the churches, which had been rather stable up to 1965, fluctuated drastically after that, in direct proportion to political factors operative during the period in each particular locale.

(9) Political instability of the period caused people to look for something stable upon which to rebuild their lives.

(10) The government's emphasis on the five-year development plan and the utilization of Indonesia's resources focused public attention on modernization. The progress of Western nations was favorably contrasted with that of Islamic nations(48). Christianity was viewed as an ally in modernization and progress.

As one church leader summed it all up: "Although they came because of such political considerations, the power of the Holy Spirit can make them firm in faith and obedience, so that many of them abandon that type of thinking. Herein lies the power of God"(49).

NOTES

1. W. B. Sidjabat, *Religious Tolerance and the Christian Faith* (Jakarta: Badan Penerbit Kristen, 1965), p. 74 (hereafter cited as *Religious Tolerance*), translates this key phrase as "the Divine Omnipotence." Another Indonesian Christian theologian, Harun Hadiwijono, *Man in the Present Javanese Mysticism* (Baara: Bosch & Keuning N.V., 1967), p. 1 (hereafter cited as *Javanese Mysticism*), suggests "The Absolute Lordship." Boland, *Struggle of Islam*, p. 38, prefers the translation "Belief in the One and Only God." Also see C. A. O. van Nieuwenhuijze, *Aspects of Islam in Post-Colonial Indonesia: Five Essays* (The Hague: W. van Hoeve, 1958), pp. 208-43 (hereafter cited as *Aspects of Islam*), for an analysis of the phrase's meaning as a "deconfessionalized" Moslem concept.

2. See Sukarno's speech, "The Pantja Sila," in *Indonesian Political Thinking*, ed. Herbert Feith and Louis Castles (Ithaca: Cornell University Press, 1969), pp. 40-49 (hereafter cited as *Political Thinking*), which he presented to the Body for Investigating Efforts in Preparation for Independence (*Dokuritsu Zyunbi Tjooksakai*), a commission established by the Japanese near the end of the war in anticipation of their defeat.

3. See Ismaun, *Problematik Pantjasila Sebagai Kepribadian Bangsa Indonesia* [The Problem of *Pancasila* as the Personality of the Indonesian People] (Bandung: Penerbit Karya-Remadja, 1971), pp. 5-10.

4. For an Indonesian historical development, see C. S. T. Kansil, *Pantjasila dan UUD 45: Dasar Falsafah Negara* [*Pancasila* and the 1945 Constitution: The Foundation of the Nation's Philosophy] (Jakarta: Penerbit Pradnja Paramita, 1972).

5. See Sidjabat, *Religious Tolerance*, p. 41.

6. Feith and Castles, *Political Thinking*, p. 45.

7. Roeslan Abdulgani, *Pantjasila, the Prime Mover of the Indonesian Revolution* (Jakarta: Prapantja, n.d.), p. 18.

8. See van Nieuwenhuijze, *Aspects of Islam*, pp. 167-79 for a chronicling of Kartosuwirjo's Islamic state.

9. Van der Kroef, *Since Sukarno*, pp. 57-64.

10. For an orthodox Moslem view of *Pancasila* as set forth by Daud Beureuth, see Polomka, *Since Sukarno*, p. 43.

11. See Donald Hindley, "Indonesia 1971: *Pantjasila* Democracy and the Second Parliamentary Elections," *Asian Student* 12 (January 1972), 56-68.

12. Soeripto, *Surat 11 Maret*, p. 25.

13. For a Christian view of *Pancasila*, see Polomka, *Since Sukarno*, pp. 183-84.

14. Tasdik, *Motives for Conversion*, p. 11. Several places in his booklet, Tasdik refers to the effect the decree had on those becoming Christians.

15. In a private interview this Ministry of Religion official explained that the procedure was to say that traditional Javanese religious practices were in reality Hindu practices, and that therefore the Javanese people were already Hindus without realizing it. He said:

"The truth is, in Central Java people still follow the Hindu religion even though they profess to be Moslems, Christians, or Catholics; they still have offerings to their ancestors . . . . Most of these people can't say that they follow Hinduism, but they do sacrifice like

Hindus. In fact, the people from antiquity have
really been Hindus, because they have sacrificed the
products that they have gotten from the soil--food
and clothes. . . . Actually, everybody who worships
like that is a Hindu whether he realizes it or not.
. . . The real reason for the growth of Hinduism is
that there was an order from the government that
everyone must purify their religion."

16. From a speech by J. L. C. Abineno given at the Indonesian
Baptist Theological Seminary, Semarang, 1970.

17. Polomka, *Since Sukarno*, pp. 182-83.

18. Ibid., p. 184.

19. Ibid., p. 185.

20. Ibid.

21. Copied from a mimeographed paper distributed by the Government to Central Java leaders, pp. 10-11.

22. See Donald McGavran, *Understanding Church Growth* (Grand
Rapids: William B. Eerdmans Publishing Co., 1970), pp.
87-91.

23. Hindley, "Fall of the Old Order," p. 60.

24. See D. S. Lev, "Political Parties in Indonesia," *Journal of
Southeast Asian History* 8 (March 1967): 52-67.

25. Van der Kroef, *Since Sukarno*, p. 216.

26. For a discussion of the conflict between Moslems and the
army, see van der Kroef, *Since Sukarno*, pp. 45-64. For a
more recent discussion of the conflict, see A. A. Samson,
"Army and Islam in Indonesia," *Pacific Affairs* 44 (Winter
1971-1972): 545-65.

27. Van der Kroef, *Since Sukarno*, pp. 214-25.

28. See "We're Not a Party, We're Functional," *Economist* 239
(26 June 1971): 45-46.

29. "Partai-Partai: Profil Disimpang Djalan" [The Parties:
Profile at the Crossroads], *Tempo*, 12 July 1971, p. 7.

30. "Ketegangan Politik Mendjelang Pemilu" [Political Tension
Approaching the Election], *Expres*, 22 February 1971, pp. 5-6.

31. Moertono, *State and Statecraft*, p. 92.

32. Ibid., p. 27. See also van Akkeren, *Sri and Christ*, pp. 194-97.

33. Ibid., pp. 8-9.

34. See "GOLKAR: Mandat Telah Diberikan" [GOLKAR: A Mandate Has Been Given], *Expres*, 19 July 1971, pp. 5-10.

35. See A. A. Samson, "Indonesia 1972: The Solidification of Military Control," *Asian Student* 13 (February 1973): 127-39.

36. Polomka, *Since Sukarno*, p. 186.

37. David B. H. Denoon, "Indonesia: Transition to Stability?" *Current History* 61 (December 1971): 338.

38. See unofficial totals on the front page of the Indonesian daily newspaper *Pikiran Rakyat*, 16 May 1977.

39. Statistics were given by the offices of each denomination, but there is room to question their accuracy because they also include estimates of congregations which did not report. The number of members added by baptism (see Figure 4) does not show the continual increase in membership in the last three years of the period as shown on the membership graph (see Figure 6). One explanation of this discrepancy is that the baptism graph does not include estimates for congregations which did not report. Membership statistics also include infants. Furthermore, they reflect more optimistic estimates of membership by synod leaders, than I have been able to substantiate from baptismal records.

40. Private interviews.

41. Interviews with denominational leaders.

42. Donald Anderson McGavran, *Church Growth in Christian Mission* (New York: Harper & Row, 1965), p. 71.

43. Ibid.

44. See Brackman, *Indonesian Communism*, p. 152, and van der Kroef, *Communist Party*, p. 65.

45. Information gained from several interviews with members, the pastor, and a missionary who works in the area.

46. Christians exert a greater influence in Indonesian society
     than their numbers would indicate. A larger percentage of
     Christians are educated, and the percentage of Christian
     students in universities today is far out of proportion to
     their percentage in society. Dr. Leimena, late founder of
     the Protestant Christian political party, held a position
     in most of the cabinets from independence until the time
     Sukarno fell. For other important posts he held, see O. G.
     Roeder, *Who's Who in Indonesia* (Jakarta: Gunung Agung,
     1971), pp. 192-93. One of Suharto's chief advisors,
     General Mareden Panggabean, is a Protestant; he heads a
     centralized Pentagon-style structure of joint chiefs of
     staff and the command for domestic security and intelli-
     gence, whose authority extensively overlaps that of the
     police. Frans Seda, A Catholic, was Suharto's first Minis-
     ter of Finance until the Moslems forced him to be relieved of
     the command, after which he was made Minister of Communications.
     See Polomka, *Since Sukarno*, p. 188. The Protestant Party was
     given credit by leaders of the East Java Christian Church for
     greatly aiding evangelization.

47. See Tasdik, *Motives for Conversion*, pp. 19, 21, 24, 32.

48. For a recent presentation of the Moslem view, see Anwar
     Hardjono, "Masa Depan Hukum Islam di Indonesia" [The
     Future of Islamic Law in Indonesia] in *Kejakinan dan Per-
     djuangan*, pp. 368-75.

49. Darmowigoto, *Pemashuran Indjil*, p. 5.

PART III

Sociological Factors

8

Extended Families
Extend the Kingdom

Sociological factors did not play a primary role in the response
of Javanese to Christianity after 1965, but they did play a
significant secondary role. Sociological factors multiplied the
response initially caused by religio-cultural and political
factors. Among influences toward conversion mentioned by our
Javanese interviewees, "Family" ranked fifth and "Society" sixth
as primary reasons (see Figure 2). But in the over-all evaluation, 60 percent listed one of these factors as contributing
to their decisions (see Figure 3). If the influence of Christians (classified under "Christian Life") is also included in
the total, 80 percent of the converts recognized the role of
sociological factors in their decisions.

Let us examine these sociological influences toward conversion from three perspectives: *communal structure of Javanese
society, divisions of class or status,* and *effects of modernization.*

COMMUNAL STRUCTURE OF JAVANESE SOCIETY

Prehistoric migrants from Indo-China who first settled Indonesia determined the patriarchal, communal structure of present-
day rural Javanese society.

Influence of the Family

In a communal society the family determines the children's
ethnic identification, religious affiliation, and social class

membership. In a Javanese family, the father as patriarch has
increasingly less frequent intimate relationships with his
children as they grow older, and, in his absence, an ideal
father-image develops. "As a consequence the child develops a
relationship of reverence for the father's authority but with a
marked disruption of warm affection"(1). The mother, in a more
subservient role, has a warmer, more intimate relationship with
her children, but she is usually assisted by other children,
close relatives, or servants who constantly watch the younger
ones. Such persons often become mother-substitutes, since the
real mother is busy with household duties, social obligations,
or business affairs. It is customary for the first male child
to be reared by paternal grandparents, and the first girl by
maternal grandparents(2). Thus a Javanese is socialized as a
member of an extended family, and maintains relationships with
a large number of relatives in the nuclear family(3).

In the traditional village, most of an individual's decisions,
including choice of a marriage partner, are made for him by his
family. At no time in his life is he thought to be free from
the guidance of older members of his family. The family plays a
major role in any crisis decision of significance, such as
changing religions. Many new Christians said, "I became a
Christian along with my family."

One hundred and sixty-nine of our Javanese interviewees were
asked, "Was your family influential in your decision to become a
Christian?" to which 84.7 percent answered yes. Only 15.3 percent said their families opposed their decisions. In order to
view the family influence from another direction we also asked
192 converts whether members of their families became Christians
before they did; 73.5 percent of those who became Christians
before 1960 answered yes, but only 43 percent of those who
became Christians after 1960 did so. This indicates that much
of the growth prior to 1960 was "biological growth," while more
of those who became Christians from 1960 to 1971 were "from the
world." (See p. 106 and note 22 in Chapter 7.)

The respondents were also asked whether other family members
became Christians after they did. Only 23.6 percent of the
converts prior to 1960 had relatives who followed their example,
in contrast to 77.7 percent of the 1960-1964 converts. Among
converts of 1965 to 1968, the percentage fell to 60.8, and it
dropped again to 36.6 for the 1969-1971 group. (Of course, some
of this drop-off can probably be accounted for by the short
period of time between these latter conversions and our interviews, which were conducted in 1972-73.)

Over-all, the people who became Christians from 1960 to 1971
were not influenced as much by their families as were the

pre-1960 converts, but they had more influence on other members
of their families becoming Christians. The fact that more of
the 1960 to 1971 converts came from non-Christian families
meant that they had more intimate contact with non-Christians,
and therefore were more effective in influencing them.

The marriage of non-Christians to Christians accounted for a
small percentage of growth "from the world," both before and
after 1960.

Influence of Friends

Eighty-six percent of the post-1965 converts had Christian
friends prior to their conversions. Of the 51.5 percent of the
total sampling who came from non-Christian families, 60.4 percent of the 1965-1968 converts and 42.5 percent of the 1969-1971
converts had Christian friends prior to their conversions.

Thus both the figures relating to friends and the figures
relating to family show that approximately 80 percent of the
post-1965 converts were influenced to some degree by one or
both of these two basic social relationships.

Influence of the Community

The Javanese learns his social position early, and adjusts to
the total of his relationships within society(4). He is more a
product of his rearing and socialization than his counterpart in
the West. He is taught to base his decisions on social approval
more than on moral rightness. Thus he develops a keen sensitivity to shame more than guilt, due to failure to internalize
moral choices(5).

Pressure to conform is continually applied on the Javanese
until he acquires the characteristics of his group. A village
lad in Java is relatively free from sanctions until the initia-
tion rite of circumcision at about the age of twelve; after this
he is expected to act like a man(6). At this time indulgence
ceases and rigid conformity is stressed, thus producing a
sudden transfer of dependency from the mother to the "arms of
collectivity"(7).

The sympathy and solidarity of the Indonesian *desa* (village)
is best exemplified by *gotong royong* (mutual assistance), "in
which a group of persons accomplish collectively something which
touches their common interests"(8). This practice of recipro-
city and redistribution has integrated the Javanese family and
village for over four thousand years, and governs all relation-
ships(9). Koentjaraningrat says the three basic ideas in *gotong
royong* are: (1) everyone in the village is dependent upon

others and should therefore maintain a good relationship; (2)
everyone must always be ready to help his fellow-man; and (3)
everyone must conform so that he does not in any way stand out
more than his fellow-man(10).

Individuality is viewed as a divisive force, causing disintegration and disorganization in traditional structures; therefore
gotong royong must be maintained at any cost(11). Van
Nieuwenhuijze says that in the "closed *desa*" one is passively
absorbed into the community life

> so much so that the concept of "an individual" hardly
> makes sense. An individual, seen in the light of these
> conditions, is someone who willfully and deliberately
> tears himself apart from his surroundings, from the world
> wherein he belongs, from the fabric of which he is a
> thread. Such a person is indeed an individual in the
> derogatory sense. He is dangerous to himself and, what
> matters more, to all others(12).

Encroaching modernization provides more mobility and flexibility
than the above description allows (see "Effects of Modernization"
later in this chapter). Yet, this remains the basic framework
in which the average Javanese lives and makes his decisions.

The democratic process is not violated in the *desa*, because
communal agreement is based on *musyawarah* (consultative deliberations) and *mufakat* (consensus), more than on authoritarian
pronouncements. The village chief is reponsible for maintaining
harmony by listening to varying viewpoints expressed in *desa*
meetings and then stating a consensus acceptable to all. He
does not have authority to state the opinion of only the
majority, for majority rule imposed upon the minority is alien
to Indonesian village society(13). If the points of debate
seem irreconcilable, a short recess allows time for leaders of
varying viewpoints to agree on a compromise which is then
announced by the village chief. If he continually makes pronouncements that are not acceptable to the community, he will
be removed from office at the next election.

The *desa*, then, is a more or less autonomous, democratic,
communal system that determines its own way of life within
bounds set by higher authorities. The village chief serves as
link between the *desa* and higher authority, with much of his
power dependent on his ability to maintain the traditions,
harmony, and way of life of the village(14).

The nature of the communal society and its traditional
religious *adat* (customs which govern life) limit the possibility
of changing religions. Sociological factors evidently caused

the Sundanese and Madurese (two other large ethnic groups who, like the Javanese, live on the island of Java) to reject Christianity. Kraemer says that Islam has been accepted as the crowning element of Sundanese *adat*, and a similar thing could be said in relation to the Madurese people as well. Kraemer continues:

> The real explanation of the great power of Islam over the Sundanese people seems to me to be that in their mind it has been completely fused with their *adat* . . . yet most of them are quite indifferent to religion in its pregnant sense. . . . In this consciousness of *adat* and their collective apprehensions referred to above, their strong attachment to the family is also embedded. . . . [and] constitutes the second great obstacle to conversion to another religion(15)

One is inclined to agree with McGavran, who maintains that "It is defensible to affirm that the chief resistance of Islam and other religions is social, not theological."

Yet, if a large enough group in an Indonesian community desires to make a change of religion, this may be done without disrupting community life. Van Akkeren shows that traditional Javanese social structure is based on a four-way system of opposites, in order to absorb diverse elements without disrupting communal ties(17). Yet, if individuals seek to introduce innovations without the agreement of a substantial number in the community, they may be summarily dismissed and, if they persist, even opposed.

People Movements

A majority of the Christians in Indonesia were converted in people movements. In describing the success of Christian missions in Indonesia, Wertheim states:

> Modern Protestant missions made special headway in religions where the *adat* chiefs could be won over to the new religion. By maintaining the aristocratic order of society, the missionaries could assure themselves of the influence of these leaders of a large part of the agrarian population. "Fishing with the net" proved in quantitative terms more efficient than "fishing with the hook," as it was called. Where missionaries, inspired by Protestant individualism, chose the latter approach which was more personal and far more penetrating, the religion spread to very limited groups only. The best propagandists proved to be Indonesian Christians(18).

Donald McGavran clearly differentiates people movements from mass movements, stating that the latter term gives "an entirely erroneous idea that large, undigested masses of human beings are moving into the Church"(19).

A people movement results from the joint decision of a number of individuals--whether five or five hundred--all from the same people, which enables them to become Christians without social dislocation, while remaining in full contact with their non-Christian relatives, thus enabling other groups of that people, across the years, after suitable instruction, to come to similar decisions and form Christian churches made up exclusively of members of that people(20).

Two-thirds of the five hundred interviewees who became Christians between 1960 and 1971 did so in people movements. Individuals, often village leaders, talked to their "in-groups" about the possibility of their becoming Christians together. Occasionally all of them did so together, but more frequently one group would be followed by related groups over a period of months or years.

These decisions were not imposed by leaders, but followed the *desa* pattern of decision-making based on *mufakat* (consensus) arrived at by *musyawarah* (mutual deliberations). They were not mass decisions, but "multi-individual" ones. A decision can be personal in a people movement without becoming individual in the Western sense. No doubt some people professed Christianity without making adequate personal commitment to Christ, but because the churches required a three- to twelve-month new members' course or study of the catechism before baptism, many of them were converted during preparation for baptism. One denominational leader said that probably twice as many people were refused baptism for failing to meet the requirements as were baptized.

A people movement began in Tlogo village near Semarang when Samusi visited a relative in a nearby *desa* and heard the gospel at a home worship service. On his return to Tlogo, he asked his brother and sister, "Why don't we become Christians?" Although no one in the village was a Christian, they decided to invite the pastor from a nearby town to explain Christianity to them. They also invited their neighbors to be a welcoming committe for their visitor.

After hearing an explanation of the gospel, five men made a decision together to become Christians. They were soon joined by their families and friends. A thriving, indigenous church took root in Tlogo, and in the years that have followed, it has been able to withstand tremendous pressure from Moslem neighbors. Samusi remarked, "Who would have ever thought there would be Christians in Tlogo? And now we even have a church. The Moslems are amazed, but we have decided together that no matter what happens, we will not retreat"(21).

People movements have not been as obvious in Indonesian cities as in Indonesian villages, because decisions among the urban groups are primarily of a different type; they consist of chain reactions centered around vocations, neighborhoods, classes, and age groups. The cities of Java are composed of hundreds of *kampungs* separated by lines of homes and stores along the main streets. Each *kampung* is little more than a compressed village of dislodged rural peasants, with village mentality and sectional identity. Although decisions for Christ in Indonesian cities have been more individualistic, they have still been greatly influenced by social and kin relationships, as the gospel spreads from area to area and group to group.

Role of the Leader

Imported religio-cultural influences of Hinduism and Islam strengthened the developing patriarchy at Javanese court centers. They also strengthened the mystically conceived cycle of individual and group continuity congenial to the pantheistic-monotheistic beliefs of Javanese villages(22).

In the Javanese state, the king was the exponent of the macrocosmos and his subjects' spiritual connection to it(23). The ruler therefore was the focal point of maximum spiritual intensity; his residence was the center from which power emanated to each person in the surrounding population(24). In terms of practical administrative policy, the ruler assumed an attitude of fatherly protective superiority over his subjects.

Much of this paternalistic feeling has been carried over to administrative authorities of the modern Indonesian state. Therefore, any command from higher authorities, communicated through the village chief, is given due consideration. This sociological relationship reinforced the governmental order for all Indonesians to profess a religion (though not specifically Christianity). Yet each village was still autonomous, being allowed to make its own decisions within boundaries set by the state(25).

DIVISIONS OF CLASS OR STATUS

Efforts to divide Indonesian society into traditional economic classes of the West have not proven very effective(26).

Van Niel says that 98 percent of the Javanese belong to the
common people, and that almost 90 percent of them are related
to the villages(27). Kahin uses the term "middle class," but
applies it to the emerging elite(28). In fact, a middle class
has begun to emerge among the Javanese, but very slowly--
probably due to Javanese discouragement of wealth-producing
activities and encouragement of expensive traditional ceremonies
which dissipate financial reserves(29).

A more helpful classification is what Clifford Geertz terms
variants in the social-structural system: the *abangan*, the
santri, and the *priyayi*(30).

Abangan may be characterized as blue-collar, rural, tradition-bound, animistic, nationalistic, Moslem peasants, subject
to higher authorities(31).

Priyayi(32) may be characterized as white-collar, city,
traditional, feudal, bureaucratic, nationalistic gentry(33).
In modern times, education, wealth, and position as well as
heredity have formed the basis for inclusion in the *priyayi*.
"The *priyayi* remained a part of Javanese society with an outlook
on the world distinct from that of the peasantry--more urbane
and cultivated, but still within the same world-view"(34).
Their refined *politesse*, high art, intuitive mysticism, and
style of life are a model for the *abangan*. This gap between
these two groups is still basically the distance of the court
center from the *desa*.

Santri, technically students of Islam, are most commonly
urban traders or wealthy peasants who devotedly follow the
Moslem ritual, doctrine, and social grouping (*ummat*)(35).
Their distinguishing feature is their adherence to the "objective, deductive, abstract law that defines a Moslem and defines
the Moslem community"(36), rather than adherence to a mixture
of belief and status like that shown by the *abangan* and *priyayi*.
The solidarity of the *ummat* is illustrated by the *santri* section
of the community, which is always located near the mosque(37).

The *santri* characteristically look to the religious leader,
teacher, or scholar, while the *abangan* look to the village chief,
who is the perpetuator of the *adat* (traditions). Although the
santri, *abangan*, and *priyayi* all claim the Moslem faith, antipathy between Javanism and Islam divides them into two sociological camps: *santri* and *abangan-priyayi*(38).

The majority of church growth among the Javanese since 1960
has come from the *abangan* sector of society. The most probable
reasons for this are: (1) they do not identify themselves with
the *ummat*, and can therefore more easily move to another

religion without being ostracized from their social group;
(2) their Islamic beliefs are lightly held, because their heart
orientation is to *kejawen* (Javanism); (3) most of them joined
nationalist or communist parties rather than Islamic parties,
and therefore were more responsive to alternatives other than
Islam when their own political parties fell into disrepute; and
(4) they sought a religion of the spirit that could effectively
help them deal with their fear of spirits.

On the other hand, the percentage of the *priyayi* becoming
Christians was smaller because: (1) more of the Javanese
churches were related to the *abangan*; (2) the *priyayi* had more
to lose in status and economic position(39); (3) their religious
orientation was toward *kebatinan* (mysticism) which is more
resistant to Christianity; and (4) they were susceptible to
group pressure only if it came from their peers; therefore,
people movements among the *abangan* exerted little influence on
them. Nevertheless, because of their antipathy to orthodox
Islam, the *priyayi* were more likely to become Christians than
the *santri* were.

A very small percentage of the *santri* became Christians
because: (1) their peers were strong Moslems, among whom there
was no people movement toward Christianity; (2) they were
already practicing their religion, and therefore felt no
pressure from the governmental decree; (3) they were more likely
to be in a better economic position, and therefore were not looking for innovations; and (4) their dogmatic, antagonistic,
polemic attitude shielded them from an effective hearing of the
gospel. Those *santri* who did become Christians usually had
encountered personal crises, dissatisfaction in their spiritual
lives, or a very persuasive witness from Christian friends or
members of their families.

Alert evangelists learned to look for signs that would lead
them to the receptive *abangan* group: a *Partai Nasional
Indonesia* sign posted at the entrance of the *desa* or *kampung*,
music of a *gamelan*, presence of a shadow-play, or a paucity of
Moslem houses of worship and P3A signs. (See p. 50.)

EFFECTS OF MODERNIZATION

Modernization(40), the countermovement to most of the
sociological norms thus far mentioned in this chapter, has just
begun to affect the traditional order, particularly the structure, of Javanese village life. Van der Kroef says, "Of the
three major cultural forces that have impinged on traditional
Indonesian society--Hinduism, Islam, and the West--only the West
has succeeded in severly threatening the stability of peasant
communalism"(41).

Modernization has brought radical changes in social groupings, institutions, and world view of the Indonesian people, including new norms, values, ideas, expectations, and attitudes. This process of transformation is moving Indonesian society "from a traditional to a rational, a rural to an urban, a static to a dynamic, a homogeneous to a heterogeneous, a communal to an associational character(42). Development of a modern, rational, pragmatic viewpoint has caused some Indonesians to look at their culture with a certain detachment. After they have once so looked, then it is too late to return to their former unreflective, traditional, prescientific viewpoint. In this sense the process of modernization is irreversible(43).

Effects of modernization in the Indonesian colonial period included the foundation of foreign commercial and administrative enclaves, the abolition of slavery, the transformation of native aristocrats into salaried civil servants, the administrative consolidation of villages, an embryonic system of education, and a gradual monetizing of the economy(44). During the Japanese occupation, authority based on tradition was gradually undermined by intellectuals, by new organizations involving millions of Indonesians, and by personal achievements of Indonesian leaders(45). Since independence, the holders of power have adopted Western status symbols(46). In recent times, the army(47) and the youth(48) have become leaders in the modernization process.

Modernization has affected the churches through: the population explosion, mobility, new economic patterns, technological advances, and a resulting measure of industrialization, urbanization, and secularization. Its fires have been fueled by the insatiable desire of Indonesians for education and its promised advancement.

The population of Java has grown from less than five million people in 1820(49) to approximately 87,500,000, with a net yearly population growth of 1,600,000(50). The Indonesian population has tripled in seventy years, and is expected to double again in twenty-four more, passing 200 million--even if government-promoted family planning programs are successful(51).

Although the percentage of increase in church membership since 1960 has been over ten times higher than the percentage of increase in population(52), the churches are still falling rapidly behind in relation to the total Javanese population increase: While 280,000 people were added to the membership of Javanese churches from 1960 to 1971, Java's population increased by approximately 20,000,000 people. The population explosion accentuates the pressure of other social problems.

A chaotic economic structure, runaway inflation, widespread unemployment, and chronic underemployment contributed to the unrest which pushed many Indonesians toward Christianity(53). The average per capita income was only eighty dollars per year during the period under consideration(54). The Labor Department reported that the number of unemployed in Central Java jumped from twelve thousand to twenty thousand in 1968, while at the same time, the number of underemployed rose from four million to six million--more than 25 percent of the province's total working force!(55). Those who had joined communist organizations hoping for economic improvement were disillusioned; some joined churches, secretly hoping for economic gain or a job(56).

Social mobility characterized those in search of education and employment(57). Although most of those moving from village to city maintained relationships with their rural kin, urbanization took its toll on their *desa* lifestyle of traditional conformity. The dislocation and alienation felt by these new city dwellers made some of them amenable to innovation, including religion. Much church growth came through city dwellers who returned to their villages with the gospel message.

Urbanization, industrialization, and technical advances resulted in a growing secularization, although the percentage of "secularized" Indonesians is still small. Problems of modernization as experienced in the West were multiplied in the lives of these secularized Indonesians by the instability of their political and economic institutions. The process of modernization based on Western education "led too much to the forming of an up-rooted, spiritually unbalanced group of suddenly Westernized intellectuals"(58). These Indonesians were detached from the spiritual life of their own culture, but found that the accoutrements of Western culture failed to produce spiritual life. "The people concerned expected no more salvation from their own tradition, but Western culture left their hearts 'stone cold'"(59).

These spiritually disenfranchised urbanites searched for new gods, but usually settled for secular substitutes. Churches located in urban areas grew rapidly if they had effective witnessing outreach programs, but in general the growth rate of city churches was much slower than that of village churches. Our research revealed almost no growth in many churches in towns and cities, while village congregations started by these same churches were growing rapidly.

This modern secular revolution in Indonesia has paved the way for the growth of Christianity--as well as of Buddhism, Hinduism, mystical sects, and a resurgent Islam(60). Christianity's relationship to the West had a positive influence on Indonesians

who wanted to get in step with the modern world. But by expos-
ing and questioning traditional religious values, the process of
modernization helped Christianity even more. Whether this
negative factor can be converted into a positive one will
depend on the type of evangelism and Christian image projected
by the churches. It is by no means an unmixed blessing: While
the modern image of the church led part of the modern minority
to accept Christianity, this same modern image caused the tradition-bound majority to reject it. The churches must learn to
appeal to this small but growing minority affected by modernization, without isolating themselves from the slow-moving
tradition-loving masses.

CONCLUSIONS

In summary several sociological factors influenced Javanese
to become Christians:

(1) The communal nature of Javanese society aided people
movements, once a small group had accepted Christianity.

(2) Village leaders often became agents of innovation and
led their people toward Christianity.

(3) Extended web-relationships of family and kinsmen became
avenues of religious innovation.

(4) The marriage of Christians to non-Christians influenced
a small percentage of the converts.

(5) Modernization brought rapid social change, causing
Javanese to search for an integrating factor.

(6) Poor economic conditions forced many Javanese to look
for a better way of life in a society that was becoming increasingly modern and urbanized.

(7) The population explosion added members to the churches
through "biological growth," but intensified other sociological
problems.

(8) The modern image of some of the churches attracted a
minority of Javanese who welcomed modernization.

(9) Social mobility helped provide new avenues and agents
for the spread of the gospel.

NOTES

1. Win, "Political Socialization," p. 77.

2. Ibid., pp. 72-76.

3. For further information on the Javanese family, see: Robert R. Jay, *Javanese Villagers: Social Relations in Rural Modjokuto* (Cambridge: MIT Press, 1969), pp. 30-187 (hereafter cited as *Javanese Villagers*); Selosoemardjan, *Social Change*, pp. 137-39; Hildred Geertz, *The Javanese Family* (New York: Free Press of Glencoe, 1961); Win, "Political Socialization," pp. 69-108; Nicholson, "Introduction of Islam," pp. 107-27; and Douglas, *Student Activism*, pp. 30-66.

4. For additional information, see: Soetardjo Kartohadi-koesoemo, *Desa* [Village] (Yogyakarta: Sumur Bandung, 1965); Jay, *Javanese Villagers*, pp. 188-452; Soedjito Sosrodihardjo, *Perubahan Struktur Masjarakat di Djawa* [Changes in the Structure of Society in Java] (Yogyakarta: Karya, 1972); Selosoemardjan, *Social Change*, pp. 105-249; Koentjaraningrat, ed., *Villages in Indonesia* (Ithaca: Cornell University Press, 1967), pp. 244-80, 386-405; and Ina E. Slamet, *Pokok-Pokok Pembangunan Masjarakat Desa* [Fundamentals for Developing Village Society] (Jakarta: Bhratara, 1965).

5. Win, "Political Socialization," p. 80.

6. Van der Kroef, *Social Evolution*, pp. 38-39, says that Indonesian society is marked by its lack of facility to transform the little child into a little adult.

7. Win, "Political Socialization," p. 90.

8. Notoatmodjo, "*Gotong Royong*," p. 11.

9. Ibid., p. 248.

10. Koentjaraningrat, *Rintangan-Rintangan Mental Dalam Pembangunan Ekonomi di Indonesia* [Psychological Obstacles to Economic Development in Indonesia] Seri I/2 (Jakarta: Bhratara, 1969), p. 35 (hereafter cited as *Rintangan Mental*). Also see Koentjaraningrat, *Some Social-Anthropoligical Observations on "Gotong Royong" Practices in Two Villages of Central Java*, trans. Claire Holt (Ithaca: Department of Far Eastern Studies, Cornell University Press, 1961), p. 29, for a summary of the seven types of *gotong royong* practices in the village.

11. Notoatmodjo, "*Gotong Royong*," p. 34.

12. Van Nieuwenhuijze, *Aspects of Islam*, p. 9.

13. Mintz, *Mohammed, Marx, and Marhaen*, p. 13.

14. Van Niel, *Modern Indonesian Elite*, p. 18.

15. Kraemer, *From Missionfield*, p. 115.

16. McGavran, *Understanding Church Growth*, p. 299.

17. This four-in-one concept is too involved to discuss here. For a detailed analysis see Van Akkeren, *Sri and Christ*, pp. 3-27.

18. Wertheim, *Society in Transition*, p. 205.

19. McGavran, *Understanding Church Growth*, p. 297.

20. Ibid., pp. 297-98.

21. Private interviews.

22. Van der Kroef, *Modern World*, p. 100.

23. Moertono, *State and Statecraft*, pp. 26-27.

24. Win, "Political Socialization," p. 148.

25. In Tasdik's research, he showed that "following others in choosing a religion" was more significant than all other factors in the villages surveyed in East and Central Java. In a Central Java small town, it ranked first, and in an East Java small town, it ranked second to "being threatened," although in neither case was the percentage as high as in the villages. *Motives for Conversion*, p. 11.

26. Van der Kroef, *Social Evolution*, p. 166, says that the social structure of the Indonesian republic is divided into various classes: peasantry, rural and urban proletariat, aristocracy, and clerics. He also states that most of these have significant sub-divisions. But Kuntowidjojo, *Angkatan Oemat Islam, 1945-1950: Beberapa Tjatatan Tentang Pergerakan Sosial* [The Islamic Forces, 1945-1950: Several Notes Concerning Social Movements] (Yogyakarta: Fakultas Sastra dan Kebudayaan Gajah Mada, Seminar Sejarah Nasional II, 26-29 August 1970), p. 9 (hereafter cited as *Pergerakan Sosial*), says that economic groupings are not applicable in Java, and that income and possessions are not of great importance in the social structure.

27. Van Niel, *Modern Indonesian Elite*, p. 16.

28. See Legge, *Indonesia*, pp. 104-6.

29. See L. H. Palmier, *Social Status and Power in Java* (London: University of London, Athlone Press, 1960), p. 8 (hereafter cited as *Status and Power*).

30. See Geertz, *The Religion of Java*, pp. 5-6. Mortimer, "Class, Social Cleavage and Indonesian Communism," p. 7, and Kuntowidjojo, *Pergerakan Sosial*, p. 9, agree with Geertz that the cleavages are more helpful than customary class divisions in understanding Indonesian society; but Legge, *Indonesia*, p. 24, warns that these are not to be thought of as separate entities, nor as the only traditional way of dividing society.

31. See Clifford Geertz, *Religion in Mojokuto: A Study of Ritual and Belief in a Complex Society* (Cambridge: Harvard University, 1956), p. 18 (hereafter cited as *Religion in Mojokuto*); and Reinhardt, "Nationalism and Confrontation," p. 157.

32. Sosrodihardjo, *Perubahan Struktur Masjarakat di Djawa*, p. 26, says that the word *priyayi* is derived from the words *para yayi*, meaning the younger brothers and sisters of the king.

33. See Koentjaraningrat, *Rintangan Mental*, pp. 37-42, for a description of the *priyayi* outlook.

34. Legge, *Indonesia*, p. 10.

35. C. Geertz, *Religion in Mojokuto*, p. 18.

36. C. Geertz, *The Religion of Java*, p. 129.

37. See Kuntowidjojo, *Pergerakan Sosial*, p. 10.

38. Moslems often object to these distinctions. They say that *santri* and *abangan* cannot be clearly divided, and that the *abangan* variant of religion in Java is really a variant within Islam and no different from nominal adherents of other religions. They object even more strongly to the distinction Geertz makes between the *priyayi* and the other two variants, because they feel that the *priyayi*, too, are members of Islam and should be judged on their devotion to it rather than on class distinctions or cultural preferences. See Boland, *Struggle of Islam*, p. 4. C. Geertz, in a book published eight years after his *The Religion of*

Java, considered characteristics of the *abangan* and *priyayi* as "mainline traditions" of Java, while the *santri* variant was a "counter tradition" which he called "scripturalism." See C. Geertz, *Islam Observed*, p. x.

39. Koentjaraningrat, *Rintangan Mental*, pp. 39-42, shows that the attitude of the *priyayi* is to go as high as he can in position and social acceptance without risking the possibility of doing anything displeasing to his superiors or to anyone else who might hurt or shame him.

40. We are using the term "modernization" instead of "Westernization," because the revolution unleashed within Western culture has spread far beyond it and formed cultural patterns that are becoming dominant all over the world in this century. S. Takdir Alisjahbana, *Indonesia: Social and Cultural Revolution* (London: Oxford University Press, 1969), pp. 13-22, says, "The term 'modern culture' has a far narrower scope than 'European culture' in that it excludes Christianity" (p. 13). By this he does not mean that modern culture is unrelated to the Christian religion, but that a clear distinction may be drawn between modern culture, which places the final responsibility for men's lives and for the world they live in on man's own intelligence and endeavor, and Christianity, which gives preeminence to God and his commandments as the basic criterion of cultural excellence. See also D. H. Burger, *Structural Changes in Javanese Society: The Supra-Village Sphere* (Ithaca: Cornell University Press, 1956), p. 27. Nevertheless, occasionally these phenomena of modernization will be referred to as "Western"--because of their source, and because of the difficulty of separating modernization from Westernization in the mind of the average Javanese.

41. Van der Kroef, *Modern World*, p. 98.

42. Cooley, *Church and Society*, p. 37.

43. Van Nieuwenhuijze, *Aspects of Islam*, pp. 16-18.

44. Donald R. Fagg, "Authority and Social Structures: A Study in Javanese Bureaucracy" (Ph.D. dissertation, Harvard University, 1958), p. 91 (hereafter cited as "Authority and Social Structures").

45. Wertheim, *Society in Transition*, p. 57.

46. Palmier, *Status and Power*, pp. 142-60.

47. Ibid., p. 60.

48. C. Geertz, *The Religion of Java*, p. 372. Also see Douglas, *Student Activism*, especially pp. 47-54 and 120-55.

49. C. Geertz, *Agricultural Involution*, p. xi.

50. Richard Critchfield, "Indonesia Heads for Violence," *Nation Magazine* 216 (25 June 1973): 810.

51. Ibid.

52. The population increase is 2.8 percent a year. See "Five More Years: Re-election of Suharto," *Time*, 2 April 1973, p. 101.

53. See Cooley, *Church and Society*, pp. 26-30, for a brief description of the chaotic economic situation of the nation during this period.

54. Critchfield, "Indonesia Heads for Violence," p. 810.

55. Van der Kroef, *Since Sukarno*, p. 234.

56. Tasdik, *Motives for Conversion*, pp. 12 and 37.

57. Most villages did not have schools past the sixth grade; students had to go into nearby towns and cities if they continued their education. The dwindling plots of arable land divided among descendents of each generation forced many to move to the cities in search of employment. See Wertheim, *Society in Transition*, pp. 95-131, for a discussion of the problem Indonesia has of being an agrarian country with an extremely low per capita production rate. For the cause of this, see C. Geertz, *Agricultural Involution*, pp. 131-45.

58. Burger, *Structural Changes*, p. 36.

59. Ibid.

60. Simatupang, "Situation and Challenge," pp. 26-27.

PART IV

Church Growth Factors

9

Churches on the
Frontier: East Java

The preceding chapters have given a broad perspective of the
relationship between Javanese church growth and religio-cultural,
political, and sociological trends in Indonesia. Chapters 9,
10, and 11 now examine the same scene from within the churches,
showing how five denominations capitalized on, or failed to
capitalize on, the situation between 1960 and 1971. These
chapters are less descriptive than the preceding chapters, but
more specific and critical, as we evaluate strengths and weaknesses in order to find guidelines of a strategy for winning
the Javanese to Christ. Let us study the *identity* of each
denomination, its *approach to evangelism*, and its *relationship
to the world*, in order to determine the effect of each on church
growth.

In these final chapters we are using the word "Church" to
refer to all Christians, or to a specific denomination. We also
refer to each denomination by the initials of its name in
Indonesian; both these usages follow common Indonesian practice.
When the word "church" is not capitalized, it usually refers to a
local organized congregation. The term "congregation" indicates a
group of baptized believers usually not yet organized and recognized as a church by its denomination.

EAST JAVA CHRISTIAN CHURCH (GKJW)

Identity

The GKJW is located in the province of East Java, center of the ancient Mojopahit dynasty and frontier for the expanding Javanese population during the last century. East Java's pioneering spirit and its distance from the later Mataram court centers of Central Java have influenced the outlook and growth of the GKJW. Its sociological and cultural background have prepared the GKJW to live and move in a Javanese world of indigenous forms and aspirations.

GKJW is a people's church. It reflects the attitude of the people of the area against the authoritarian rule of feudalism and colonialism. It is characterized by built-in resistance to an authoritarian clergy, by initiative of the laity, and by syntonic members oriented toward evangelism(1).

The GKJW was born in 1843 with the baptism of the first Javanese converts; Coolen and Emde served as midwives (see pp. 30-31). It began to take form with the establishment of the Christian village of Mojowarno by Paulus Tosari in 1846(2). Jellesma, a missionary of the Netherlands Missionary Society, moved to Mojowarno in 1851 and assisted Tosari in giving excellent leadership to the church and its nine branch congregations, which counted a total of 1,100 members by 1854(3).

Jellesma's death and the missionary society's disappointment with the quality of Christians in Mojowarno precipitated the coming, in 1864, of J. Kruyt, who took control of the *desa* and began an era of missionary tutelage. The generation of missionaries succeeding him followed his example of concentrating on education as the primary means of developing congregations(4). This resulted in: (1) Christians being isolated from the masses of Javanese and losing touch with the Moslem world around them; (2) Christians losing their urge to share the gospel and their secret *ilmu* (knowledge); (3) the missionary's becoming the administrator and educator of the village rather than its preacher and pastor; and (4) Christian villages established by missionaries failing to offer an appealing lifestyle to Javanese.

Nortier says, "Spontaneous joy over the treasure found in the Gospel, and consequently much of the spontaneous expansion, fell into the background"(5). The Christian enclaves were viewed as foreign possessions, and the missionaries as landowners instead of spiritual leaders. In contrast, villages started by Javanese Christian pioneers survived and became the strength of the GKJW(6).

FIGURE 6

CHURCH MEMBERSHIP GROWTH IN FIVE DENOMINATIONS

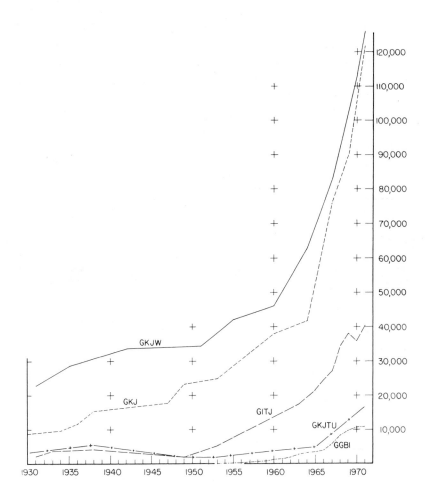

Javanese pioneers continued to open Christian villages in the sparsely settled areas south and east of Mojowarno. Around 1900 they also began to migrate to urban areas. These two sociological shifts helped break the isolation of Christian villages, and paved the way for future growth(7).

The independence of the GKJW from the missionary society in 1931, the internment of the remaining missionaries during World War II, and Indonesia's independence from the Netherlands served to break the bonds of missionary tutelage. Yet, the GKJW still follows the theology and structure of Dutch Reformed churches.

Approach to Evangelism

The membership of the GKJW increased by 273 percent in eleven years, a growth rate of 12.7% per year, average. (See Figure 6 and Figure 4 showing number of baptisms during this period.) Such a growth rate demands investigation into methods used to take advantage of political, cultural, and sociological currents.

The Rev. Mr. Sukrisno, chairman of the GKJW's evangelism division, said his denomination really began to grow in 1957 with the institution of new evangelistic methods, although it was 1960 before these methods began to take effect. (Note that the growth rate pictured in Figure 6 was even higher from 1951 to 1955 than from 1955 to 1960.) The methods included the role of every Christian as an evangelist, a new emphasis on the laity, family worship and Bible study in small groups, effective leadership by elders, a program of pastoral leadership to prepare church members for these tasks, and a better use of social ministries such as polyclinics and agricultural assistance(8).

Ten years later, in 1967, the GKJW revised its constitution and ecclesiology after a three-year debate between two groups: one represented by the former moderator of the synod, Marjosir (1946-1949 and 1952-1961); and the other by the new moderator, Ardi Suyatno (1961-1973). The former argued from John's idea of *logos* and emphasized the fellowship of the believers, mystic communion, and the traditional approach of Christians separated from the world. The latter contended that the emphasis should be on the Kingdom of God dynamically and innovatively penetrating society with the gospel.

The latter approach was adopted, and a new program of evangelism--*Pilot Proyek Jumaat Missioner* (Missionary Church Pilot Project)--was launched to help local congregations accomplish their mission as light "concentrated" on the world and salt "dissolved" into it. Its goals were: to make Jesus Christ, rather than "inherited religion" or a "folk religion," the cornerstone of their lives; to emphasize the fellowship of

Christians; to supply spiritual food based on the Word and the sacraments, rather than "devotional reflections;" to be a pilgrim church spread throughout society; and to build Christian homes. All of these were designed to contribute to the over-all goal of developing a stronger, more influential Christian presence in society(9).

The new program of evangelism was implemented in the cities in 1969. Surabaya, a city of 1,556,232(10), was divided into nine districts with ten to twenty-five groups (composed of ten to twenty families) in each. These small groups, led by their natural leaders, conducted regular Bible study and prayer meetings in members' homes and invited non-Christian neighbors to attend. Offerings received were divided three ways: for refreshments, for *diakonia* in the community, and for expenses of the mother church. With the *diakonia* funds, expenses were paid for the child of a communist prisoner, a pedicab was purchased to provide work for a refugee, capital was supplied for small home industries, and so on. Of the 450 groups in Surabaya, 150 met weekly.

The effectiveness of the program is shown in Figure 7 on the following page, which contrasts growth of the church in Surabaya with growth of the church in Mojowarno. In 1960, Surabaya had 2,094 members compared to 4,688 in Mojowarno. The static traditional Christian village of Mojowarno recorded an increase of baptisms from 1964 to 1967, with its highest totals coming after the attempted communist coup of 1965. But beginning in 1969, baptism totals fell back to around the 1964 level, and continued to decrease slightly with each succeeding year. On the other hand, Surabaya showed a marked increase for the three years following the coup, and then dropped back to its 1963 level in 1969, following the general trend. But after the new program of evangelism was begun in 1969, Surabaya's rate of baptisms ran counter to the general trend, increasing dramatically, even surpassing the 1967 high.

The emphasis on dividing the constituency into small groups meeting in homes of church members in each area is one of the secrets of growth of the GKJW. In addition to its ninety-two organized congregations, this denomination has over three hundred unorganized congregations with 25 to 70 families each, and a multitude of small groups. The program implemented in Surabaya is an organized version of a spontaneous rural pattern. (See pp. 15-16 and 21-22 for examples of such growth in rural areas of East Java.)

Preparation of the laity for leadership has contributed much to church growth. The GKJW has traditionally faced a scarcity of trained pastors; thus, laymen have taken an active part. A

FIGURE 7

BAPTISMS OF GKJW IN MOJOWARNO AND SURABAYA

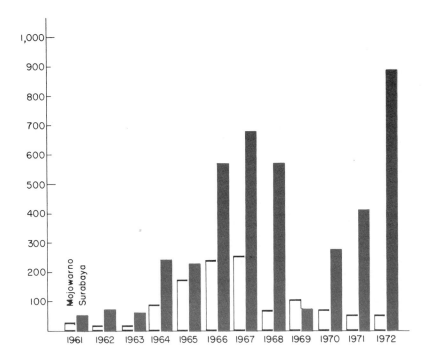

theological institute, established in 1929, has sought to understand and use Javanese cultural patterns probably better than
any other in Indonesia. After candidates for ordination began
to attend ecumenical seminaries in Jakarta and Yogyakarta(11),
the purpose of GKJW's institute was changed to upgrade lay church
workers through short-term retreats. The Church Member Development Center, an ecumenical institute, was established in Malang
in 1969 to bring together those of the same professions, for
training that would enable them to minister through their respective professions.

GKJW's evangelistic approach is reflected in the conviction
of synod leaders that the influence of Christian lives is the
most important factor in their growth. (See pp. 16-17.) Sixty-
one percent of the GKJW members interviewed said that the
influence of Christian lives was a factor in their conversions,
ranking it second only to "Spiritual need." This is in stark
contrast to the evaluation of members of the other four denominations, who ranked "Christian life" tenth, with only 12 percent
of them even mentioning it.

Freytag reports that the reason most frequently given by
Asians for their becoming Christians is

that Christians have another life. This other life is
almost indiscernible to outsiders, yet not to neighbours.
. . . What astonishes the neighbours is the fact that
Christians have "a life in another dimension, a life which
stands incontestably under another norm, even if this norm
is not obeyed, a life in which another power is at work,
which finds expression perhaps only in signs, but always
again in a surprising way"(12).

GKJW has not emphasized "dissolving as salt" into the world
to the exclusion of "concentrating the light" on the world: A
significant part of its success lies in the balance of the two.
Cooley says,

The actual outreach is done by members of the missionary
commission of the local congregation, largely laymen, who
make use of family gatherings and festivals, Christian
holidays, and the like to hold evangelistic meetings in
homes of Christians to which all neighbors are invited.
Since 1960 the Church has held each year a Church-wide
Proclamation of the Gospel Week, seeking to reach every
village in East Java(13).

GKJW's spirit of evangelism has involved them in several
mission efforts, including the sending of Tartib Eprajim to Bali
in 1934, only three years after gaining their independence from

the Netherlands Missionary Society(14). Yet, regrettably, this
zeal has raised a problem, because church leaders have felt they
must try to regulate the activities of pioneer Javanese evangelists. Representing the ancient tradition of freedom and independence of the autonomous *desa*, these evangelists have found it
difficult to fit into the institutional church and its discipline
(15). Tensions have arisen when they have baptized candidates who
have not fulfilled all the catechism requirements, or when they
have started congregations in virgin territory without approval
of the pastor who considers the area his parish, even if he has
never ministered there(16). This has resulted in some new congregations suffering from lack of leadership and acceptance. If
church leaders could have allowed these free spirits to evangelize and lead congregations, or could have provided pastoral
leadership for these village congregations, growth would have
been much greater.

GKJW has engaged in service ministries through polyclinics,
schools, and public school religion classes, but on a much
smaller scale than the Javanese denominations in Central Java
(17). Their male nurses have been very effective foundation
stones on which new churches have been built. Nevertheless,
GKJW converts rated "Service" as the least important factor in
their conversions.

Relationship to the World

Due to its birth in a Javanese village, the GKJW has related
the gospel to Javanese culture better than any of the other four
denominations. Traditional Javanese values, such as *gotong
royong* (mutual assistance), *musyawarah* (mutual deliberations),
and *mufakat* (consensus), are viewed by GKJW members as a fulfillment of Christ's commandment to love. *Slametans*, such as the
bersih desa (purifying of the village), have been adapted to
emphasize Christian beliefs(18). (See pp. 40-41.) Christian
puppeteers have presented aspects of the Christian faith through
the medium of shadow-plays.

The relationship between culture and the gospel has not been
institutionalized, and a dynamic confrontation will continue(19).
The GKJW's relationship to the culture has been one of the most
significant reasons for its growth.

Several sociological factors contributed to growth of the
GKJW. Christianity, in contrast to other religions, was not
accepted as the religion of the ruler, and thus did not arrive
in the *desa* via a detour through the feudal upper crust. It was
viewed as a new foundation for rural life in East Java(20), and
the GKJW, with its roots in the peasant class, has remained
rural in outlook even though 25 percent of its members have

moved to the city(21). Research reveals that 76.3 percent of
the converts became Christians in people movements.

The sociological composition of the ninety-two GKJW churches
is as follows:

Location:	City	2
	Large town	17
	Small town	18
	Village	24
	Christian village	31
Established:	Before 1931	45
	1931-1955	19
	1955-1960	12
	1960-1971	16
Economy:	Prosperous	3
	Adequate	35
	Potentially adequate	18(22)
	Poor	36

Most of the GKJW's growth has come on the edges of its territory, among new settlers in general, and in areas of economic
depression(23). Suyatno stated, "It appears that the responsiveness of the Javanese occurs when there is a vacuum or displace-
ment, either geographical or religious"(24).

The family in East Java plays an important role in the spread
of Christianity, through its traditional rural concern for all
members of the nuclear family. Sukrisno gave his own family as
an example: His only brother became a Christian before he did;
and in the ten years since then, seventeen nieces and nephews
(some of whom have lived with Sukrisno), two uncles and aunts,
and seven servants who worked for them have become Christians
and started Christian families. In his wife's family, four of
the eight children are married; three married non-Christians who
later became Christians.

The impress of modernization is being felt less in the *desa*
than in the cities. Christian villages, in general more progressive than non-Christian villages(25), are often cited by the
government as examples of advanced development and organization
(26). Although the constituency of the GKJW is basically rural
and lower class, its leaders are well educated and seem capable
of leading the Church into the modern era without pulling its
roots from Javanese soil.

The GKJW has faced and met church growth challenges presented to it by: (1) adjustment to the culture, (2) emphasis on the laity, (3) use of sociological contacts, (4) innovative methods, and (5) strong leadership.

On the other hand, the GKJW still faces significant problems:

(1) Many of the Christian villages are still static, traditional, satisfied, and dependent on farm land owned by the churches, rather than actively teaching and practicing stewardship.

(2) For some, Christianity is a folk religion inherited from their parents with more political connotations than religious ones.

(3) Too much dependence was placed on the now-merged Protestant Christian political party as an aid to evangelism and missions.

(4) Emphasis on the Christian life and Christian presence has been very effective in East Java, but it presents the danger of such witness becoming unbalanced or dissolving into the world if proclamation does not accompany it.

(5) Freedom in evangelism and church planting has been curbed hindering spontaneous expansion.

NOTES

1. Research notes of interviews with church leaders by Frank Cooley. (Unpublished.)

2. Van Akkeren, *Sri and Christ*, p. 97.

3. Bentley-Taylor, *The Weathercock's Reward*, p. 86.

4. Van Akkeren, *Sri and Christ*, pp. 108-9.

5. C. W. Nortier, "A 'Younger Church' Grows into Maturity: The Role of the Laity in the Life and Mission of Christ's Church in East Java, Indonesia," *Laity* 4 (November 1957): 21.

6. Van Akkeren, *Sri and Christ*, pp. 109-10.

7. Ibid., pp. 114-18. On p. 210, van Akkeren says that 9.5 percent of the members lived in urban areas by 1938. By 1962, between 20 and 25 percent lived there.

8. Private interview with Sukrisno, Office of Evangelism, GKJW, Surabaya, 16 May 1973.

9. "Pedoman Pelaksanaan Pilot Projek Djumaat Missioner" [Manual for the Missionary Church Pilot Project] (Badan Pekabaran Indjil Sinode GKDW, 1969). (Mimeographed.)

10. Statistics from the *Badan Perkumpulan Statistik* [Bureau of Statistics], Jakarta, 1971.

11. *Sekolah Tinggi Theologia* and *Sekolah Tinggi Duta Wacana*.

12. Weber, *Ecumenical Movement*, p. 170.

13. Cooley, *Church and Society*, pp. 89-90.

14. See Weber, *Ecumenical Movement*, pp. 170-77.

15. "As the *desa* feels itself free from the State, they feel free from the church and were [*sic*] convinced of having received their charge directly from the Lord" (van Akkeren, *Sri and Christ*, p. 162).

16. See the diaries of David Bentley-Taylor, *The Prisoner Leaps* (London: Lutterworth Press, 1965), and *The Great Volcano* (London: Lutterworth Press, 1967), and comments on them by van Akkeren, *Sri and Christ*, pp. 160-62.

17. For a description of GKJW's service ministries, see ibid., pp. 181-84 and 201-3.

18. See ibid., pp. 166-68 and 181-82.

19. See ibid., pp. 210-13, for some theological approaches to Javanese cultural forms in present-day Indonesia. Yet, Ismanoe Mostoko, "Report of Badan Pekabaran Indjil Sinode Geredja Kristen Djawi Wetan," 19 October 1969 in "Pedoman Pelaksanaan Pilot Projek Djumaat Missioner," pp. 1-2, laments the fact that some of the old customs, such as circumcision and the *slametan* for the dead, are still being practiced even though Christian emphases have replaced the original ones.

20. Van Akkeren, *Sri and Christ*, pp. 149-51.

21. Synod leaders say that only one local church has a modern
    viewpoint; between 64 and 72 have a traditional viewpoint;
    and from 16 to 28 fall somewhere in between. See Frank
    Cooley, notes of interviews with leaders at GKJW Synod
    office, Malang, 18 November 1972.

22. These eighteen congregations own church lands that with
    proper management would provide for their needs.

23. The most responsive areas are the Malang II *klasis*, the
    southeast corner of the Basuki *klasis*, and the areas north
    of Purwokerto, west of Wiyung, south of Lamongan, and east
    of Madiun, near the Malang-Surabaya county line, and Pare.

24. Frank Cooley, notes of interview with Ardi Suyatno, GKJW
    synod office, Malang, 18 November 1972.

25. Van Akkeren, *Sri and Christ*, pp. 204-5.

26. Ibid., pp. 205-6.

10

Churches in the Heartland: Central Java

All who study about Indonesia (and even knowledgeable tourists) know that the heartland of the nation's dominant Javanese culture is located in Central Java. Here one of the world's few remaining sultans, Hamengkubuwono IX of Yogyakarta, still maintains his ancestral palace (although he himself is more often elsewhere, busily serving as Vice-President of the Indonesian Republic). Here is the world-famed Hindu temple of Prambanan, spectacular backdrop for the equally famous Ramayana dances. Here is Borobudur, the world's largest Buddhist shrine (now undergoing a long-needed restoration, with international financial backing).

Three of the five Javanese Churches are almost exclusively located in this Javanese heartland. Let's study them one by one, using the same threefold pattern introduced in the previous chapter: first the *identity* of each denomination, then its *approach to evangelism*, and finally its *relationship to the world*.

JAVANESE CHRISTIAN CHURCHES (GKJ)

Identity

The GKJ churches cover the province of Central Java, particularly the southern region, heart of the former Mataram kingdom. The cities of Yogyakarta and Surakarta (Solo) are considered the cradle of Javanese culture. Residents of this area follow rigid traditional patterns more closely than other Javanese.

Islamization was never completed here, and the peasantry was an easy target for communism.

The first Christians in Central Java were baptized in 1858, as a result of the work of laymen and laywomen(1). Congregations were formed, and the work flourished after Sadrach Suropranoto began working with Mrs. Johannes C. Philips (see pp. 32-34). When the first Dutch missionaries of the Christian Reformed Missionary Society entered in the late 1880's, there were already nine thousand Christians and scores of congregations under Sadrach's leadership.

The missionaries sought to take over leadership of these congregations. Conflict developed, and only 150 people followed the missionaries. "Thus the opportunity of building on a broad, indigenous foundation was lost, and the missionaries had to start from the beginning"(2).

These well-meaning Dutch missionaries were determined to establish churches modeled on their sending churches in the Netherlands. Their distinctives are still evident in the GKJ: emphasis on independent churches with local autonomy, the Heidelberg Confession, a high liturgy, city-centered work, and social services as instruments of evangelism(3). The connection of local churches in the Netherlands with local churches in Java has provided large sums of money for service ministries. With few exceptions, the GKJ has adhered to the conservative *Gereformeerde* theology and structure.

The GKJ gained its independence in a series of steps: A GKJ synod was organized by 1931. Javanese leaders were left with sole responsibility for the work during World War II. The churches stated their independence from the missionaries in documents promulgated in 1947 and 1950. These two documents stated the relationship of missionaries to Javanese leaders as that of equal partners, but a further statement in 1958 limited the missionaries to working only in service ministries(4).

Approach to Evangelism

Since 1960 the membership of the GKJ has more than tripled-- from 38,000 to 121,500(5). These members are distributed among 174 independent congregations and 615 subsidiary congregations in 16 *klasis*(6). They are served by 134 ordained pastors and 90 *guru Injil* (Gospel teachers, i.e., unordained lay or assistant pastors). Although the number of pastors has almost doubled since 1960, the number of *guru Injil* has increased by only three(7).

The GKJ, with a different methodology, polity, and theology from the GKJW, has grown at about the same rate. This indicates that religio-cultural, political, and sociological factors produced response among the Javanese, regardless of evangelistic approach. Yet a closer look reveals that the two situations are different, and that the methodology used by the GKJ was as effective in evangelizing its area as that used by the GKJW in East Java. The GKJ began in towns and cities among the *priyayi* (gentry), and through them spread to the *abangan* (peasantry) in towns and villages. This social structure fitted Central Java's feudal background.

The GKJ concept of evangelism changed radically between 1959 and 1969. At their first synod meeting in 1959, evangelism was defined as "the work of Jesus Christ himself who gathered men into Christian churches . . . and then gave this task to his apostles and the Christian churches until the end of the age" (8). The eleventh synod meeting in 1969 said that evangelism was "the spreading of the gospel of the Kingdom of God," interpreted as meaning not "the salvation of individuals only, but on the other hand, the salvation and regeneration of all society according to the laws and norms of the kingdom of God(9).

Initially the GKJ exhibited a positive response to rapid growth following the attempted coup of 1965. But some church leaders showed an increasingly negative reaction as large numbers of people could not be adequately nurtured. "Mass repentances" had become such a problem by 1967 as to occasion an evangelism consultation. These "mass conversions" had occurred in almost all the churches, and had polarized leaders on the question of quantity versus quality. Some pastors complained about the multitude of problems caused by large numbers of new members with only a shallow understanding of the Christian faith. The Rev. Mr. Darmowigoto, director of the GKJ's evangelism division, contended that the sociological situation demanded mass evangelism methods in addition to conventional ones, in order to meet the challenge of millions of former communists and others who were left without an adequate foundation in life(10). (See pp. 20-21.)

The result of this consultation on evangelism had both a positive and a negative effect on church growth. The positive response was a new program to solve the pressing need for trained leaders to teach and serve new converts. It included the establishment of a theological education institute to train one class of *desa* pastors for two years, and the addition of special courses in a mobile training program to equip church members for service(11). The negative result was that 70 to 80 percent of the synod members were unhappy about rapid church growth because of the shallowness of new members and the

financial burden placed upon the churches. Thus they concentrated on the newer concept of evangelism (as adopted in 1969,
p. 157), and emphasized consolidation to the detriment of
evangelization(12).

Soegiri's evaluation of the GKJ's response to evangelism was
that pastors seldom pioneered in starting churches in new areas
but were preceded by the laity(13). Sardi Karjoredjo's evaluation was:

> One thing is clear: Growth came from external forces,
> not internal ones, and in fact, we think that GKJ was not
> ready to receive such growth due to a lack of coordination
> and a firm strategy to wrestle with the problem of nur-
> ture. . . . In reality, without our realizing it, the
> reception of these new members changed the evangelism
> strategy from a pastor-centered to a lay-centered orien-
> tation, because of the mobilization of great numbers of
> laymen(14).

Thus the growth of the GKJ was made possible by the response
of members and local pastors rather than by a program planned
by the synod, although the evangelism division did give
encouragement and guidance to this spontaneous expansion. The
effect of the "new theology of evangelism" adopted in 1969 has
yet to be seen, because it has not yet permeated the local
churches or the average church members, who are still emphasizing the direct proclamation of the Gospel(15).

GKJ church growth was unevenly distributed: The greatest
response was in south Central Java near Yogyakarta, Surakarta,
Salatiga, and Purwodadi. Growth in west Central Java, along the
south coast from Yogyakarta to Banyumas was excellent, but then
began to show signs of slowing. The north coast area, where
Moslems first gained control, has been characterized by slow
growth with the exception of the metropolitan area of Semarang.
Areas of previous communist concentration have shown the most
rapid growth. And growth in villages has far exceeded growth in
cities.

One example of good growth is in the area near Purwodadi,
where church membership grew from 1,900 in 1957, to 3,500 in
1965, to 9,000 in 1969, and to 10,418 in 1972, not including
7,000 who were still candidates for membership. The Tegowanu
church grew from one family in 1950, to four families in 1960,
to four hundred families in 1970. The Gundih church began with
two families in 1961, and had grown to four congregations and 23
Bible study groups by the end of the 1960's(16).

However, in many areas the lack of trained leaders and the emphasis on quality resulted in the tragic loss of a monumental opportunity to lead many more thousands to Christ.

Missionary outreach to Javanese who have cooperated with the Indonesian government's program of moving rural transmigrants from overcrowded Java to sparsely settled outer islands has resulted in three *klasis* in South Sumatra and scattered congregations on other islands.

Service ministries were originally established as instruments of evangelism. But since 1967 all medical services have been under the Christian Foundation for Public Health, with the emphasis changing from direct evangelism through health-care facilities to service and visitation of the patients in their homes. Serious questions have been raised by synod members concerning the efficiency and evangelistic thrust of the new program in GKJ's three hospitals, five family planning clinics, six health centers, seven obstetric clinics, and sixteen polyclinics (17).

The GKJ taught 69,999 students in 472 schools in 1969(18), in addition to placing 265 teachers of religion in public schools(19). Other services include ministries to youth, university students, women, orphans, refugees, prostitutes, and social projects in agriculture, animal husbandry, fisheries, and home industries.

One would expect church growth in the GKJ to be greatly influenced by these vast service ministries. Yet, less than 2 percent of the interviewees credited "Service" as being a primary influence in their conversions, and only 10 percent even mentioned such ministries as having any influence on their decisions. Although these deeds of mercy no doubt contributed to the image of Christianity in Central Java, failure to proclaim the gospel to those who were served greatly weakened the contribution of GKJ's service ministries to church growth(20).

Relationship to the World

The GKJ has made an honest attempt to adjust to the culture and, at the same time, hold to their distinctive beliefs. Marriage *adat* is no longer a problem because it has been recognized as acceptable tradition shorn of its original religious implications(21), but pregnancy and birth *adat* with the attendant *slametans* are not generally practiced by GKJ members.

In 1951 the synod prohibited circumcision (based on Col. 2:11-12) except for clear medical reasons; but the problem was still being discussed in the synod meeting of 1971. Informants said that some new Christians became inactive when they realized they could not be circumcised like their neighbors.

GKJ members have developed a custom of giving Bible or foreign names to their children, with the result that many call them "*Landa Jawa*" (Javanese Hollanders), thus presenting a barrier to non-Christians who are determined to remain Javanese(22).

To communicate the gospel, the GKJ occasionally uses traditional shadow-plays, a type of folk opera, Javanese clown acts, and classic and modern dances with biblical themes.

Although the GKJ has related to the culture as far as they feel their theology will allow, their insistence on no circumcision and the giving of Christian names has hindered their growth. On the other hand, cultural substitutes (such as a thanksgiving service to replace the *slametan*) have helped keep lines of communication open to society in general(23).

Even though the GKJ began among upper classes in the cities, their rapid growth in rural areas (especially since 1965) has produced a sociological configuration similar to the GKJW, which began in rural areas and moved toward the cities.

Modernization has affected the GKJ more than the GKJW, due to GKJ's higher educational level, their use of modern media, and their geographical location. The population explosion, economic depression, urbanization, and democratic ideals are affecting the churches, threatening to modernize them even faster than those of the GKJW in East Java. This process, however, had aided growth in such urban areas as Semarang and Yogyakarta.

Problems and opportunities listed by GKJ leaders in their self-study included:

(1) Educating lay workers to take advantage of evangelistic opportunities.

(2) Making maximum use of educational institutions to provide the kind of leaders needed.

(3) Redistributing leaders to areas of greater need.

(4) Developing new methods of follow-up.

(5) Reconciling the difference between church structure as written and church structure as practiced.

(6) Distinguishing between the church as an institution and the church as an organism in relation to service institutions.

(7) Re-evaluating positive and negative aspects of church institutions being largely supported by foreign funds(24).

In addition to problems listed by their own denominational leaders, the GKJ needs to face the fact that, partly due to their reticence to accept large numbers of converts and partly due to their new concept of evangelism, they are missing one of their finest opportunities to reach thousands of Javanese who are in the process of moving toward a permanent religion. Their emphasis on training their entire membership, particularly the leadership, is excellent. But the question remains whether these newly trained workers can be guided to reap the harvest and build up new Christians so that evangelism becomes a perennial part of GKJ's church life.

NORTH CENTRAL JAVA CHRISTIAN CHURCH (GKJTU)

Identity

The GKJTU built on the work of Gottlob Brückner, Sadrach Suropranoto, Ibrahim Tunggul Wulung, and the Dutch missionary Hoezoo (see pp. 31-32). The first members were led to Christ by Mrs. LeJolle of the Simo estate near Salatiga, and were baptized by Hoezoo at Semarang in 1857. A Christian village was established at Ngemoh, with Petrus Sedojo, an evangelist from Mojowarno, as their pastor. Mrs. LeJolle enlisted the help of the Ermelo church on her return to the Netherlands, and their first missionary, DeBoer, arrived in Ngemoh in 1868.

In Neukirchen, Germany, a faith mission alliance was organized, composed of members of Lutheran, Reformed, Baptist, United, and Free churches; their first missionaries arrived in 1889. They had no confession of faith or catechism but emphasized the role of every Christian as an evangelist who provided his own support through faith or a secular vocation(25). German evangelical missionaries cooperated in the task of evangelism through building complexes of churches, hospitals, and schools in each city(26). By 1940 the GKJTU consisted of five organized churches, 42 unorganized congregations, and 60 preaching points (27) with 4,000 to 6,500 members led by eight missionaries and twelve *guru Injil* (unordained assistants)(28).

Although the missionaries themselves lived by faith, they failed to teach the congregations to support and lead the work, leaving them poorly prepared to face the rigors of war. The Japanese confiscated their institutions during World War II, and Dutch forces occupied their territory during the Revolution of

1945-1949. This caused many GKJTU members to move to south
Java, seeking safety and employment(29).

The Dutch, considering property of the German faith missions
to be spoils of war, gave all GKJTU institutions to the GKJ,
which still had connections in the Netherlands. Pastors from
the GKJ even used GKJTU buildings for worship services(30).

In 1949 these two denominations inaugurated merger plans,
which were only partially successful due to misunderstandings
about GKJTU property and GKJ church order. As a result, in 1953
sixteen churches with two thousand members decided to remain
independent and continue the GKJTU tradition.

As a result of a visit by K. Middelsted of the mother church
in Neukirchen, hospitals and polyclinics of the German faith
mission were surrendered to the GKJ, and church buildings,
parsonages, and schools were returned to the GKJTU. But the
problem has never been satisfactorily solved: The GKJ still
refuses to vacate buildings to which the GKJTU holds legal
title.

Most GKJTU churches of today are located in north Central
Java, from Tegal to Bojonegoro. The GKJTU finally was permitted
to become a member of the Indonesian Council of Churches in 1972,
after the GKJ withdrew their objections(31).

The original structure of loose congregationalism led by
laymen has evolved toward a strong synodal pattern directed by
the clergy. A group of young pastors led by Paulus Sujoko, head
of the synod since 1969, directed the GKJTU through a transition
period toward a clearer statement of theology and ecclesiology
(32).

Approach to Evangelism

GKJTU showed little growth from the time of their new beginning in 1953 until 1965, when membership began increasing. From
an estimated 2,400 in 1965, their numbers reached 16,846 in
1971 (see Figure 6). They met in 43 organized churches and
35 unorganized congregations, served by fourteen ordained
pastors, eight *guru Injil*, 22 *guru Injil* helpers, and 33 candidates for *guru Injil*. Twenty-seven of the 43 churches have been
started since 1965. The six city churches had many members from
the higher classes, but 60 percent of the members of the 37 *desa*
congregations were landless farmers, while 30 percent owned
their own farms(33).

Accurate statistics kept by the Semarang GKJTU church show
growth from 173 members in 1956 to 1,828 in 1971. This gives a

picture of church growth similar to the pattern of other
churches in Java, except that the peak year for baptisms was
1968 instead of 1967.

The GKTJU growth generally parallels the growth of the other
churches. From 1960 to 1965, membership grew 52.8 percent, or
8.8 percent annually. From 1966 to 1970, it grew 105 percent,
or 19.7 percent per annum. In 1971, it only grew 1.6 percent,
even less than the birth rate. The percentage of growth actually dropped each year from 1962 to 1966, increased dramatically
in 1967, and then began to drop again.

The most spectacular growth in the GKJTU has taken place around
Mount Merbabu near Salatiga, where 24 churches with seven thousand members have been started since 1965. (See pp. 112-113, for
a description of conversions in Cuntel village near the top of
Mount Merbabu.) In response to this rapid growth, the GKJTU was
able to use the first German missionaries to come and serve
among them in 25 years, to begin training leaders. Iugo Garthe
reopened a training school in Salatiga in 1965, which five years
later was put under the direction of Seidlitz, the second
missionary to come from Germany. Garthe then began a new training program in 1970, with an emphasis on aiding indigenous
leaders in villages near Salatiga. These leaders came down the
mountain to school for one week of intensive training every
three months, and returned to become effective leaders of new
congregations during the rest of the quarter(34).

Methodological reasons given for this rapid growth are
(1) the emphasis on evangelism by every member, (2) the acculturation of the gospel, and (3) the training of the laity(35).
Much of this growth has been made possible by GKJTU's flexible
attitude. Pastors organized lay groups to teach catechism
classes in each of the villages for a twelve-month period, but
some of the converts were baptized sooner because of pressure
felt from the governmental decree.

GKJTU converts ranked the government's decision on religion
higher than any other denomination as a factor in conversion,
with 41.2 percent saying it was the primary cause and 76.2 percent giving it as one of the factors. "Spiritual need" was a
distant second, but in the total evaluation, "Society" outranked
all factors except "Government." When added together, political,
spiritual, and social factors played an almost equal role in
this denomination's conversions, with other factors being almost
negligible.

Relationship to the World

Its rather vague theological stance has given the GKJTU
flexibility in relationship to the culture. Nevertheless, its
traditions have come into conflict with cultural practices of
new Christians:

+ Circumcision is allowed for health reasons, but is not
acceptable on cultural or religious grounds. It is discouraged
by explanation rather than by prohibition.

+ Traditional ceremonies on the third, fortieth, hundredth,
and thousandth day after the death of a relative are often
replaced by prayer meetings, but GKJTU has never set a policy
on such practices.

+ Opinions on attending *slametans* is divided, although many
Christians attend in order to maintain harmonious social relationships.

+ Polygamy is a problem with new Christians. But those who
have had more than one wife prior to conversion are accepted,
although with reservation. Christians are prohibited from
taking a second wife(36).

Cultural art forms have been adapted for Christian use on
special occasions, but a Western-style liturgy is used in
regular worship services(37). Most of the new GKJTU congregations conducted their services in the open front porch of
Javanese homes, until they were able to construct church buildings. (Ten indigenous buildings have now been erected on Mount
Merbabu.) Members of such churches sat on the floor, wore the
sarong and Javanese turban or Indonesian national fez (*peci*),
and used Javanese chants to sing passages of Scripture. A type
of Javanese folk opera was often used as a vehicle for Bible
stories. In these congregations, leaders were not insistent on
the prohibition of circumcision, although most of them person-
ally thought it best not to allow circumcision.

Modernization's impact has been felt on church structure
through the influence of six younger men among the GKJTU's
pastors. An attempt to modernize the structure failed in 1967,
when eight older pastors adhered to the German faith mission's
traditional concept of charismatic spiritual leadership as
opposed to organization and structured administration. The
younger group in 1969 elected Sujoko Paulus as head of the
synod, and under his leadership the GKJTU has pushed forward
with innovative methods in spite of the generation gap.

The only other noticeable effect of modernization on the GKJTU was the pressure on some new Christians by increased gambling when the Indonesian government began a lottery. (The government-sponsored lottery has since been discontinued.)

The GKJTU has made a remarkable contribution to evangelism in spite of tradition-bound leadership, controversy with the GKJ, and the loss of much property. Their emphasis on the laity, lay training programs, adaptation to the culture, and use of social, political, and religious currents in Indonesia has greatly aided their growth. Nevertheless, they face the problems of too few trained leaders, an undefined theology and ecclesiology, a distorted church image as a result of their problem with the GKJ, and poor churches having difficulty supporting themselves.

GKJTU church growth has slowed since 1969, particularly in mountain areas. The methodological reason most responsible for this is the emphasis by the GKJTU on consolidation. In 1971 they devised plans to consolidate the gains they had made, until 1976, at which time they planned to begin evangelizing again. In so doing, they failed to reap the harvest of many receptive villages surrounding their churches. At the same time, they inadvertently taught those eager new congregations that their primary task was nurture, instead of both nurture and evangelism(38).

JAVA EVANGELICAL CHURCH (GITJ)

Identity

The GITJ is located around Mount Muria on the northern coast of Central Java, the domain of the former Islamic kingdom of Demak. The population of the area is more strongly Islamic than that of any other area studied, although animistic practices are still observed(39).

Ibrahim Tunggul Wulung established successful Christian villages in this area beginning in 1863, but the missionaries who established the GITJ did not build on his foundation. Pieter Jansz was sent from the Netherlands to begin working in the area in 1853(40). The fanatical Moslems in the area did not accept his isolationist Mennonite views, so in the next twenty years only forty persons were baptized(41).

Jansz and his son began establishing Christian colonies in 1878, after seeing the success of such colonies in East Java. But their villages were neither open to non-Christians (unless they agreed to attend worship services and refrain from working on Sunday) nor led by Javanese; therefore, they remained small and isolated from Javanese culture. In 1928 missionaries shifted their emphasis more to the towns where Christian nurses, teachers, civil servants, and youths had moved.

Due to the predominant role of missionaries, the GITJ was not prepared for independence which was forced upon them by World War II. They took a step toward maturity after the Netherlands was attacked, by organizing the "Conference of Javanese Congregations in Pati, Kudus, and Jepara Residences," consisting of twelve congregations and about two thousand adult members(42).

Traumatic experiences during the following decade helped break the isolationist syndrome of the GITJ. Their suffering began when local Moslems attacked them prior to the Japanese invasion, destroying their buildings and killing many church members. Then the Japanese confiscated all mission property and inflicted more suffering on GITJ members. During the Revolution of 1945-1949, they were caught between the Dutch and the nationalists, each of whom suspected them of being spies for the other side. In spite of loss of members and property, the GITJ was able to survive and even to prove its patriotism by fighting the Dutch, although this meant transgressing Mennonite pacifist principles(43).

GITJ leaders, along with those of other Javanese denominations, declared their independence from the missionaries in 1950. In the GITJ's desire to establish its identity and relationship with other churches, it joined the Indonesian Council of Churches and has been greatly influenced by the GKJ. They borrowed ecclesiastical terms from the GKJ, along with their synod model. Nevertheless, they maintained their distinctive church polity by having representatives to the synod meeting come from local churches rather than from the *klasis* (although in recent years their structure has evolved until synod decisions are now binding on both the *klasis* and the local churches)(44).

The GITJ has twice as many churches in villages as in towns or cities. The village churches consist of poor farmers and fishermen who hold tenaciously to traditional views, while the city churches, composed of better educated members, welcome innovations(45).

The outlook of the GITJ in relation to culture, church structure, traditions, and spiritual movements has changed radically since 1940, but the leadership still feels that progress is hindered by attitudes inherited from missionary tutelage. Members of the traditional churches have not been taught to support the church, take initiative without a dominant leader, or integrate with society(46). In spite of opposition from the

older generation, GITJ leaders have been able to take great
strides in the last two decades, resulting in increased growth.

Approach to Evangelism

   GITJ has grown rapidly, from 2,000 members in 1949 to 7,000
in 1960, at an annual rate of 12.1 percent, and 40,150 in 1971--
a net growth of 473.5 percent during the latter eleven years,
or an annual average of 17.2 percent(47). After a revival in
1963 (see pp. 18-19 for an account of it), church growth
accelerated to a higher rate per year than after the attempted
communist coup of 1965, although the number of baptisms after
1965 was larger. (See Figure 8 for baptisms per year.)

   Since 1963 the number of organized GITJ churches has grown
from fourteen to 23, the number of ordained pastors from 27 to
49, and the number of lay pastors from seventeen to 45(48). The
growth figure of GITJ shows a steady increase in membership
since 1953 (see Figure 6). Their missionary spirit has led to
mission work in Sumatra and West Irian.

   The three reasons given by GITJ for its rapid growth are:

   (1) The political, social, and economic situation pushed
people to find a new way of life.

   (2) The Church had been prepared for this work. The seed of
the gospel had been planted, and following the revival of 1963,
spiritual gifts were used to reap the harvest.

   (3) The principle of personal evangelism was practiced by
ordinary members as the People of God(49).

   My research supports the above-mentioned reasons. More
GITJ members listed "Protection" as the primary cause for their
conversions than any other motivation. The influence of the
"Christian life" ranked second; "Church" and "Miracles" tied
for third place as primary causes. In the overall evaluation,
"Christian life" and "Church" tied for the lead in times
mentioned, followed by "Protection" and "Miracles." Evidently
the daily witness of Christian villages accounted for the high
ranking of "Christian life" and "Church." Fanatical Moslem
neighbors accounted for the high ranking of "Protection." And
the revival of 1963, with its attendant charismatic manifestations, made GITJ the only Javanese denomination claiming
"Miracles" as a significant factor in its growth.

   The response of the GITJ to this challenge of rapid growth
resulted in 23 organized churches and 116 unorganized congregations by 1971. The growing need for leadership was revealed by

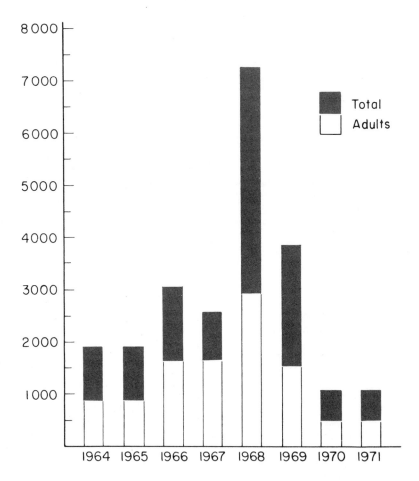

FIGURE 8

NEW MEMBERS OF GITJ

Total
Adults

the fact that each pastor or *guru Injil* was responsible for 277 persons in 1953, 399 persons in 1963, and 544 persons in 1969 (50). In order to provide leaders for new congregations, the synod established a Christian academy in Pati in 1965, added a two-year program in 1967 to train pastoral assistants to fill pressing needs, and instituted short-term courses for church officers(51).

According to the GITJ philosophy, service cannot be separated from evangelism, but it can be differentiated: Service is the witness of actions motivated by love, and evangelism is a verbal witness(52). GITJ operates eighteen schools with 157 teachers and 2,586 students. In addition, they have 175 part-time teachers of religion who began teaching in 1968 in public schools in direct response to the government's emphasis on religion(53). In contrast to the GKJ, the GITJ uses its hospital at Tayu as an instrument of evangelism, although efforts are made not to offend Moslem patients.

GITJ has identified itself with the needs of the people and the aspirations of the government by establishing (in cooperation with Mennonites in Canada and Europe) economic self-help projects such as irrigation, commerical fishing, transportation, animal husbandry, farming cooperatives, and small home indus-tries. The synod estimated that 50 percent of the projects were successful, but it discontinued some, such as a low-priced rice store, because they were producing "rice Christians."

Originally these projects were to have increased the income of the churches. When they did not, the emphasis was placed instead on serving the public, thus helping GITJ to overcome its previous isolationism(54). Although the role of service ministries was stressed by Church leaders, GITJ converts ranked "Service" only tenth in the list of primary causes of conver-sions, and seventh in the total evaluation.

Relationship to the World

Conflicts which the GITJ has gone through in the last three decades have opened up its attitude and its relationships with society. No longer are all connections with the world thought to be evil nor all its arts sinful. With the exception of a few traditional congregations, GITJ churches have begun to identify with the culture.

Adat related to birth and the giving of names is still practiced in rural areas, but the more educated church members in towns do not follow it. Some tension is evident concerning circumcision; the Mennonite Mission strictly prohibited it because it was the initiatory rite for Moslems. GITJ has gone

on record as prohibiting it on the same grounds, but has not
enforced this decision because circumcision is also viewed as a
sign of manhood, and the ceremony provides an avenue of communication with society. Enforcement of the prohibition is left to
local churches, which are usually lenient in new areas and among
new Christians(55).

Marriage *adat* is still followed by Christians in the *desa*,
but those in towns use only the traditional decorations. Death
and burial customs have not caused many problems among GITJ
members; most funerals become opportunities for evangelism.
Adat surrounding planting and reaping does not generally affect
Christians, except for the annual harvest festival, in response
to which a thanksgiving service filled with Christian meaning
has been substituted.

GITJ does not seek to use art forms, but allows its members
to do so as long as they do not violate Bible teachings.
Members near Jepara are widely known for their religious wood
carvings. Others have used traditional dances and Christian
drama to communicate the gospel(56).

The fact that no large city is in the area served by GITJ
has affected its sociological configuration and its adjustment
to modernization. A majority of its people live in villages or
small cities. Only a small percentage are "middle-class" (civil
servants, merchants, and those with commercial interests). Since
the 1930's a continual exodus of GITJ young people from *desa* to
small town and city (to become teachers, nurses, midwives, and
students) has provided membership for congregations in these
more urban areas. In the Jepara church, about 90 percent of
the members have such a Christian village background. Therefore, the church has not attracted many truly urbanized members
(although it has started several village congregations).

The greatest problems caused by modernization are the
mobility of GITJ youth who do not return to help in the *desa*,
and the influence of improper films and gambling. Gambling was
viewed as the most difficult problem, because it was sanctioned
for a time by the Indonesian government and people around Mount
Muria liked to go to the *dukun ramal* (seer) to obtain winning
lottery numbers(57).

GITJ sees its needs as: (1) overcoming the dependency
syndrome, (2) a theological answer to problems presented by the
culture, (3) a deeper understanding of the church, (4) a need to
educate and minister to church members, (5) better administration, and (6) an improved attitude by church members toward
other religions(58).

This Mennonite-oriented denomination has exhibited resiliency in suffering, dynamic life in tension with traditionalism, and quick response to challenges presented after the abortive communist coup. The problem of having enough trained leaders of the right kind is a critical one; there is still too much dependence on synod leadership.

NOTES

1. Cooley, *Church and Society*, p. 90.

2. Ibid., p. 91.

3. Müller-Krüger, *Sedjarah Geredja*, pp. 180-185.

4. Iman Soegiri, *Study dan Penelitian Gereja-Gereja Kristen Jawa Tengah* [Study and Research of the Central Java Christian Churches] (n.p., 1970; hereafter cited as *Study dan Penelitian*), sec. 5, p. 6.

5. Cooley, "Church in Indonesia." But Soegiri, *Study dan Penelitian*, sec. 7, p. 2, gives 40,127 for 1959 and 90,176 for 1969. See Figure 6.

6. Soegiri, *Study dan Penelitian*, sec. 3, p. 2.

7. Ibid., sec. 5, p. 1.

8. Ibid., sec. 7, p. 6.

9. Probowinoto, "Memorandum on Cooperation in Evangelism between *Geredja Kristen Jawa, Gerdja Kristen Indonesia,* and *Geredja Kristen Nederland*" (1969), as quoted in Soegiri, *Study dan Penelitian*, sec. 7, p. 6.

10. Darmowigoto, "P.I. Setjarah Massal." Darmowigoto himself organized a Gospel Proclamation Committee with several sub-committees--into small groups according to their ages, and began preparations for baptism.

11. See Soegiri, *Study dan Penelitian*, sec. 3, pp. 3-6, and sec. 7, p. 3, for further information.

12. Ibid., sec. 7, pp. 8-9.

13. Ibid.

14. J. Sardi Karjoredjo, "Perkembangan Jumaat G.K.J. [The Growth of the GKJ Church]" (Den Haag: January 1973); mimeographed.

15. Indicated by several leaders in private interviews.

16. Private interviews.

17. See Soegiri, *Study dan Penelitian*, sec. 8, pp. 5-6, for an evaluation.

18. From the field notes in the *Gereja Kristen Jawa* files of the Department of Study and Research, Indonesian Council of Churches, Jakarta.

19. Soegiri, *Study dan Penelitian*, sec. 3, p. 1. Thirty of these teachers are full-time (sec. 5, p. 2).

20. A notable exception was the service ministry to prisoners. Ibid., sec. 2, pp. 53-54.

21. The GKJ synod in 1935 and 1967 established norms for Christian marriage. Ibid., sec. 9, p. 3.

22. Ibid., sec. 9, p. 7.

23. For a discussion of these cultural elements, see ibid., sec. 1, pp. 1-7, and sec. 10, pp. 1-10.

24. Ibid., sec. 13, pp. 1-2. When word came that subsidy was going to be discontinued in 1974, these churches were shaken, because they had not learned to operate on their own resources as well as the GKJW churches had. (Private interviews.)

25. Müller-Krüger, *Sedjarah Geredja*, pp. 184-87.

26. Frank Cooley, "Memperkenalkan Gereja Kristen Jawa Tengah Utara" [Introducing the North Central Java Christian Church], typescript of report, February 1974, p. 4 (hereafter cited as "Memperkenalkan GKJTU").

27. Müller-Krüger, *Sedjarah Geredja*, p. 188.

28. Cooley, "Memperkenalkan GKJTU," p. 5. For more detailed information concerning the same general period, see J. I. Parker, ed., *Interpretive Statistical Survey of the World Mission of the Christian Church* (New York: International Missionary Council, 1938), pp. 89-90.

29. Cooley, "Memperkenalkan GKJTU," p. 6.

30. Ibid., p. 7.

31. Ibid., pp. 7-11.

32. Frank Cooley's unpublished interview notes.

33. The GKJTU did not keep records or statistics until 1971. See Cooley, "Memperkenalkan GKJTU," chap. 3, for statistical reports and estimates from various sources. The statistics for 1971 were reported to the government's Department of Religion by GKJTU early in 1972.

34. Private interviews with Iugo Garthe and Sujoko Paulus.

35. This evangelistic emphasis is not reflected in the GKJTU synod organization by the presence of a section or division of evangelism. Minutes of the 1972 synod meeting list difficulties encountered in evangelism, indicating the lack of an organized program of evangelism. See Cooley, "Memperkenalkan GKJTU," part 3, n.p.

36. Cooley, "Memperkenalkan GKJTU," part 4, pp. 2-4.

37. Ibid., pp. 4-5.

38. Sujoko Paulus, interview held at the Indonesian Baptist Theological Seminary, Semarang, 13 March 1973.

39. In 1970 Pati County reported 772,744 Moslems, 15,167 Protestants, and 4,580 Catholics. Martati Kumaat, *Laporan Self-Study Gereja Injili Tanah Jawa* [Self-Study Report of the Javanese Evangelical Church] (Pati: GITJ Synod, 1973), p. 77 (hereafter cited as *Laporan Self-Study*).

40. Ibid., pp. 3-4.

41. Cooley, *Church and Society*, p. 92.

42. Ibid., p. 93.

43. Kumaat, *Laporan Self-Study*, pp. 7-9.

44. Ibid., pp. 10-24.

45. Ibid., p. 25.

46. Ibid., p. 79.

47. Ibid., p. 11. The latter figure is actually for 1972, but
     does not include five organized congregations. No figure
     was given for 1971. These statistics include children who
     have not yet been baptized. This is unusual for Mennonites
     who only baptize adults, but total figures are given as a
     result of the influence of other Javanese churches.

48. Kumaat, *Laporan Self-Study*, pp. 10-11, 46-48.

49. Ibid., p. 50.

50. Ibid., p. 48.

51. Ibid., pp. 31-36.

52. Ibid., p. 50.

53. Ibid., statistics for the 1969-1970 year. See p. 32 for
     information on the establishing in 1970 of a teacher
     training school for these teachers of religion.

54. Ibid., pp. 56-57.

55. Ibid., p. 69.

56. Ibid., pp. 68-78.

57. Ibid., pp. 73-74.

58. Ibid., pp. 80-81.

11

Churches Looking for
a Home: Baptists of Java

All four of the Javanese denominations studied in Chapters 9 and
10 had their roots in the previous century. All four are now
considered "old-line Churches" in Indonesia.

During the tumultuous years since World War II, many other
denominations (and non-denominational missions) have begun
work in Indonesia. They range across almost the entire spectrum
of Christianity, including some movements usually considered to
be Christian heresies.

Only one of these comparative newcomers to Indonesia has
built up a majority of its constituency among the dominant
Javanese. This exception to the rule is the one with which I
have been associated, as church member, pastor, missionary, and
theological educator.

Baptist churches in Indonesia had no national organization
until the formation of the *Gabungan Gereja-Gereja Baptis
Indonesia* (Union of Indonesian Baptist Churches, or GGBI) in
1971. However, we will use both "Baptist" and "GGBI" in refer-
ring to this denomination, even before the fact of their organizational entity. As with the other Javanese denominations
studied, we will consider Baptist *identity, approach to evangelism,* and *relationship to the world.*

INDONESIAN BAPTIST CHURCHES (GGBI)

Identity

Baptists arrived late on the Indonesian scene in December
1951, in the person of three former China missionaries representing the Foreign Mission Board of the Southern Baptist Convention,
USA(1). The first converts were baptized on 23 November 1952,
the day the First Baptist Church of Bandung was organized. Since
then Baptists have spread to four provinces in Sumatra, and to
all the provinces of Java; but over 80 percent of the church
members live in Central and East Java(2). (See Table 1.)

The missionaries concentrated in the cities of Java, establishing churches similar to Southern Baptist churches in
theology, structure, methodology, and outlook. With an influx
of manpower and money, they erected church buildings in strategic locations, subsidized pastors when necessary and established
service institutions such as the Indonesian Baptist Theological
Seminary in Semarang (1954), and the Baptist Hospital in
Kediri (1955).

This approach initially attracted mostly youth, urbanites,
and Indonesians of Chinese descent. A conscious effort was made
to use the Indonesian language (rather than Chinese, which the
early Baptist missionaries already spoke), in order not to limit
growth to the Chinese minority(3). An effort was also made to
establish conglomerate churches, composed of several ethnic
groups, but directed toward the educated middle class. Few
responded, except in the case of the Indonesian Chinese. Instead,
the Baptist approach attracted students, plus some from the
lower classes(4).

As Baptists grew, the composition and outlook of its membership greatly changed. The response of Javanese in rural areas
after the attempted coup of 1965 forced GGBI and the Indonesian
Baptist Mission (IBM) to reconsider their approach and their
relationship to cultural and sociological shifts. Responsiveness
occurred largely among the *abangan* element of the population.
Javanese Baptist churches generally reflect the sociological
structure of the masses, with a very small percentage of upper-
class members (and even these few are usually not Javanese)(5).

Conservative theology, congregational ecclesiology, modern
methodology, and Western pedagogy characterize the image projected by Baptist churches.

In 1971 at least 56 percent of Baptist church members were
reported as formerly having had no religion, or having been

"statistical Moslems." Another 30 percent listed themselves as "formerly Moslem," without further clarification(6).

The organizational structure of the GGBI is still in a state of flux. The development of Baptist work has slowly shifted from a mission-directed program toward a national convention-directed program, but not without problems.

The chaotic political situation in mid-1965 occasioned the first *Musyawarah Antara Kaum Baptis* (Baptist Consultative Conference). The IBM feared that communists might pressure American missionaries into leaving Indonesian churches without adequately prepared leadership or clearly defined property rights. In this conference representatives from the churches made no decisions, but only gave suggestions as to how the IBM might solve these problems. The meeting resulted in inclusion of Indonesians on boards of Baptist institutions, formation of some local associations of churches, and plans to surrender legally Mission-held property to the churches as they were able to assume responsibility for it.

The growing desire of pastors for a more direct role in leadership, plus an awareness on the part of both Indonesian Baptists and missionaries of inappropriate and inadequate strategy for evangelism and church development, resulted in two more significant meetings held within a six-month period in late 1967 and early 1968.

In November 1967 the Mission conducted a strategy conference (for its missionaries only). At that time R. Keith Parks (who has since been promoted to high positions as a Baptist world mission executive) outlined mission methodology used by Baptists in Indonesia up to that time. He said the work had been characterized by initiative, planning, and finances being provided by the Indonesian Baptist Mission. These usually included a place to meet (missionary residence or church building erected with IBM-channelled funds), missionary personnel to lead in the work, and a full program of church life patterned after activist American churches. He noted a dependence on modern equipment, revival meetings, contacts attracted by the English language, and financial support supplied through the Mission(7).

The IBM considered revisions in strategy, recommended further research, and proposed another *Musyawarah* with representatives from the churches in order to consider the next steps. Results of this second Baptist *Musyawarah* (which was held in May 1968) included formation of the *Badan Kerja Sama Kaum Baptis* (Baptist Board for Cooperative Work, usually abbreviated BKS) composed of nine Indonesian Baptists and five missionaries. Its tasks included planning and carrying out programs of evangelism, church development, and research; appointing board members of institutions; and being a channel for gifts from the churches to these institutions.

The BKS was established for a set period of three years only, after which another *Musyawarah* was to be held. Furthermore, it had little influence on local churches or Mission-sponsored projects, and therefore was severely limited as to what it could accomplish(8). Nevertheless, 24 Indonesian Baptist churches actually joined this loose confederation, and other churches added their support, especially when the BKS sent Indonesian Baptists' first home missionary, A. B. Sarbini, to Banyuwangi, East Java, in 1971.

The next triennial *Musyawarah*, on 12 August 1971, organized the *Gabungan Gereja-Gereja Baptis Indonesia*. This move came as a result of important developments both in the national constituency and in the Mission. A group of national leaders had met unofficially in Sukabumi in June 1971 to propose a permanent structure for Baptist churches(9). And missionaries, in their annual meeting held in July 1971, had also radically changed their approach. (More will be told about these events in the next section of this chapter.)

These two unilateral developments left the relationship between the GGBI and the IBM unclear, particularly in regard to institutions which had hitherto been primarily financed through the Mission, and evangelistic work which had been conducted primarily in cooperation with local pastors, who by this time were all Indonesians. Nevertheless, it was at least clear that with the organization of the GGBI, Indonesian Baptists had reached a new plateau in national leadership and internal development.

Approach to Evangelism

Numerical growth of Indonesian Baptist churches is shown in Figure 9, Table 1, and Figure 6. In Table 1 the average annual membership growth rate is 20.8% between 1960 and 1965, and 21.6% between 1965 and 1971.

Evangelistic methodology used during most of the 1960-71 period was based on the experience of Baptists in America:

(1) Churches begun in missionary homes, rented quarters, or buildings bought by the Mission.

(2) Strong missionary direction, with a growing national leadership who worked with, and were usually paid by, the missionary.

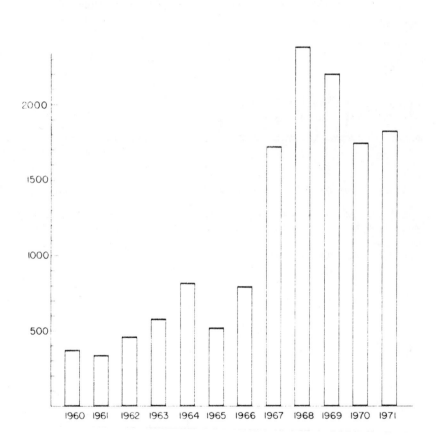

FIGURE 9

BAPTISMS OF GGBI

TABLE 1

NUMERICAL GROWTH OF INDONESIAN BAPTISTS(10)
1960-1971

	1960	1965	1971
Membership	1,317	3,391	10,948
Organized churches	9	17	34
Unorganized churches	13	34	185
Ordained pastors	8	14	28
Unordained pastors	4	39	65
Missionaries	55	77	103
Percentage of membership in East and Central Java	61.3	70.8	81.3

(3) Modern means of mass media such as movies, literature, television, and radio.

(4) Personal evangelism and house-to-house visitation, with an emphasis on confronting people with the claims of the gospel.

(5) Home worship services conducted by Indonesian pastors in rural areas, many of which grew into churches that met in buildings purchased or rented by the Mission.

(6) Large-scale evangelistic campaigns.

The concept of evangelism as stated by the leadership of GGBI is personal witnessing, sowing gospel seed in mass meetings, and establishing churches. To the average member, evangelism is sharing one's personal experience of conversion and the love of God revealed in Christ, in order that persons will believe in Him as Savior and Lord(11). Eighty-three percent of the members of Indonesian Baptist churches have never been related to a church of another denomination, most of them having been won "from the world" by an aggressive evangelistic program(12).

The response of GGBI to the growth situation following the attempted coup of 1965 was commendable: Local churches opened their doors to those who were motivated by religio-cultural, political, and social factors. Many new congregations and preaching points were opened, particularly in the *desas* (note

the figures for "Unorganized churches" in Table 1). The number
of young people entering Christian service doubled. Laymen took
the initiative in beginning new congregations and nurturing them.
Several local churches grew to maturity and were organized.

The Indonesian Baptist Mission opened new stations, added many
new missionaries, sponsored denomination-wide evangelistic campaigns in 1967 and 1970, and opened new training opportunities
for Indonesians. The Indonesian Baptist Theological Seminary in
1962 added a two-year program for junior high school graduates,
and expanded it to a four-year diploma program in 1968 (to
correspond to the degree program). Lay training, formally
begun in 1960 with the institution of a "Preachers' School" in
Kediri(13), has not been a continuous program, but short-term
courses for laymen have been conducted periodically in cities
where Baptists have work. The East Java Baptist Bible School,
designed to train village and lay pastors in Kediri and the
surrounding area, began to operate in 1970 under the direction
of Ebbie C. Smith. Further developments in theological education resulted from IBM decisions to restructure and decentralize
theological education(14).

As a follow-up to the 1967 mission strategy conference mentioned earlier, three surveys were conducted to determine the
effectiveness of Baptist work in light of growth opportunities:
The *Survey Usaha Baptis* was led by the writer, in cooperation
with the Indonesian Council of Churches, from 1969 through 1973.
A McGavran-type survey of Baptist growth was led by Ebbie C.
Smith in 1971. Cal Guy and Bryant Hicks (professors of missions
at Southwestern Baptist Theological Seminary, Fort Worth, Texas,
and Southern Baptist Theological Seminary, Louisville, Kentucky,
respectively) were asked to conduct interviews with missionaries,
pastors, and lay people, and help evaluate data gathered in the
other two surveys. Their recommendations were presented to the
Mission at the annual meeting in July 1971.

All three surveys revealed serious problems resulting from
faulty methodology, rapid growth, and the socio-cultural
situation(15). All three agreed that the most critical problems
included:

(1) Dependence of churches, pastors, and programs on
Mission initiative and funding.

(2) Poor working relationships resulting from inadequate
organizational structures of the Mission, of the national body,
of churches, and of institutions.

(3) Failure of American missionaries and Westernized pastors
to relate well to Javanese culture.

(4) Limitations in methodology and finances threatening to slow the rate of growth in the face of expanding opportunities.

(5) Lack of direction in planning for the future.

(6) Deficiencies in spiritual life, zeal, and life-style of missionaries and pastors.

Concurrent with the surveys, Baptist missionaries experienced in 1971 a spiritual renewal marked by prayer, repentance, confession, love, joy, and witnessing(16). In their "New Pattern of Work" statement adopted in July 1971, the missionaries confessed failures in their spiritual lives and in many aspects of their methods of work which had imposed a Western pattern of Christian life not in keeping with the national culture, economy, and aspirations upon the Indonesian Baptist churches. The New Pattern of Work included:

(1) The priority and urgency of evangelizing the masses of Indonesia through the establishment of thousands of house churches--led by their natural lay leaders, centered around the reading of the Bible, and without the imposition of Western forms.

(2) An emphasis on the freedom and responsibility of every believer to be a priest before Christ--in spreading the gospel, leading family worship, and establishing other house churches.

(3) The missionary's role as ministering in the Spirit--in building up Christians to minister to others, itinerating in new areas, and serving as a teacher in Christian leadership training.

(4) Phasing out all subsidies to churches or pastors for salaries, housing, equipment, transportation, or meeting places.

(5) Discontinuation of the "present program of seminary training" and redeployment of missionary professors with major responsibilities in developing leadership training programs en loco.

(6) A new approach to Mission structure, coupled with making institutions responsible to their respective boards instead of to IBM.

(7) Other structural changes in cooperation with Indonesian Baptist brothers(17).

The response of Indonesian Baptist leaders to problems revealed by the surveys and to the Mission's "New Pattern of Work"

included the above-mentioned organization of the Union of Indonesian Baptist Churches' (GGBI) plans to begin an academy to
provide resident theological education, and further deliberations with the IBM concerning the over-all structure of Baptist
life. They reacted to the unilateral nature of the Mission's
decisions and disagreed with several proposals in the New
Pattern. Decisions of both these groups were in response to
the growth situation: The missionaries' decisions were more
closely related to radical changes in the size, composition,
and outlook of the Baptist constituency. The nationals'
decisions were more closely connected with the growing maturity
of Indonesian leaders and churches. These internal struggles in
1971 and thereafter absorbed much of the energy formerly devoted
to church growth.

Baptist service institutions are all related to evangelism.
Church growth in the Kediri and Semarang areas is directly
related to evangelism programs sponsored by the hospital and the
seminary(18). The student centers, radio and TV ministry,
Baptist publishing house, church loan board, and six elementary
schools begun by local churches all state that their *raison
d'être* is evangelism and service.

Baptist interivew respondents ranked "Spiritual need" first,
"Protection" second, and "Government" and "Church" third as
primary causes for their conversions. But in the over-all
evaluation, the order was almost reversed, with "Church" first,
"Government" second, "Spiritual need" third, and "Gospel"
fourth. In contrast to the GKJW, "Christian life" was named
as a primary cause for conversion by less than 1.0 percent of
Baptist interviewees, with only 10 percent even mentioning it.
In contrast to the GITJ and GKJTU, which ranked political,
social, and religious factors about evenly, Baptists mentioned
spiritual factors 201 times, political factors 89 times, and
social factors 76 times, indicating that Baptist growth was more
directly related to their methodology than to political,
cultural, or social factors. This is commendable; but it also
reveals that Baptists did not take as much advantage of
currents flowing through society as did the other Javanese denominations. Had they done so, the churches would probably have
grown even more.

In the *Survey Usaha Baptis*(19), church growth factors
credited were: the increase of missionaries and national
pastors, responsive areas in Semarang and Yogyakarta, the evangelism program of the seminary, the Sunday School campaign in
1966, and the evangelism campaign in 1967 at the peak of response
throughout Indonesia.

Baptist leaders, who analyzed this report in June 1973, said
that Baptists did not begin to grow in 1964 as several other
churches working among the Javanese had, because: the churches
were young, the political situation was not favorable for
American missionaries, Baptist churches were in the cities while
other denominations were growing in the villages, and Baptists
were not related to politics as were the other denominations.

Reasons given for growth between 1965 and 1969 were: protection; government; the nature of Christian worship in comparison to Islamic ritual; receptivity of the churches; the fact
that Baptist preachers were generally young and unmarried and,
therefore, more courageous; the emphasis that God protected
Christians during the coup; and economic advantages anticipated
by the converts(20).

Laymen, though active, did not play as important a role in
Baptist growth as in other denominations, partly because the
seminary provided an adequate supply of pastors for the traditional pattern. Yet, due to the reluctance of seminary graduates to return to the *desa*, the laity did lead many congregations. (Note Table 2 at the beginning of the next chapter,
which shows only 93 pastors to serve 219 congregations.)

Relationship to the World

The shift of response from the city to the *desa* changed
GGBI's sociological structure in regard to race, class, and
location. A majority of the new converts were *abangan* Javanese
(peasants) in new territories. Social influences were far less
important in Baptist churches than in other denominations, with
only 33.3 percent becoming Christians in people movements, in
contrast to an average of 70 percent in the other denominations.
The Baptist emphasis on individual conversion and adult baptism
accounted for part of this difference, but failure to use
sociological currents was probably a bigger factor.

Baptists ignored Javanese culture for more than a decade.
They concentrated on conglomerate churches with members from
many ethnic backgrounds, and expected Indonesians to adjust to
the "Baptist way of doing things." No official pronouncements
have ever been made about Javanese *adat* relating to marriage,
birth, name-giving, the *slametan*(21), or circumcision. Instead,
the churches (except for a few individuals) have been indifferent
toward such matters.

Individual missionaries and pastors have experimented with
Javanese dance forms, bamboo musical instruments, and the
Javanese *gamelan* orchestra. (One pastor even invented a *gamelan*
instrument which allowed music to be played on the Western

eight-note scale, rather than the five-note Javanese scale.)
However, no efforts have been made to use shadow-plays, folk
operas, or Javanese chants.

Only since rapid growth began have services been conducted
in the Javanese language on a regular basis, in sharp contrast
to the other Javanese denominations that use it almost exclusively, seldom conducting more than one service a month in Indonesian. Baptist Javanese churches in rural areas now use
Javanese in at least one worship service a week. Missionaries
engaged in direct evangelism in Central and East Java began to
study the Javanese language near the end of the 1960's.

In other words, Baptists on the whole have ignored lessons
that might have been learned from over one hundred years of
cultural adaptation by other denominations. They have Westernized the members of their churches. Their emphases on youth,
"Western democracy," freedom from restraint of social mores
between the sexes, modern church music, large numbers of
activities, a wealthy image, and large buildings--these are
often cited as problems by older Javanese in the *desas*, although
they do not present such difficulty in the cities. The modern
image of Baptist churches has attracted youth and those affected
by modernization; but it has also hindered the masses, who still
like the old traditional ways(22).

The IBM and GGBI have both taken radical steps to rectify the
problems each thinks most important. Nevertheless, many
problems are still unsolved, including: good working relationships among missionaries, pastors, and laity; a structure that
will allow for ordered development on a national scale and yet
allow spontaneous expansion; appropriate religious and theological education for both members and pastors of the churches;
an adequate approach to the total life situation; the maturation
of church members and churches to support their work; a program
for city churches, facing modernization and moral decadence; and
a different program for *desa* churches, still steeped in tradition.

Growth dependent on foreign funds and foreign initiative has
reached its limit. If Indonesian Baptist churches are to
continue to grow, the initiative in evangelism, methodology, and
church development must be seized by mature Indonesian leaders
who can effectively take advantage of cultural trends, social
relationships, and available resources, including the large
corps of Baptist missionaries still serving in Indonesia.

NOTES

1. For a description of Baptist beginnings, see John L. Nance, "A History of the Indonesian Baptist Mission: 1950-1960" (M.A. thesis, Baylor University, 1969; hereafter cited as "Indonesian Baptist Mission"); and Smith, *God's Miracles*, pp. 124-43.

2. See "Minutes of the Nineteenth Annual Session of the Indonesian Baptist Mission" (mimeographed, 1971), and Ebbie C. Smith, "What Did the Questionnaires Say?" (mimeographed report, 1971; hereafter cited as "Questionnaires"), who says that 81 percent of the Baptists are Javanese, 13 percent are Chinese, and 6 percent are from other ethnic groups (p. 5).

3. See "Minutes of the Second Annual Session of the Indonesian Baptist Mission," p. 15.

4. Smith, "Questionnaires," p. 9, says that in 1971, 46 percent of Indonesian Baptists were between twelve and 23 years of age, and 63 percent were under 30. Only 11.8 percent could be designated as middle-class economically.

5. Smith, "Questionnaires," p. 9, said in 1971 that 78.6 percent of Indonesian Baptists earned less than three thousand rupiahs a month ($7.91).

6. Ibid., p. 11.

7. From notes taken at the meeting.

8. Avery T. Willis, Jr., *"Survey Usaha Baptis: Konsep Pertama"* [Survey of Baptist Work: First Draft] (1 November 1970), pp. 66-68 (hereafter cited as *"Survey Baptis I"*). (Mimeographed.)

9. See Julianus E. Tarapa, *"Pertemuan Sukabumi"* [The Sukabumi Meeting], 1 June 1971. (Mimeographed pamphlet.)

10. All statistics in Table 1 are from "Minutes of the Indonesian Baptist Mission" for the years indicated, except for membership, organized churches, unorganized churches, ordained pastors, and unordained pastors for 1971, which are from Eddy Wiriadinata, *"Survey Usaha Baptis: Konsep Kedua"* [Survey of Baptist Work: Second Draft] (June 1973), sec. 7, p. 1, and sec. 5, p. 1 (hereafter cited as *"Survey Baptis II"*). (Mimeographed.)

11. Ibid., sec. 7, p. 4.

12. Smith, "Questionnaires," p. 2.

13. Nance, "Indonesian Baptist Mission," p. 139.

14. See Avery T. Willis, Jr., "Base Design of the Indonesian Baptist Theological Seminary" (June 1973). (Mimeographed.)

15. See Willis, "Survey Baptis I"; Wiriadinata, "Survey Baptis II"; Smith, "Questionnaires"; and Cal Guy and Bryant Hicks, "Report to the Indonesian Baptist Mission," July 1971. (Mimeographed.)

16. See "Central Java Prayer Retreat" in "Minutes of the Nineteenth Annual Session of the Indonesian Baptist Mission," pp. 193-97; William N. McElrath, "Has the Movement Gone Worldwide?" *Home Missions*, June-July 1971, p. 69; and Avery T. Willis, Jr., "Spiritual Breakthrough in Indonesia," two tapes (Holland, Mich.: Portable Recording Ministries, 1971).

17. From "New Pattern of Work: Indonesian Baptist Mission," in "Minutes of the Nineteenth Annual Session of the Indonesian Baptist Mission," pp. 310-13.

18. See "Minutes of the Fifteenth Annual Session of the Indonesian Baptist Mission," pp. 81-7, for "village worship program" (in Kediri), and Smith, *God's Miracles*, p. 133, for the seminary evangelism program.

19. Wiriadinata, *"Survey Baptis II,"* sec. 7, pp. 1-2.

20. Notes taken at the meeting.

21. Smith, "Questionnaires," p. 7, reports that 43 percent felt it was improper for a Christian to attend a *slametan*, and 15 percent were uncertain.

22. Willis, *"Survey Baptis I,"* pp. 58-60.

PART V

Retrospect
and Prospect

12

How the Churches Grew

All five of the Indonesian denominations having a majority of Javanese church members experienced great growth in recent years. That fact is clear from Table 2 on the following page. The table also clearly shows the comparative growth experienced by each of the five Javanese Churches.

But statistical comparison by itself is not enough. In this chapter we will try to draw some conclusions based on a comparative analysis of church growth in the five denominations. We will point out methodology which helped church growth and methodology which hindered it. We will further delineate this comparison by a study of several coordinates arranged along an axis of the intensive-extensive nature of church growth.

Before continuing to read this chapter, take a moment to study the data in Table 2, which underlies much of what follows. Note that Baptist (GGBI) statistics for membership do not include children of believers, as do figures for the other four denominations. In order to get a roughly comparable estimate, we should perhaps double GGBI membership totals.

COMPARATIVE CONCLUSIONS

(1) The higher the ratio of congregations to total membership, the higher the annual growth rate. Note that GGBI, with the fewest average members per congregation, had the best percentage of growth. The same pattern holds true for each of the other four.

TABLE 2

COMPARATIVE GROWTH OF JAVANESE CHURCHES(1)

CHURCH		GKJW	GKJ	GKJTU	GITJ	GGBI
	Mission Background	Dutch Reformed	Christian Reformed	Faith Alliance	Mennonite	Baptist
G	1971 membership[a]	126,000	121,500	16,846	40,150	10,939
R	Gain since 1960[b]	80,000	83,500	13,846	33,150	9,622
O W	Annual increase[c] 1960-1964	8.1%	2.4%	6.1%	28.4%	24.5%
T H	Annual increase[d] 1965-1971	10.6%	15.5%	22.2%	11.1%	21.6%
C H	Organized churches[e]	92	174	43	23	34
U R	Congregations[f]	300	615	36	116	185
C H	Total[g]	392	789	79	139	219
E S	Membership per[h] Congregation	321	153	213	296	50
L	Ordained pastors[i]	71	134	14	49	28
E	Unordained pastors[j]	16	30	8	10	65
A	Lay leaders[k]	31	90	47	45	43
D E	Total national[l] leaders	118	254	69	104	136
R	Members per[m] leader	1067	476	244	386	80
S	Missionaries[j]	4	34	4	15	106

TABLE 3

MEMBERSHIP GROWTH IN FIVE DENOMINATIONS

Date	GKJW	GKJ	GKJTU	GITJ	GGBI
1930		7,547			
1931	22,904			2,134	
1933		9,701		3,712	
1935	28,551				
1936		11,179			
1938		15,377	5,680	4,284	
1940					
1942	33,937				
1945					
1946					
1947		17,875			
1948					
1949		23,126	2,000	2,000	
1950					
1951	34,239				
1953		24,813	2,000	5,260	39
1954					64
1955	42,140				126
1956					282
1957					538
1958					793
1959			3,500		967
1960	46,000	38,000	3,715	(7,000)	1,317
1961	8.1%	6.1%	6.1%	28.4%	1,580
1962					1,979
1963				17,562	2,843
1964	62,890	41,760	(4,711)	(19,027)	3,169
1965	(68,984)	(51,097)	5,000	21,386	3,391
1966				24,428	3,965
1967	83,000	76,500		27,000	5,834
1968	10.6%	15.5%	22.2%	34,351	8,186
1969	107,379	90,176		38,094	9,779
1970	113,917			36,000	10,748
1971	126,000	121,500	16,678	40,150	10,939

GGBI percentages: 24.5% (1961–1963), 21.6% (1967–1970); GITJ 11.7% (1967–1970).

Stated another way, the more congregations a denomination established, the faster it grew. A Church that desires to grow should concentrate on establishing congregations.

(2) The higher the ratio of leaders to members, the faster the growth rate. Table 2 substantiates this conclusion, with the exception of GKJ. But GKJ had three types of leaders not shown in the table: 265 teachers of religion (30 full-time) in public schools, plus teachers (a majority of whom were Christians) in 472 Christian schools established for the expressed purpose of evangelism(2). and also (in former years) a large force of colporteurs sowing the seed(3). This large number of leaders, plus those in medical and other service ministries, when added to leaders counted in our table, confirms the principle verified in the other Churches: The higher the ratio of leaders to members, the faster the growth(4).

(3) All five denominations benefited from the political situation, and were basically open to the possibilities of massive growth. They actively identified with the government's five-year development program (except for Baptists, who only tacitly supported it).

(4) None of the denominations were prepared for such rapid growth. This is clearly seen in the lack of trained pastors and mature lay leaders: Those available were soon overworked and spiritually fatigued. Baptists had more prepared leaders per capita than any other denomination, but many of them lacked the needed maturity.

(5) All the denominations grew, regardless of methodology used or concept of evangelism followed. Religio-cultural, political, and sociological factors played a larger role in church growth than methods; but methodological factors played a significant role in slowing or speeding the rate of growth.

(6) No denomination capitalized fully on opportunities presented to it, due to varying factors in different denominations.

(7) Christianity had been identified with Javanese culture enough to make it a viable alternative when the opportunity presented itself. Most of the denominations used the culture to increase growth. (Baptists had a more tenuous relationship to Javanese culture, so Javanese entered other Churches more easily.)

In our research, 265 people were asked whether the culture helped or hindered in their becoming Christians; 70 percent said their Church's relationship to the culture helped them become Christians, while 30 percent said it was a detriment.

When broken down by Churches, the percentage approving each
Church's relationship to Javanese culture was as follows:
GKJW - 94.5; GITJ - 86.6; GKJTU - 84.2; GKJ - 77.7; GGBI - 63.3;
other denominations - 66.6. (This latter group was a random
sampling of 45 people from other denominations, mostly pente-
costals and non-Javanese churches, that served as a control
group for the five denominations studied.) The four ethnic
denominations had an average of 84.8 percent approving their
relationship to the culture, while Baptists and other denominations had only 65.3 percent.

These results could cause some of the denominations to feel
satisfied. But a random sampling of non-Christians who were
generally synpathetic to Christianity revealed that 93.4 percent said lack of acculturation by the Churches was a hindrance
to their becoming Christians. This fact, in addition to the
sizeable minority of 30 percent who felt that the lack of
acculturation was a hindrance even though they had become
Christians in spite of it, should cause the Churches to rethink
their relationship to Javanese culture.

(8) All the denominations benefited from the sociological
composition of society, with Baptists and GITJ benefiting least.

(9) The most effective methods used to capitalize on church
growth opportunities in 1960-71 were: an emphasis on the responsibility of every Christian to be a witness; establishing new
congregations, including small groups of all kinds; widespread
initiative and use of the laity in evangelism and nurture;
training leaders to meet the opportunity; active evangelistic
programs such as prison services, evangelistic campaigns, and
new members' classes (in which many "converts" actually became
Christians); and service institutions which helped prepare the
soil but did not play a determinative role in the increase of
members.

(10) The rate of growth in all five denominations slowed
after 1969. Although total membership figures continued to
rise, an examination of baptismal increases shows a definite
slowing and even a retreat in some years(5).

Sixty-seven pastors and denominational leaders gave the
following reasons for the slowing of the growth rate in their
denominations:

Poor follow-up	23.9 percent
Change of political situation	16.4 percent
Insincere converts	16.4 percent
Persecution	15.0 percent
Moral failure	12.0 percent
De-emphasis on evangelism	6.0 percent
High standards of church	4.5 percent
Economic situation	4.5 percent
Disappointment with church or leaders	1.3 percent

The GKJW, GKJ, and GKJTU placed their emphasis on consolidation of gains already made. In the case of the latter two, numerical growth was de-emphasized for the last several years of the period. The same trend was apparent in the GITJ and GGBI, but it was not as pronounced.

(11) Rapid growth resulted in internal changes in all the denominations, as well as a rethinking of identity, structure, philosophy, and methodology.

METHODOLOGY THAT HELPED CHURCH GROWTH

A summary of methods which contributed to each Church's growth shows that the most effective ones included:

(1)   Acculturation that allowed Christians to remain Javanese.

(2)   Evangelical theology.

(3)   Effective Christian presence as the Community of Love.

(4)   Spiritual renewal in many churches.

(5)   Spontaneous witness of Christians.

(6)   Prophetic call of the Churches for justice.

(7)   Demonstration of love.

(8)   Receptivity to seekers.

(9)   Emphasis on responsive groups.

(10) Extensive use of the laity.

(11) Effective use of the catechism and new members' classes.

(12) Nurturing of people movements.

(13)   Planting of hundreds of new congregations.

(14)   Use of small groups for Bible study, prayer, and nurture.

(15)   Training programs for the laity.

(16)   Special evangelistic emphases.

(17)   Missionary spirit.

METHODOLOGY THAT HINDERED CHURCH GROWTH

Methods used by the Churches that hindered church growth included:

(1)   Neglect of proper identification with, and use of, Javanese culture.

(2)   Lack of trained leadership.

(3)   Inability to nurture, assimilate, and train new converts.

(4)   Inadequate discernment of converts' motives, resulting in an indiscriminate reception of some members and an over-cautious rejection of others.

(5)   Slackening of evangelistic thrust--due to spiritual fatigue, doubts about the sincerity of converts, emphasis on quality, and involvement with mundane duties.

(6)   Failure to evangelize "to the fringes" (McGavran's term for evangelizing all those related to a tribe, clan, class, or segment of society in a people movement)(7).

(7)   Insufficient perception of embryonic people movements, trends, and causes of conversion.

(8)   Restriction of spontaneous expansion.

(9)   Lack of physical and spiritual resources to meet needs.

(10) Miscalculation of opportunities.

Ebbie C. Smith's analysis of questionnaires filled out by Baptists provides a sad example of miscalculation of opportunities: When the greatest response was coming in Javanese villages, only 9.0 percent of Baptist pastors thought village people were the most strategic group to reach, and only 4.0

percent thought heads of villages were the most strategic. It
should be noted that 54 percent saw heads of families as most
strategic, and 23 percent cited students(8).

Our analysis of church growth among the Javanese has revealed
some dangerous trends which, if allowed to continue, will impede
church growth. The best church growth occurs when a dynamic
tension exists between opposite, but equally valid, emphases:
poor church growth, or no growth at all, occurs when either
extreme is overemphasized. These pairs of opposite, but actually
valid emphases, may be viewed as coordinates arranged along an
axis of the intensive-extensive nature of church growth. The
ones that appear on the left side in the following list relate
to internal growth, and the ones on the right side relate to
external growth:

CHURCH GROWTH COORDINATES

In Philosophy of Growth

(1) Consolidation versus expansion

(2) Nurture versus evangelism

(3) Quality versus quantity

(4) Presence versus proclamation

In Organization

(5) Structure versus spontaneity

(6) Clergy versus laity

(7) Scholars versus pastors

(8) Theology versus culture

In Programs

(9) Classes versus masses

(10) Individual conversions versus people movements

(11) Urban versus rural

(12) Modern versus traditional

(13) Future versus present

In debates on methodology, each proponent usually overstates his side of the equation and discounts the importance of the other side, thereby resolving the tension of the paradox. This polarization characterizes the debate now raging in theology, ecclesiology, and missiology(9).

The Javanese Churches have done precisely this; they have overreacted to the growth situation and are currently over-emphasizing church growth coordinates on the intensive (or left-hand) side of the equations. As a corrective, therefore, the following analysis emphasizes the extensive (or right-hand) side of the equations, in order that both coordinates may be put in proper perspective. The ultimate solution does not lie in the exclusion of either side, nor in a synthesis of the two, but in careful assessment of the situation and proper application of priorities at a given time. Internal and external church growth occurs when a dynamic tension exists between these coordinates in *philosophy*, *organization*, and *programs* of church growth.

TRENDS IN PHILOSOPHY OF GROWTH

Consolidation Versus Expansion

Following the initial acceleration in growth, the Javanese Churches began to emphasize consolidation. This probably influenced the decline in growth more than stabilization of the political situation. The GKJTU program of consolidation until 1976 inadvertently excluded thousands of Javanese who were responsive to a gospel witness during those years. It also allowed thousands of others to fill a spiritual vacuum by moving in the direction of another religion.

Interviews with members of GKJTU churches in 1973 revealed that, as far as they knew, surrounding villages were still responsive, but efforts were not then being made to establish new congregations. Leaders may discover when (according to plan) they begin emphasizing evangelism again, the difficulty of motivating their members to evangelize after years of consoli-dation. They may find once-responsive prospects no longer interested.

It is normal to have a period of consolidation after a period of rapid expansion. But if church leaders emphasize consolidation to the exclusion of expansion, church growth is circumscribed. It is the task of leadership to plan for the future while living in the present. With astute planning, churches can be rescued from their natural inclination to over-react after a period of stress.

Nurture Versus Evangelism

This coordinate expresses the *means* of accomplishing objectives stated in the first coordinate. One of the weaknesses exhibited by all the denominations was their inability to nurture thousands of new Christians. But then came overreaction, as shown by de-emphasis on evangelism.

Certainly all churches need to prepare adequate follow-up programs for new converts, and continuing programs of nurture for all their members--but not to the exclusion of evangelism. To emphasize nurture only, will produce a mind-set which will be very difficult to erase later when church leaders want to emphasize evangelism.

The coordinates of nurture and evangelism are not enemies, but partners. It is significant that Jesus nurtured his disciples as they followed him through the harvest fields.

Quality Versus Quantity

This coordinate expresses the *results* desired in the consolidation versus expansion coordinate. The emphasis of quality over quantity is presently in vogue among many churchmen(10). Winter exposes the fallacy of emphasizing one over the other(11),

> because all quantities are measurements of certain qualities! . . . The crucial issue in missions in connection with quality arises when it is assumed that either any numerical measurement of quality must be superficial or that any important quality cannot be measured(12).

The emphasis on quality versus quantity was especially apparent in the attitude of some leaders of the GKJ. One of them said:

> I think we have grown more qualitatively since 1969, even though we haven't grown quantitatively. I went to an Easter service in Wonosari in 1967 attended by five thousand people. The local leader said that in previous years, there had been only a few hundred people in attendance, but now there were five thousand! I had to tell him and the crowd that they should not just look for numbers; I contrasted the former times [favorably] to the present(13).

Such attitudes curtail numerical church growth.

Presence Versus Proclamation

This coordinate expresses the *manner* or *procedure* of accomplishing the above-mentioned coordinates. It is an outgrowth of another coordinate--mission versus missions--which has been controverted for several years. If everything that the Church does is mission, then proclamation no longer occupies center stage; therefore, "presence" became the maxim of mission, much as "proclamation" had of missions. But the problem arises, neither with "mission" nor with "presence" as the means of spreading the Kingdom of God, but with their becoming ends rather than means, as in the present trend.

It is evident that the current emphasis originated in the West. Herbert Neve says:

It is true that Christian presence thinking is uniquely a product of the West, formerly Christian, and now secular. It is based on the presupposition that in a post-Christian culture, mission must take the form of renewal, regardless of whether this be of a revolutionary or of an evolutionary kind(14).

If "presence" receives the same emphasis in the East as in the West, this bodes ill for church growth and extension of the Kingdom of God in Asia(15). "Presence" has already been adopted as the basic thrust of evangelism in the GKJW and GKJ; but one cannot tell yet whether their traditional understanding of it as preparation for proclamation will continue to be used, or whether the recent emphasis on Christian presence will, for practical purposes, eliminate proclamation by these Javanese Churches. The basis for its formulation in the so-called "Christian West" is not valid in the Javanese situation, where 99 percent of the people have never been Christians. This poses one of the greatest dangers for the future of church growth among these two largest Javanese denominations. The only effective way to reach the Javanese masses is through a balanced emphasis on presence and proclamation.

GKJW was the only denomination in which "presence" (in the form of Christian lives) had much effect on growth. In the light of statistics which show that their growth rate between 1965 and 1971 was lower than that of any of the other denominations, the question needs to be raised: "If a greater emphasis had been made on proclamation in conjunction with the GKJW's strong witness by presence, would not their rate of growth have equaled or even surpassed that of the other denominations?"

TRENDS IN ORGANIZATION

Structure Versus Spontaneity

The Javanese respect for authority and structure tends to
curtail spontaneity. This dependence on structure and on those
in authority has resulted in many Javanese Christians' suppress-
ing the impulse to take the initiative in establishing new
congregations. Yet, a large number did break through prescribed
structures during the period of rapid growth. Church leaders
wisely relaxed some of the stringent protocol during the period
of rapid growth; but immediately afterward, leaders in all five
denominations began to strengthen church structure and increase
the control of governing bodies.

Although the Javanese have a tradition of respect for those
in authority, they also have a spirit of independence born in
the autonomous *desa* which often expresses itself in spontaneous
Christian witness. The uniqueness of being a Christian in the
midst of a non-Christian world probably has made them more
consciously evangelistic than their counterparts in the West.
If an increasing rate of growth is to be regained, leaders must
design structures which allow spontaneity(16) and yet provide a
stamp of authority.

Clergy Versus Laity

Organizational lines are most clearly drawn between clergy
and laity. Imported ecclesiastical structures, plus the Hindu
social system with the *pandito* (priest) as the most revered
caste, combined to contribute the elevation of the clergyman
(*pendeta*) in Indonesia. Yet, we have shown the pivotal role of
the laity in growth of churches in Java, particularly after 1965.

If the churches can recapture the doctrine of the People of
God, with the clergy and the laity recognizing their common
nature and function as one people with a common task (even
though some are given the responsibility of equipping the Church
so that all might minister), then there is hope for great church
growth in Indonesia(17). This is not a plea for the elimination
of pastors, but for their concentration on the equipping of the
whole People of God for their God-given responsibility to
minister to the world.

Scholars Versus Pastors

Present church structures and theological curricula emphasize
the training of scholars more than the training of pastors to
shepherd and build up their flocks. Of course scholarly
Indonesian theologians are needed, to help the churches

interpret their role and theology in context. But the education
of all ministers to be scholars is a misappropriation of
resources and a disservice to the churches served.

Theological institutions need to define clearly the kinds of
leaders they are training. McGavran says that Churches need
five kinds of leaders: (1) local unpaid leaders who primarily
minister to the Church; (2) local unpaid leaders who primarily
minister to the world in the expansion of the Church; (3) paid
or partly-paid pastors of small congregations; (4) well-trained
paid pastors of larger churches; and (5) international leaders.
He contends that the number of class one, two, and three
leaders is more important to church growth than the number of
class four and five leaders; but theological schools almost
exclusively teach the latter two(18).

The basic approach of most theological schools in Indonesia
is to train men as full-time, fully-supported, scholarly-
inclined clerics, while the bulk of the leaders in expanding
churches are part-time, voluntary or partially paid, lay leaders.
Winburn Thomas says, "Nine-tenths of the ministerial functions
in Indonesia are performed by unordained, part-time preachers
who earn some or all of their income as teachers, farmers,
etc"(19). Most of them are inadequately trained. The Churches
and theological institutions of Indonesia must face the questions, "Who is to be trained?" and "For what?"

Theology Versus Culture

This coordinate relates to the content present in theological training programs, and to the structures of society. In
the early stages of church growth in Indonesia, theology was
often viewed as the antithesis of culture. This conflict is
seen in the approaches of Tasdik and van Akkeren. According to
Alan Thomson's evaluation,

> Mr. Tasdik, taking his cue from Hendrik Kraemer, is insis-
> tent that conversion means a radical rejection of all
> reliance upon animistic ways of thinking. Van Akkeren,
> who regards himself as being in the tradition of Kraemer
> and B. M. Schuurman . . . seems to take clear exception
> to this. He feels that such traditional practices as the
> *selamatan* ceremonial meal in fact represent and also
> guarantee the solidarity of village life upon which the
> whole social fabric depends(20).

For the Christian theologian, the Bible is authoritative in
matters of faith and practice(21), but the theologian versed in
anthropology realizes that many church practices are more
closely related to culture than to the Bible. Charles Kraft

has attempted to wed these coordinates into an "ethnotheology"
(22). He says,

> From theology such a discipline would draw understanding
> of eternal (absolute) truths relating to each of the areas
> it treats. From anthropology, it would draw cultural
> (relative) truths and perceptions concerning these
> areas(23).

We have continually pointed to the need for acculturation,
so that the average Javanese may learn of God through forms he
can understand. Such a Javanese ethnotheology would present
the purity of the gospel without offending Javanese tastes
because of Western accretions.

TRENDS IN PROGRAMS

Classes Versus Masses

Christians as a minority group tend to seek acceptance by
influencing the higher classes of society rather than the
masses (even though it often happens that the masses are influenced more by accident than the classes are by design!). The
presence of Christians in the upper classes and in influential
positions in Indonesia lends credence to the idea that this is
a better strategy . . . until one discovers that the majority
of these leaders originally came from the masses and worked
their way into these positions.

The tendency of modern society to emphasize education,
wealth, and power has distracted the leadership of many Javanese
Churches from the masses of responsive Javanese in rural areas.
These masses need to be evangelized now, even though the
Churches continue to prepare leaders for higher positions in
society. Those who emphasize reaching the higher classes first,
fail to realize that in Indonesia, no leader is any stronger
than his mass following. When enough people become Christians,
they more strongly influence leaders by their numbers, than
leaders without a strong base influence the masses. Neither
classes nor masses should be slighted; but the priority should
be placed on reaching responsive masses now.

Individual Conversions Versus People Movements

The Churches of Indonesia have understood the importance of
people movements better than their missionaries. Yet, it is not
a choice between people movements and the gathered church, but a
question of whether personal conversions are made within people
movements--that is, multi-individual decisions made within the
groups.

One of the most urgent needs in Indonesia today is for the
Javanese Churches to design a strategy which uses people movements of all kinds to multiply their witness.

Urban Versus Rural

The worldwide trend toward urbanization is influencing the
direction Indonesian society is moving. Yet, over 80 percent
of Indonesia's population still lives in rural areas, and the
majority will probably continue to live there for the remainder
of this century.

Therefore, the Javanese Churches cannot allow their emphasis
to center only in urban areas. They must continue to go to
rural areas, where the Javanese people live in greatest numbers,
and where they are most responsive.

Modern Versus Traditional

The trend toward modernization has influenced some denominations to seek a new image, but they must be careful not to
forsake their traditional constituencies and the responsive
traditional masses in an attempt to be leaders in modernity.
They must learn to appeal to the futuristic-thinking urbanite
in the city churches, while at the same time flowing with the
traditional cultural currents which appeal to the masses.

The traditional mind-set is not confined to rural areas, for
large numbers of urbanites are emotionally still rural peasants.
Peacock says,

Underneath the Western overlay, the elite maintain
indigenous or mestizo private habits. They wear the
sarong at home, consume rice as their staple, and bathe
by splashing themselves with water from a square tiled
basin rather than a shower or tub(24).

And Bakker states, "Most cities are nothing else than shapeless
agglomerations of villages with a mentality of a psuedo-village
community"(25).

Future Versus Present

Although Indonesian churches need to plan for the future,
they must live in the present. They are in perhaps the best
potential church growth area in the world (of which their own
record in the period under study is proof), but to dream of the
future to the neglect of the present is comparable to Nero's
fiddling while Rome burned.

In summary, a perusal of these coordinates reveals that factors listed on the left-hand side relate more to internal development of the Church, while those on the right-hand side relate more directly to its expansion. Both sides are essential.

The reader will note that during the period of rapid church growth, the pendulum swung to the right (extensive) side. But after a brief period of massive growth, it began to swing back toward the left (intensive) side. The shift to the right resulted more from the general situation, and from the large numbers of converts, than from a planned strategy by the Churches. But the shift to the left resulted more from strategy designed by pastors and church leaders in reaction to massive growth.

In the final chapter we will consider further the issues involved and offer recommendations for a church growth strategy for the Javanese.

NOTES

1. GKJW statistics a, b, c, d, and e are from Cooley, "Church in Indonesia"; statistics f, i, k, n are from GKJW synod records. The GKJW office of evangelism cited a total of 61,726 for 1960; Suyatno, head of the synod, estimated 50,000; both totals contrast with Cooley's Indonesian Council of Churches figure of 46,000. For consistency, and in light of evaluations of several leaders, Cooley's figure is used as the basis for figuring the rate of growth.

   GKJ statistics a, b, d, are from Cooley, "Church in Indonesia"; statistics e and f are from Soegiri, *Study dan Penelitian*, sec. 3, p. 2; i and k, ibid., sec. 5, p. 1; j, ibid., sec. 5, p. 2; and n, ibid., sec. 5, pp. 7-8. Other sources give conflicting totals for the GKJ in 1960. Soegiri, *Study dan Penelitian*, sec. 7, p. 2, quotes Natan Daldjuni, who credited GKJ with 40,127 members in 1959 and 59,451 in 1964 but failed to cite his sources. If this were correct, the rate of growth per annum would be as follows: 1954-1959, 8.49 percent; 1959-1964, 9.63 percent; and 1965-1969, 10.34 percent. This would explain the great difference between the 1960-1964 period and the 1965-1971 period in this chart, but it fails to coincide with other evidence which shows a much higher growth rate after 1965. An accurate figure probably lies somewhere between these two, but since synod records are incomplete, the statistics listed here most nearly agree with the other evidence.

GKJTU statistics are all from Cooley, "Memperkenalkan GKJTU."

GITJ statistics a and d are from Kumaat, *Laporan Self-Study*, p. 11; e, f, i, j, ibid., p. 17; n, ibid., pp. 35-36; and k, ibid., p. 31. Statistic b is from Cooley, "Church in Indonesia."

GGBI statistics a and k are from Wiriadinata, "Survey Baptis II," sec. 7, p. 1; e and f, ibid., sec. 5, p. 1; i and j, ibid., sec. 5, p. 1-2; statistic b is from Smith, "God's Miracles," p. 145; and statistic n is from "Minutes of the Nineteenth Annual Session of the Indonesian Baptist Mission," p. 207.

Statistics not specifically cited were calculated from the above sources.

2. Soegiri, *Study dan Penelitian*, sec. 8, pp. 1-2.

3. Ibid., sec. 1, pp. 4-5. In 1938, 83 GKJ colporteurs were circulating throughout Central Java.

4. Figures are unavailable for lay leaders not counted in church statistics, but general observation of their numbers and zeal supports the same principle.

5. See Figure 4, Figure 7, Figure 9, and Figure 10.

6. Alan R. Tippett, *Verdict Theology in Missionary Theory* (Lincoln, Ill.: Lincoln Christian College Press, 1969), emphasizes a conversion theology. George W. Peters, "Indonesia: An Evaluative Study of East and Central Java" (typescript of unpublished article), p. 6 (hereafter referred to as "Indonesia: An Evaluative Study"), proposes that Reformed missiology and Reformed theology have been predominant in most of the great Christward movements in the modern history of missions.

7. McGavran, *Understanding Church Growth*, pp. 212-13.

8. Smith, "Questionnaires," p. 3.

9. See Donald McGavran, *Eye of the Storm* (Waco, Texas: Word Books, 1972).

10. See several articles from McGavran, *Eye of the Storm*: Walter J. Hollenweger, "Church Growth: A Faulty American

Strategy," pp. 108-14; Jordan Bishop, O. P. "Numerical
Growth--An Adequate Criterion of Mission?" pp. 121-27,
J. G. Davies, "Church Growth: A Critique," pp. 128-35; and
J. C. Hoekendijk, "The Call to Evangelism," pp. 41-54.

11. See Ralph D. Winter, "Quality or Quantity," in Donald
McGavran, *Crucial Issues in Missions Tomorrow* (Chicago:
Moody Press, 1972), pp. 175-87 (hereafter cited as *Crucial
Issues*).

12. Ibid., pp. 177-78.

13. Private interviews.

14. See Herbert Neve, "Christian Presence: One of Its Critics,"
in McGavran, *Eye of the Storm*, p. 169.

15. Space limitations prevent an exhaustive study of this
debate. Fortunately the primary sources are available in
McGavran, *Eye of the Storm*.

16. See Roland Allen, *The Spontaneous Expansion of the Church*
(Grand Rapids: William B. Eerdmans Publishing Co., 1962).

17. See Suzanne DeDietrich, *The Witnessing Community* (Philadel-
phia: Westminster Press, 1958); Hendrik Kraemer, *A
Theology of the Laity* (Philadelphia: Westminster Press,
1958); Georgia Harkness, *The Church and Its Laity* (New York:
Abingdon Press, 1962); and Niel Braun, *Laity Mobilized:
Reflections on Church Growth in Japan and Other Lands*
(Grand Rapids: William B. Eerdmans Publishing Company,
1971).

18. Donald A. McGavran, "Five Kinds of Leaders," tape of a
lecture at Colombia Bible College (South Pasadena: William
Carey Library, n.d.).

19. York Allen, Jr., *A Seminary Survey* (New York: Harper
Brothers, 1960), pp. 218-19.

20. Tasdik, *Motives for Conversion*, p. 3.

21. See Lloyd Kwast, "Christianity and Culture: Biblical
Bedrock," in McGavran, *Crucial Issues*, pp. 159-71.

22. Charles H. Kraft, "Toward a Christian Ethnotheology," in
Alan R. Tippett, *God, Man, and Church Growth* (Grand Rapids:
William B. Eerdmans Publishing Co., 1973), pp. 109-26.

23. Ibid., pp. 110-11.

24. Peacock, *Indonesia: An Anthropolitical Perspective*, p. 138.

25. J. W. M. Bakker, "Indonesia 1970: A General Survey of Society" (Yogyakarta, 1969). (Mimeographed paper for private circulation.)

13

What Is God Saying to the Churches?

The more than two million baptisms in Indonesia, the fantastic growth of churches ministering to the Javanese, and the eleven reasons cited for that growth support our basic thesis that God prepares peoples and countries for response to the gospel through a confluence of anthropological, political, sociological, economic, cultural, and religious factors. God is moving in history, and his redemptive concern includes the totality of the human condition(1).

The concept of a sovereign God who is at work in all these areas harmonizes well with the Javanese view of life. Their religious outlook colors all other aspects of life. They do not compartmentalize life into separate categories as Westerners do, but see spiritual reality pervading the mental, physical, social, moral, cultural, political, and economic aspects of life.

The situation in Indonesia had been prepared by all these forces for many centuries. But the convergence of divergent factors in the twentieth century unleashed dynamic currents in Javanese culture that caused people to search for something to fill the vacuum of an empty soul, for an intimate relationship with the God of the macrocosmos, for *slamet* (safety) and peace in the microcosmos, for power to deal with malevolent forces, and for a harmonious relationship with their fellow-men. Instead of finding these, they experienced the chaos of revolution, the strife of religious hostility, and the emptiness of unfulfilled dreams inspired by communism, nationalism, and freedom.

This disillusionment left them scrambling for a foothold that would give meaning to life.

Christianity had been introduced to the Javanese by lay Christians and had begun to acclimate itself by the 1940's, at precisely the time society was disintegrating. Thus, "in the fullness of time" Christians stretched out a hand to seeking Javanese, and both struggled together toward freedom. The Javanese denominations had begun to evidence growth after 1931, when their embryonic independence preceded that of the nation. When national freedom was born during the travail of the Indonesian Revolution of 1945-1949, the churches offered spiritual freedom that was congruent with national aspirations. The churches began to reap a harvest from some of the seed that had been sown through service, witness, and acculturation. They grew rapidly from 1945 to 1953 during the quest for freedom. But they grew very slowly during the next eight years while the nation searched for a viable political system; this period of time was used to deepen their roots and to identify with "nation and character building" (a slogan of the Indonesian government, stated in English).

The convulsions of the 1960's provided a foil for display of Christianity's panoply of virtues. Political events of that decade became the *agent provocateur* for dramatic growth of the Christward movement already underway. The government's decree on religion in 1966 was the turning point. The ministry of the churches was the coadjutant in church growth.

Indonesian interviewees listed eleven factors involved in their decisions for Christ. (See details in the Appendix.) "Spiritual need" was cited first by more people, but "Government" was mentioned more often. If these eleven factors are grouped into religious, political, and social categories, religious factors (including "Church," "Spiritual need," "Gospel," "Christian life," "Service," "Miracles," and "Reaction [against Islam]") were mentioned first by over one-half of the respondents (50.6 percent), and even more (52.6 percent) rated them higher in the total evaluation. Political factors ("Government" and "Protection [during the massacre]") were mentioned first by more than one-third (35.6 percent) of the respondents, but in the over-all evaluation, they accounted for only 25.2 percent of the total. Social factors ("Society," "Family," and "Christian life" [which was also included in the social factors because a social dimension was involved as well as a spiritual one]") were mentioned as the first cause by only 13.8 percent, but in the over-all evaluation, they received almost as much emphasis (23.2 percent) as political factors. In summary, an evaluation of motivations for Javanese becoming Christians

reveals that approximately one-half were based on spiritual
factors, one-fourth on political factors, and one-fourth on
social factors.

Looking at it from another perspective, decisions were ini-
tiated by political factors 35 percent of the time, which supports
the hypothesis that political factors were the actuators of a
vast potential response that had been created by religious and
social factors. It also implies that 65 percent of the motivating factors continue to operate today, even though the dynamics
involved in the political factors have begun to wane.

Such a situation has a high potential for growth in the
future, even during political stability; but the Church itself
must become the stimulus which evokes decisions. If it does
not, dynamics of the Christward movement will wane and church
growth will decline. It is at this point that the Javanese
Churches' concepts of evangelism and methodology play a most
vital role. The Churches must do what Javanese farmers have
done for centuries: When the rain is not falling, one learns
to irrigate.

We come now to propose the outlines of a strategy of church
growth for the Javanese Churches, based on our study of methods
that have helped and hindered church growth. Such a strategy is
needed to prevent the Javanese Churches from becoming encysted,
tolerated minorities. Each part of this brief design is to be
enacted simultaneously, providing for a balanced, integrated
approach.

RENEWAL OF THE PEOPLE OF GOD

In Spiritual Life

To be effective, the Church should be a fellowship (*koinonia*),
should perform a service (*diakonia*), and should present a witness (*marturia*): but the only way the present-day Church can do
so is through repentance (*metanoia*). (See Revelation 2:1
through 3:22.) Such repentance reopens the channels of divine
power that issue in a renewed people. The renewal of the Church
involves a radical shift to the image of the New Testament
People of God, whose life revolved around fellowship with Christ,
service for Christ, and witness to Christ, as the result of
being led by the Holy Spirit to search the Scriptures daily, to
pray, and to be the Body of Christ in the world. The Javanese
Churches stand in need of this kind of renewal.

In Theology

A relevant theology for Indonesia must speak to a nation in
search of a soul. It must relate religion to the whole of life,
including home, employment, and place in society. It must
speak of God's sovereignty and power, his immanence and love,
his forgiveness and peace, and his offer of a new life for this
world and the next. It must speak to the deepest longings of
the Javanese heart by embodying the eternal truth of God in
Indonesian clothes.

In Structure

An appropriate church structure in the indigenous context
must allow for the functioning of the entire People of God as
parts of Christ's Body who have been given spiritual gifts to
perform Christ's acts in the world. It must involve all of
God's children as ministers dispersed into the world to participate in the *missio Dei*. Some of them will exercise gifts of
administration, some of wisdom, some of knowledge, some of
evangelism, some of special powers. All of them will minister
as humble servants in cooperation with Christ, who is establishing the Kingdom of God in the world.

In Training

Training in this context means equipping the followers of
Christ through man-to-man training, through leaders training
congregations, and through teachers equipping leaders. In
brief, it means the contextualization of theology for all the
People of God. It involves programs of religious education,
short-term institutes, Theological Education by Extension(2),
and seminaries as ethnotheological laboratories.

The renewal of the People of God will replenish the Churches'
spiritual resources for presence and proclamation in the
Javanese world.

CONTEXTUALIZATION

Contextualization is the practical expression of the inter-
relatedness between culture and theology which is indicated in
the term "ethnotheology." It involves identifying and understanding the elements of a given culture and of the supra-
cultural revelation of God, so that truth may be clothed with
the thought patterns of that culture.

Kraft says that theology is typically mono-cultural in its
perspective, due to the influence of Greek culture on Western
patterns of thought. He adds that we need to understand the

eternal revelation of God as God expresses himself in different cultures. This does not mean there are different revelations in different cultures, but rather, that we need to learn the perception of the one revelation in each given culture(3).

Contextualization is the incarnation of Christ through his Body in a given context. Adolfs says,

> A kenotic Church will also make the spread of the Gospel on a worldwide scale possible for the first time. The Church in the form of service will no longer be bound to Western forms of Christianity and will be able to be present, as a servant, in the non-Christian cultures of Asia and Africa and to make use of all the achievements of these cultures(4).

Such an incarnate theology will make religion a part of all of life, and will express itself through Javanese forms, ideals, and longings. Contextualization, then, involves the use of acceptable religious practices and attitudes in the Javanese context, which perhaps would involve meditation, fasting, set times for prayer, ceremonies, special days, spiritual power for dealing with evil spirits, and the use of Javanese art forms to communicate the revelation of God in Christ.

All five Javanese denominations generally follow a Western liturgy and style of worship, which sometimes fails to appeal to Javanese spiritual tastes. Hadiwijono stated that the churches should appeal more to the desire for contact with God. He said,

> I took a friend to church. After the pastor prayed, my friend said, "I do not feel that he is in communion with God; he is only teaching about God." I was very much ashamed and embarrassed. We must go past the dogmatic stage to the feeling stage, and help these people have contact with God(5).

When the revelation of Christ comes into conflict with culture, the Truth is not to be bent to fit the culture; but it is to penetrate and permeate elements of that culture, thereby transforming them or developing functional substitutes that fulfill both cultural needs and revelational requirements.

In a practical sense, contextualization means establishing indigenous churches. This process has been going on in some of the Javanese denominations for over a century, but it needs to be deepened and broadened.

Tartib Eprajim, the first missionary of the GKJW to Bali, provides a good illustration of contextualization with his three principles:

+ His first principle was to use cultural backgrounds common to Javanese and to Balinese (centered in the Hindu Mojopahit kingdom) as a means of introducing the gospel. He worked "in the Mojopahit way" as a friend, brother, and *guru* from a common heritage. He offered spiritual advice and information for those who asked. Tartib Eprajim said,

> After a time when they have come to know me, the Balinese themselves will ask me to become their spiritual adviaor on the basis of what *I have already done* for them, a situation quite different from being their spiritual advisor on the basis of appointment by a foreign power outside Bali(6).

+ The second guiding principle was that "from the beginning maturity must be the criteria. We need not repeat the mission history of Java and first begin with tutelage(7). Therefore, the Balinese Church was an independent Church from the beginning, and never asked for financial assistance from either the Javanese missionaries or Hendrik Kraemer, their advisor.

+ Tartib Eprajim's third principle was to teach that the Christian faith implied suffering for Christ's sake. Christians were to suffer willingly for Christ, being intransigent in only one thing:

> Under no condition must they agree to being excluded from the village community, because such an isolation would be fatal to the spread of the Gospel. All minor persecution which is implied in this we accept, because Christianity *within* Balinese society is of such importance for the future, that all other considerations become secondary(8).

Such contextualization did not imply syncretism, but a determination to maintain contact with their own people in their own cultural setting, so that the power of the gospel could be experienced by them.

A contextualization of evangelism in Java would mean that the gospel would be shared through normal, natural lines of communication in Javanese culture. It would seldom manifest itself in spectacular evangelistic campaigns, but more often in a quiet chat beside the road after the evening bath, a calm testimony at funerals, a prayer of thanksgiving on special feast days, and Christian teachings in the didactic portions of a shadow-play. The lack of boisterousness and display would mean no

lessening of conviction, but rather, a deepening of it, as one
Javanese shares his *ilmu*--his secret knowledge of Jesus Christ--
with his Javanese brother.

SPONTANEOUS GROWTH

Renewal of the People of God and contextualization of their
faith will issue in spontaneous mission to the world--through
fellowship (*koinonia*), service (*diakonia*), witness (*marturia*),
and proclamation (*kerygma*). This spontaneity will flow from a
renewed Church. It does not preclude planning and strategy:
Proper strategy should produce a church situation conducive to
spontaneous expansion, resulting from church members' relationship with Christ through the Holy Spirit.

All complementary strategies will seek to channel this
spontaneity, so that the Kingdom will spread through:

Proclaiming Christ

This proclamation of the gospel by the one percent of Javanese
people who are Christians to the 99 percent who are not demands
the highest priority. This means proclamation in every acceptable form in the Javanese world, including distribution of the
Scriptures, personal testimonies, preaching, and propitious use
of cultural forms and mass media.

Multiplying Indigenous Congregations

Christian presence is most obvious in worshipping, serving,
proclaiming churches. These congregations should also gather in
homes as house churches, or as small groups related to larger
churches. These churches should be Javanese in image, expression, leadership, support and propagation. Churches of all
sizes, classes, and types should be multiplied throughout all
sectors of Javanese society.

Ministering of the Laity

The People of God must be trained and released to minister to
their fellow Christians and to the world. The most critical
problem at the moment is proper training for the laity--that
they may be equipped to minister, guarded from error, and
refreshed spiritually. Peters says,

> The mobilization and training of an adequate core of
> laymen in the right methodology with the right message
> to the community becomes the most burning issue and most
> urgent call to the Church. It is my firm conviction that
> East and Central Java hold the potential of yielding

millions of people to the Lord if the present opportunity
is wisely and fully exploited for Christ and His Kingdom(9).

Seeking Responsive Groups

One can no longer say, as Kraemer said in 1931, that
"Javanese people and Javanese society as a whole are, generally
speaking, as impervious and inaccessible to Christianity as the
Sundanese world"(10). Although pockets and groups in Javanese
society are still resistant to the gospel, the large majority
are open to a witness, because of religio-cultural and social
factors. Churches should concentrate on those who are presently
receptive to Christianity.

Using Social Relationships

Churches should use web-relationships of families and social
ties of communities to multiply the impact of the gospel, both
qualitatively and quantitatively. The late Mulus Budianto, an
outstanding leader among Javanese Baptists, once said, "One must
note that in the *desa*, the people come in groups and, therefore,
are surer and will last longer"(11). Efforts should be made by
Christians to contact all members of their extended families,
cultivate them, and witness to them. Influence of community
leaders and group processes of decision-making should be wisely
used.

These three emphases of *renewal, contextualization,* and
spontaneous growth may be compared to Christ's incarnation,
death, and resurrection, which released the power of the Holy
Spirit to flow through Christ's Church to the world. Although
one may change the metaphor and think of these three proposals
in terms of stimulus, contact, and response, they should in
fact be developed simultaneously.

OPPORTUNITIES FOR GROWTH

Fresh guarantees of religious freedom, sociological shifts,
and current sensitivity to religion present the possibility of
the Christward movement among Javanese becoming a flood. The
dissatisfaction of most Javanese with their economic, political,
physical, intellectual, and religious situations is leading
them on a search. Modernization and the failure of traditional
structures have impinged on them and created aspirations that
will not be fulfilled in this generation. The masses are on the
move, looking for a new way of life and determined to find one.
The question remains, which way they will choose? Ideologies of
the modern world and ancestral spirits of a long-past golden age
hawk their wares side by side—in market place, crowded *kampung*,
busy street, and quiet lane. Indonesia is a nation in ferment.

She is in the process of making national decisions which will
last for decades or centuries. No one can predict which way
she will go.

The Christward movement was at full tide from 1945 to 1953,
at ebb tide from 1953 to 1960, at flood tide from 1960 to 1968,
and receding again from 1968 to 1976, with only occasional
waves splashing on the shore. What does the next period
promise? At whose shrine will one hundred million Javanese
worship in the year 2000? The fluctuation of response and the
potentially explosive cultural, political, and social factors
will help determine the answer to this question. But the
Javanese Churches bear the heaviest responsibility, because
their use of other factors will determine the outcome.

We might sum up the feelings of the present-day Javanese
concerning his religion as follows:

Religion is the key to all of my life, not just my soul,
and not just life after death. My religion must relate
to my country, my neighborhood, my community, my family,
my health, and my work. I want it to integrate my life,
to give me an understanding of how I relate to my microcosmos and the macrocosmos, so that I can have peace
(*slamet*).

I am looking for a way of life. Communists offered me
one, but it failed. *Santris* at the village mosque have
offered me one, but I don't think it fits. Technocrats
in my nation's government are offering me another, and
though it appears to be the best at present, it seems to
lack a soul. Perhaps *kejawen* (Javanism) or *kebatinan*
(mysticism) offers me the best opportunity. Yes, perhaps
that is what I need to do--go back to the religion of my
ancestors, but . . . I doubt if it will fit any more,
either.

If I choose a new way, it will have to be enough like
what I know now that I will feel at home in it. But at
the same time, it will have to offer more satisfaction
and more future than I have now.

I am Javanese, and whatever way I accept will have to be
Javanese. I need to recapture the ethos of being Javanese
. . . or perhaps find a new way of life for this age without losing my identity. Therefore I'm open, but cautious.
What do you church members have to offer?

NOTES

1. See Bustavo Guiterrez, *A Theology of Liberation* (New York: Orbis Books, 1973), p. 205.

2. See Ralph Winter, ed., *Theological Education by Extension* (South Pasadena: William Carey Library, 1969); Ralph R. Covell and C. Peter Wagner, *An Extension Seminary Primer* (South Pasadena: William Carey Library, 1971); and Wayne C. Weld, *The World Directory of Theological Education by Extension* (South Pasadena: William Carey Library, 1973).

3. See Kraft, "Toward a Christian Ethnotheology," pp. 113-25.

4. Robert Adolfs, *The Grave of God: Has the Church a Future?* trans. N. D. Smith (New York: Harper and Row, 1967), p. 115.

5. Private interview.

6. Weber, *Ecumenical Movement*, pp. 174-75.

7. Hendrik Kraemer, as reported in ibid., p. 177.

8. Ibid., p. 178.

9. Peters, "Indonesia: An Evaluative Study," p. 10.

10. Kraemer, *From Missionfield*, p. 103.

11. Notes taken at the analysis meeting of the *Survey Usaha Baptis*, 27 June 1973.

APPENDIX:
Field Research

Field Research as reported in this book was designed to gather a representative sampling of opinion on reasons for church growth among the Javanese from 1960 to 1971. The following methods were used:

(1) In-depth interviews were conducted by the writer with leaders of all five denominations studied, and with individuals from all walks of life. Interviews were held in the Indonesian language; notes were taken in Indonesian, with evaluations in English. A total of 54 denominational leaders and representative pastors were interviewed to interpret the situation and the data.

(2) A random sampling, totaling 203 interviews, was made by students of the Indonesian Baptist Theological Seminary, Semarang, in the spring of 1972. They used questionnaires designed by the writer to garner information from people of varying backgrounds. The students interviewed 140 persons who had become Christians since 1965, and 44 who had become Christians prior to 1965. This included 129 persons from the five denominations studied, 55 from other denominations, and 19 non-Christians. The non-Christians and members of other denominations served as a control group on answers given by members of the Churches studied.

(3) In-depth unstructured interviews in specific locations were conducted by Indonesian Baptist Theological Seminary students in the spring of 1973. These open-ended interviews probed the dynamics of church growth in varying sociological sites picked by leaders of the denominations. Interviews were held in Javanese

or Indonesian, and transcribed in Indonesian within 24 hours.
Interviewees included 136 new Christians, 82 mature Christians,
and 40 leaders. The writer also interviewed some of the same
people at a later date to verify the accuracy of the students'
interviews.

The writer recorded all information available from the interviews on IBM System 3 data cards. The following information
verifies that the sampling was representative:

CHURCHES

GKJW	66
GKJ	95
GKJTU	63
GITJ	62
GGBI	112
Other denominations	68
Non-Christians	28
Unspecified	6
TOTAL	500

RELIGIOUS BACKGROUND

Animist/Communist	9
Animist	48
Buddhist/Confucianist	9
Islam/Animist	133
Islam/Communist	4
Islam	113
Christianity	165
Christian/Animist	4
None	2
Other	11
TOTAL	500

PERIOD IN WHICH THEY BECAME CHRISTIANS

Before 1960	126
1960-1964	17
1965-1971	338
Non-Christians	28
TOTAL	500

Two hundred respondents were from urban areas, and 229 from
rural areas; 206 were from traditional or older churches, and
223 from new churches; 272 were from large churches, and 157

from small churches. Of the 500 respondents, 101 were pastors
or denominational leaders, 93 were board members, 69 were lay
pastors or workers, and 186 were average church members; data
was incomplete on 51 interviews.

A primary aim of the research was to discover the motivations
of those who became Christians during the various periods following 1965. Each respondent usually listed several reasons, but
except in the case of those who used questionnaires, a specific
number of reasons or a ranking of them was not requested. Of the
respondents, 495 gave a first motivation, 459 gave a second, 363
a third, 219 a fourth, and 148 gave five motivations.

Figure 2 shows which motivations were mentioned first. Figure
10 shows a total evaluation based on ten points for the first-
mentioned motivation, nine for the second, eight for the third,
and so on. The latter approach affords insight into the influence of each factor and whether it was a primary or secondary
motivation.

The following categories were used to sum up motivations
referred to in the interviews; the explanation of each describes
and limits that category.

Government:

The decision of the Indonesian government in 1966 that
every Indonesian must believe in God and must profess a
sanctioned religion. Only a very small percentage referred to an actual decree, but the presence and policy of
the government was listed as a determining factor in their
conversions, or at least in their beginning a search for a
religion.

Church:

Any effort or activity of the institutional church that
was a determinative factor, including pastors, evangelistic
campaigns, special programs, Sunday Schools, catechism
classes, etc. This does not include service ministries of
the church, such as schools, hospitals, or other social
ministries.

Spiritual Need:

A spiritual need felt by the person, often stated as
inner need, emptiness of soul, or *not at peace.* This
excludes physical needs and needs listed in reaction to
other religions.

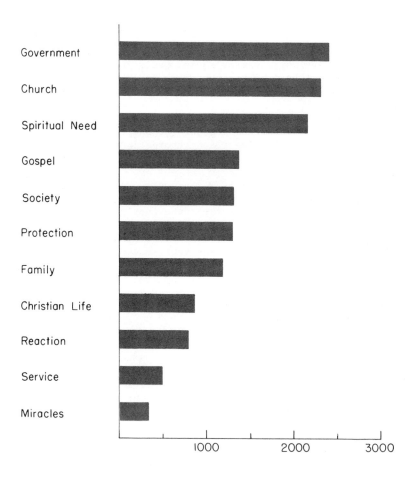

FIGURE 10

RESULTS OF INTERVIEWS:
TOTAL EVALUATION OF MOTIVATIONS

Gospel:

> The message of the Good News and its appeal to human
> hearts. The emphasis was placed upon what was said,
> rather than on who said it or the agents that brought it.

Society:

> Any social relationship that was determinative, including
> influence of village leaders, social groups or sub-groups,
> and personal witness of Christians if the respondent
> emphasized the social relationship more than the message.

Protection:

> Fear of losing their lives, social positions, or employ-
> ment because they were not members of a sanctioned
> religion. It was often stated as "seeking a refuge," or
> "running away." In most cases, it meant the person was
> afraid of being accused of being a communist. It
> included a few who had no communist connections, but who
> were afraid that for some reason the government's decree
> would cause them problems.

Family:

> A member or members of the immediate family played a
> determinitive role in the decision to become a Christian.
> Usually this was a family member who was already a Chris-
> tian, but at other times respondents said that they
> became Christians as a family.

Christian Life:

> Testimony of Christian life in day-to-day activities,
> even in times of stress and ridicule.

Reaction:

> Anything in a former religion that repelled people or
> failed to answer their needs, causing them to look else-
> where for spiritual help.

Service:

> Any service ministry performed by a Christian institu-
> tion, including education, medical aid, or other physical
> needs that were met by these institutions.

Miracles:

A supernatural event that caused people to be aware of the power of God, in contrast to the powers of evil. It includes the power to burn fetishes, exorcise demons, and perform healings.

Glossary

abangan - animistic peasants who are generally statistical
   Moslems
adat - customs; tradition
agama - religion

Badan Kerja Sama Kaum Baptis (BKS) - Cooperative Work Committee
banting stir - a sudden turning of a steering wheel
bapak - father or father-figure
batin - the inner life; the subjective (see *kebatinan*)
Belanda - Dutch
bersih desa - cleansing of the village (of evil spirits)
Budi Utomo - Noble Endeavor Study Club, the first national organization in this century to begin striving for independence

Confrontation - Sukarno's term for opposition to the newly-formed
   nation of Malaysia

Darul Islam - an Islamic party; in Indonesia, an extremist
   guerilla organization of the post-war years
desa - village
Dewan Gereja Indonesia - Indonesian Council of Churches
dualisme - dualism
dukun - shaman, medicine man, healer, sorcerer
dukun ramal - seer

Gabungan Gereja-Gereja Baptis Indonesia (GGBI) - Union of
   Indonesian Baptist Churches
gamelan - Javanese percussion orchestra
Gereja-Gereja Baptis Indonesia (GBI) - Indonesian Baptist
   Churches
Gereja-Gereja Kristen Jawa (GKJ) - Javanese Christian Churches
Gereja Ingili di Tanah Jawa (GITJ) - Java Evangelical Church
Gereja Kristen Jawa Tengah Utara (GKJTU) - North Central Java
   Christian Church
Gereja Kristen Jawi Wetan (GKJW) - East Java Christian Church
GESTAPU - shortened form of *Gerakan September Tigapuluh*, 30th
   of September Movement, the name given the abortive communist
   coup of 1965
gotong royong - mutual assistance or cooperation
guru - teacher
guru Injil - Gospel teacher; i.e., unordained pastor with
   limited education

ilmu - knowledge; esoteric understanding or information
Irian - New Guinea

jihad - Islamic holy war
jumaat - religious congregation

kafir - infidel
kampong or *kampung* - village-like residential area within a city
kaum feodal - feudalists
kabatinan - Javanese mysticism (see *batin*)
kejawen - Javanism; the primitive Javanese religion; indigenous
   Javanese animism
Ke-Tuhanan Yang Maha Esa - the Highest Lordship; belief in one
   God; the first principle of *Pancasila*
klasis - classis; a governing body in Reformed churches corres-
   ponding to a presbytery
komunisme - communism
kris - dagger
Kristen-Jawa - Javanese Christian
Kristen-Londo - "Christian Hollander," or Dutch-like Christian

Landa Jawa (Javanese) - Javanese Hollander (Dutch)
Lubang Buaya - Crocodile Hole; location (near Jakarta) of an
   abandoned well where the bodies of the murdered generals were
   placed

mahdi - a coming savior (in Moslem thought)
Masyumi - a major Islamic party, banned by President Sukarno in 1959
mufakat - consensus
Murba - Islamic party outlawed by President Sukarno in 1964
musyawarah - mutual deliberations
Musyawarah Antar Agama - Inter-Religion Consultation
Musyawarah Antara Kaum Baptis - Baptist Consultative Conference

Nahdatul Ulama (NU) - Moslem Scholars' Party
NASAKOM - Sukarno's term for combining nationalism (*NAS*ionalisme), religion (*A*gama), and communism (*KOM*unisme) into the state ideology
nasionalisme - nationalism
NEKOLIM - (Sukarno's term for) neo-colonialists, colonialists (*KOL*onialis), and imperialists
ngelmu (Javanese) - knowledge; esoteric understanding or information

Orde Baru or *Orba* - New Order; the term given to the Suharto government
Orde Lama or *Orla* - Old Order; the term given by the Suharto administration to Sukarno's government

Pancasila - the five basic principles of the Republic of Indonesia
Partai Komunis Indonesia (PKI) - Indonesian Communist Party
Partai Muslimin Indonesia (PMI, PARMUSI) - Indonesian Moslem Party
Partai Nasional Indonesia (PNI) - Indonesian Socialist Party
peci - national fez which has become identified with Islam
pendeta - Indonesian word for "pastor," coming from the Hindu word *pandito* (priest) or *pundit* (scholar)
Pilot Proyek Jumaat Missioner - Missionary Church Pilot Project
Pilot Proyek Pembinaan Mental Agama (P₃A) - Pilot Project for Fostering Religious Mentality
priyayi - Javanese gentry; aristocrats of former days; relatives of Javanese rulers

Ratu Adil - Just King (an expected messianic figure in Javanese thought

sajen - offering to the spirits
santri - a student at a traditional type of Moslem school; in
    Java, a person consciously and exclusively Moslem
Sarekat Islam - an Islamic political party
sarong - men's traditional wrap-around skirt
SEKBER GOLKAR - Joint Secretariat of Functional Groups, which
    represented the Suharto government's program in the 1971 and
    1977 elections
Shafi'ite - a fairly conservative school of Islamic thought
sikat - brush; to sweep, massacre, wipe out, clean out
slamet or *selamat* - safe; welfare, happiness, prosperity; happy,
    pleasant; state of well-being, free from defect or danger
slametan or *selamatan* - religious feast, to mark important events
    in one's life and to bring *slamet*
Sufism - a form of Islam influenced by mysticism
Sunni - a traditionalist sect in Islam
Survéy Usaha Baptis - Survey of Baptist Work

Thirtieth of September Movement - attempted communist coup
    d'etat in 1965
Tuhan - the Lord God

umat, *ummat* - a religious community

Selected Bibliography

BOOKS

Abdulgani, Roeslan. *Pantjasilia: The Prime Mover of the Indonesian Revolution*. Jakarta: Prapantja, n.d.

Abdurrachim, Iih. *Dasar-Dasar Anthropologi Indonesia* [Foundations of Indonesian Anthropology]. Jakarta: Penerbit Wijaya, 1962.

Adams, Cindy. *Sukarno: An Autobiography*. New York: Bobbs-Merrill Co., 1965.

Adolfs, Robert. *The Grave of God: Has the Church a Future?* Translated by N. D. Smith. New York: Harper and Row, 1967.

Aghnides, Nicolas P. *The Background Introduction to Mohammedan Law*. Solo: Sitti Sjamsijah, n.d.

Ali, Mukti. *Dialoog Antar Agama* [Dialogue among Religions]. Yogyakarta: Yayasan Nida, 1970.

_____. *Faktor-Faktor Penjiaran Islam* [Factors in the Spread of Islam]. Yogyakarta: Yayasan Nida, 1971.

_____. *Pelbagai Persoalan Islam Di Indonesia Dewasa Ini* [Various Problems of Islam in Indonesia Today]. Yogyakarta: Yayasan Nida, 1971.

Ali, Mukti. *The Spread of Islam in Indonesia*. Yogyakarta: Yayasan Nida, 1970.

Alisjahbana, S. Takdir. *Indonesia: Social and Cultural Revolution*. London: Oxford University Press, 1969.

_____. *Values as Integrating Forces in Personality, Society, and Culture*. Kuala Lumpur, Malaysia: University Press, 1966.

Allen, Roland. *The Spontaneous Expansion of the Church*. Grand Rapids: William B. Eerdmans Publishing Co., 1962.

Allen, York, Jr. *A Seminary Survey*. New York: Harper Brothers, 1960.

Anderson, Benedict R. O'G. *Mythology and the Tolerance of the Javanese*. Ithaca: Modern Indonesia Project, Monograph Series, Cornell University, 1965.

_____, et al. *A Preliminary Analysis of the October 1, 1965 Coup in Indonesia*. Ithaca: Southeast Asia Program, Cornell University, 1971.

Anderson, Gerald H. *Christ and Crisis in Southeast Asia*. New York: Friendship Press, 1968.

Arsalan, Al-Amier Sjakieb. *Mengapa Kaum Muslimin Mundur dan Mengapa Kaum selain Mereka Madju?* [Why Is Islam Retreating and Why Are Other Religions Advancing?]. Translated from Arabic to Indonesian by H. Moenawar Chalil. Jakarta: Bulan Bintang, 1967.

Atjeh, Abubkar. *Sekitar Masuknja Islam ke Indonesia* [Concerning the Entrance of Islam to Indonesia]. Semarang: Ramadhani, 1971.

Bakri, Hasbullah. *Nabi Isa Dalam Al Quran dan Nabi Mohammad Dalam Bijbel* [Prophet Isa in the Koran and Prophet Mohammed in the Bible]. Solo: Sitti Sjamsijah, 1968.

Barnett, A. Doak, ed. *Communist Strategies in Asia*. New York: Frederick A. Praeger, 1963.

Benda, Harry J. *Continuity and Change in Indonesian Islam*. New Haven: Yale University, 1965.

_____. *The Crescent and the Rising Star*. The Hague: W. van Hoeve, 1958.

Benda, Harry J. *Reflections on Asian Communism*. New Haven: Southeast Asia Studies, Reprint Series, Yale University, October 1966.

Bentley-Taylor, David. *The Great Volcano*. London: Lutterworth Press, 1967.

_____. *The Prisoner Leaps*. London: Lutterworth Press, 1965.

_____. *The Weathercock's Reward*. London: Lutterworth Press, 1967.

Bidney, David. *Theoretical Anthropology*. New York: Columbia University Press, 1953.

Boland, B. J. *The Struggle of Islam in Modern Indonesia*. The Hague: Martinus Nighoff, 1971.

Bosch, F. D. K. *Selected Studies in Indonesian Archaeology*. The Hague: Martinus Nighoff, 1951.

Brackman, Arnold C. *The Communist Collapse in Indonesia*. Singapore: Asia Pacific Press, 1970.

_____. *Indonesian Communism: A History*. New York: Frederick A. Praeger, 1963.

_____. *Southeast Asia's Second Front: The Power Struggle in the Malay Archipelago*. New York: Frederick A. Praeger, 1966.

Bradshaw, Mac. *Church Growth Through Evangelism-in-Depth*. Pasadena: William Carey Library, 1969.

Braun, Neil. *Laity Mobilized: Reflections on Church Growth in Japan and Other Lands*. Grand Rapids: William Eerdmans Publishing Co., 1971.

Burger, Dionijs H. *Structural Changes in Javanese Society: The Supra-Village Sphere*. Ithaca: Cornell University, 1956.

Bustin, G. T. *Dead, Yet . . . Live*. Westfield, Ind.: Bustin's Books, Publishers, n.d.

Coedes, G. *The Indianized States of Southeast Asia*. Singapore: University of Malaya Press, 1968.

Cooley, Frank L. *Indonesia: Church and Society*. New York: Friendship Press, 1968.

Bibliography

Crawford, Don. *Miracles in Indonesia*. Wheaton, Ill.: Tyndale House, Publishers, 1972.

Dahm, Bernhard. *History of Indonesia in the Twentieth Century*. Translated by P. S. Falla. New York: Praeger Publishers, 1971.

_____. *Sukarno and the Struggle for Indonesian Independence*. Ithaca: Cornell University Press, 1969.

Daniel, Norman. *Islam and the West: The Making of an Image*. Edinburgh: University Press, 1960.

Daradjat, Zakiah. *Islam dan Kesehatan Mental* [Islam and Mental Health]. Jakarta: Gunung Agung, 1971.

Darmowigoto, Soesilo. *Iman Kristen* [The Christian Faith]. Solo: n.p., 1972.

Day, Clive. *The Policy and Administration of the Dutch in Java*. Kuala Lumpur, Malaysia: Oxford University Press, c. 1966.

Dayton, Edward R. *Mission Handbook: North American Protestant Ministries Overseas*. 10th ed. Monrovia, Cal.: Missions Advanced Research and Communication Center, 1973.

DeDietrich, Suzanne. *The Witnessing Community*. Philadelphia: Westminster Press, 1958.

Development: Summary of Indonesia's First Five-Year Development Plan, April 1, 1969-March 31, 1974. Jakarta: Garuda, n.d.

Douglas, Stephen A. *Political Socialization and Student Activism in Indonesia*. Chicago: University of Illinois Press, 1970.

Duyvendak, J. Ph. *Pengantar Ethnologi Kepulauan Indonesia* [Introduction to the Ethnology of the Islands of Indonesia]. Jakarta: Tavip Study Club, 1965.

40 Hari Kegagalan "G. 30. S" [Forty Days of Failure for the Thirtieth of September Movement]. Jakarta: Staf Angkatan Bersendjata, 1965.

Eskelund, Karl. *Indonesian Adventure*. London: Burke, 1954.

Feith, Herbert. *The Decline of Constitutional Democracy in Indonesia*. Ithaca: Cornell University Press, 1962.

Feith, Herbert, and Castles, Lance, eds. *Indonesian Political Thinking, 1945-1965*. Ithaca: Cornell University Press, 1970.

Fischer, H. Th. *In Leiding Tot De Culturele Anthropologie Van Indonesie*. Haarlem: De Erven F. Bohn, N. V. Translated into Indonesian by Anas Markruf. *Pengantar Anthropologi Kebudajaan Indonesia* [Introduction to the Cultural Anthropology of Indonesia]. Jakarta: P. T. Pembangunan, 1954.

Fisher, Charles A. *South-East Asia: A Social, Economic, and Political Geography*. London: Methuen and Co., 1964.

Freeman, Roger A. *Socialism and Private Enterprise in Equatorial Asia*. Stanford: Hoover Institute, 1968.

Gallaher, Art. *Media and Educational Innovation*. Lincoln: University of Nebraska Press, 1954.

Geertz, Clifford. *Agricultural Involution: The Process of Ecological Change in Indonesia*. Berkeley: University of California Press, 1966.

_____. *The Development of the Javanese Economy: A Socio-Cultural Approach*. Cambridge: Harvard University, 1956.

_____. *Islam Observed: Religious Development in Morocco and Indonesia*. New Haven: Yale University Press, 1968.

_____. *Peddlers and Princes: Social Change and Economic Modernization in Two Indonesian Towns*. Chicago: University of Chicago Press, 1963.

_____. *Religion in Mojokuto: A Study of Ritual and Belief in a Complex Society*. Cambridge: Harvard University, 1956.

_____. *The Religion of Java*. Glencoe, Ill.: Free Press, 1960.

_____. *The Social Context of Economic Change: An Indonesian Case Study*. Cambridge: Harvard University, 1956.

Geertz, Hildred. *Indonesian Cultures and Communities*. New Haven: HRAF Press, 1963.

_____. *The Javanese Family*. New York: Free Press of Glencoe, 1961.

Gerber, Vergil, ed. *Missions in Creative Tension: The Green Lake '71 Compendium*. South Pasadena, Cal.: William Carey Library, 1971.

Gibb, H. A. R., ed. *Mohammedanism: An Historical Survey*.
London: Oxford University Press, 1953.

Guiterrez, Bustavo. *A Theology of Liberation*. New York: Orbis
Books, 1973.

Hadiwijono, Harun. *Agama Hindu dan Agama Budha* [The Hindu
Religion and the Buddhist Religion]. Jakarta: Badan Penerbit
Kristen, 1971.

_____. *Kebatinan dan Indjil* [Mysticism and the Gospel].
Jakarta: Badan Penerbit Kristen, 1970.

_____. *Man in the Present Javanese Mysticism*. Baarn:
Bosch and Keuning N.V., 1967.

Hamka. *Pengaruh Muhammed 'Abduh Di Indonesia* [The Influence of
Muhammad 'Abduh in Indonesia]. Jakarta: Tintamas, 1958.

Harkness, Georgia. *The Church and Its Laity*. New York:
Abingdon Press, 1962.

Hatta, Mohammad. *Sekitar Proklamasi 17 Agustus 1945* [Concerning
the 17 August 1945 Proclamation]. Jakarta: Tintamas, 1970.

Higgins, Benjamin, with Higgins, Jean. *Indonesia: The Crisis
of the Millstones*. New York: D. van Norstrand Co., 1963.

Hindley, Donald. *The Communist Party of Indonesia, 1951-1963*.
Los Angeles: University of California Press, 1966.

Holt, Claire, ed. *Culture and Politics in Indonesia*. Ithaca:
Cornell University Press, 1972.

Hughes, John. *Indonesian Upheaval*. New York: David McKay Co.,
1967.

The Indonesian Armed Forces and the New Order. Jakarta:
Department of Defense and Security, Institute of History,
1968.

Ismaun. *Problematik Pantjasila Sebagai Kepribadian Bangsa
Indonesia* [The Problem of *Pancasila* as the Indonesian
Personality]. Bandung: Carya Remadja, 1971.

Jay, Robert R. *Javanese Villagers: Social Relations in Rural
Modjokuto*. Cambridge: MIT Press, 1969.

_____. *Religion and Politics in Rural Central Java*. Yale
University: Southeast Asia Studies, 1963.

Kahin, George McTurnan. *The Asian-African Conference, Bandung, Indonesia, April 1955.* Ithaca: Cornell University Press, 1956.

_____. *Nationalism and Revolution in Indonesia.* Ithaca: Cornell University Press, 1952.

Kansil, C. S. T. *Pantjasila dan Undang-Undang Dasar 1945: Dasar Falsafah Negara* [Pancasila and the 1945 Constitution: Foundation of the Nation's Philosophy]. Jakarta: Pradnja Paramita, 1972.

Kartohadikoesoemo, Soetardjo. *Desa* [Village]. Yogyakarta: Sumur Bandung, 1965.

Kennedy, Raymond. *Bibliography of Indonesian Peoples and Cultures.* Rev. ed. Vol. 2. Edited by Thomas W. Maretzks and H. Th. Fischer. New Haven: Yale University Press, 1962.

Khalidy, Mustafa, and Farrukh, Omar A. *Missi Kristen dan Pendjadjahan* [The Christian Mission and Colonialism]. Surabaya: C. V. Faizan, 1969.

Knowles, Ruth Sheldon. *Indonesia Today: The Nation That Helps Itself.* Los Angeles: Nash Publishing, 1973.

Koch, Kurt. *The Revival in Indonesia.* Grand Rapids: Kregel Publications, 1970.

Koentjaraningrat. *Rintangan-Rintangan Mental Dalam Pembangunan Ekonomi di Indonesia* [Psychological Obstacles to Economic Development in Indonesia]. Seri I/2. Jakarta: Bhratara, 1969.

_____. *Some Social-Anthropological Observations on Gotong Rojong Practices in Two Villages of Central Java.* Translated by Claire Holt. Ithaca: Southeast Asia Program, Modern Indonesia Project, Department of Far Eastern Studies, Cornell University, 1961.

_____, ed. *Villages in Indonesia.* Ithaca: Cornell University Press, 1967.

Kraemer, Hendrik. *The Christian Message in a Non-Christian World.* Grand Rapids: Kregel Publications, 1938.

_____. *The Communication of the Christian Faith.* Philadelphia: Westminster Press, 1956.

Kraemer, Hendrik. *From Missionfield to Independent Church*.
     London: SCM Press, 1958.

_____. *Religion and the Christian Faith*. London: Lutter-
     worth Press, 1956.

_____. *A Theology of the Laity*. Philadelphia: Westminster
     Press, 1962.

Latourette, Kenneth Scott. *The Expansion of Christianity*.
     7 vols. New York: Harper and Row, 1962.

_____. *The Twentieth Century Outside Europe*. Vol. 5:
     Christianity in a Revolutionary Age. New York: Harper and
     Row, 1962.

Latuihamallo, P. D.; Matondang, V.; Anwar, H. Rosihan; Ojong,
     P. I.; Hoetaoeroek, M. *Kejakinan dan Perdjuangan* [Conviction
     and Struggle]. Jakarta: BPK Gunung Mulia, 1972.

Legge, J. D. *Central Authority and Regional Autonomy in
     Indonesia: A Study in Local Administration, 1950-1960*.
     Ithaca: Cornell University Press, 1961.

_____. *Indonesia*. Englewood Cliffs, N. J.: Prentice-Hall,
     1964.

LeMay, Reginald. *The Culture of South-East Asia*. London:
     George Allen & Unwin, 1954.

Lev, Daniel S. *The Transition to Guided Democracy: Indonesian
     Politics, 1957-1959*. Ithaca: Southeast Asia Program,
     Department of Asian Studies, Cornell University, 1966.

Lewis, Reba. *Indonesia: Troubled Paradise*. London: Robert
     Hale, 1962.

Lovestrand, Harold. *Hostage in Jakarta*. Chicago: Moody Press,
     1969.

McGavran, Donald A. *Church Growth Bulletin*. 5 vols. South
     Pasadena: William Carey Library, 1969.

_____. *Church Growth and Christian Mission*. New York:
     Harper and Row, 1965.

_____. *How Churches Grow*. New York: Friendship Press, 1959.

_____. *Understanding Church Growth*. Grand Rapids: William
     B. Eerdmans Publishing Co., 1970.

McGavran, Donald A., ed. *Eye of the Storm*. Waco, Texas: Word Books, 1972.

McVey, Ruth T., ed. *Indonesia*. New Haven: HRAF Press, 1967.

_____. *The Rise of Indonesian Communism*. Ithaca: Cornell University Press, 1966.

Majur, Gusti. *Sedjarah Ringkas Indonesia* [A Short History of Indonesia]. 9th printing. Jakarta: Pendidikan Umum, n.d.

Manikam, Raja B., and Thomas, Winburn T. *The Church in Southeast Asia*. New York: Friendship Press, 1956.

Margull, Hans. *Hope in Action: The Church's Task in the World*. Philadelphia: Muhlenburg Press, 1959.

Mataram, Tjantrik. *Peranan Ramalan Djojobojo dalam Revolusi Kita* [The Role of the Prophecy of Joyoboyo in Our Revolution]. Bandung: Masa Baru, 1966.

Mintz, Jeanne S. *Mohammed, Marx, and Marhaen: The Roots of Indonesian Socialism*. New York: Frederick A. Praeger, 1965.

Mintaredja, H. M. S. *Masjarakat Islam dan Politik di Indonesia* [Islamic Society and Politics in Indonesia]. Jakarta: Permata, 1972.

Moertono, Soemarsaid. *State and Statecraft in Old Java: A Study of the Later Mataram Period, 16th to 19th Century*. Ithaca: Modern Indonesia Project, Cornell University, 1968.

Muhammady, Usman E. *Anthropologi-Religi dan Pantjasila: Penuntun bagi Pelaksanaan Agama dan Pantja Sila dalam Masjarakat* [Religious Anthropology and *Pancasila*: A Challenge to Practice Religion and *Pancasila* in Society]. Jakarta: Pustaka Agus Salim, 1969.

Müller-Krüger, Th. *Sedjarah Geredja Di Indonesia* [A History of the Church in Indonesia]. Jakarta: Badan Penerbit Kristen, 1966.

Nasution, Abdul Haris. *Menegakkan: Keadilan Dan Kebenaran* [Establishing Justice and Truth]. Jakarta: Seruling Masa, 1967.

_____. *Kekarjaan ABRI* [The Work of the Indonesian Armed Forces]. Jakarta: Seruling Masa, 1971.

Natsir, M. *Islam dan Kristen di Indonesia* [Islam and Christianity in Indonesia]. Bandung: Peladjar dan Bulan Sabit, 1969.

Negara Berketuhanan dan Agama-Agama [A Nation of Belief in God and Religions]. Jakarta: Sekretariat Nasional, 1970.

Neill, Stephen. *Christian Faith and Other Faiths*. London: Oxford University Press, 1965.

Nichols, Buford L. *Echoes from Indonesia*. Nashville: Convention Press, 1958.

Nida, Eugene A. *Customs and Cultures*. New York: Harper and Row, 1954.

Nitisastro, Widjojo, and Ismael, J. E. *The Government, Economy and Taxes of a Central Javanese Village*. Ithaca: Cornell University, 1959.

Njoto. *PKI dan Pantjasila* [The Indonesian Communist Party and Pancasila]. Jakarta: n.p., 1958.

North American Protestant Ministries Overseas. 8th ed. Waco, Texas: Word Books, 1968.

Notonagoro. *Beberapa Hal Mengenai Falsafah Pantjasila* [Several Factors Concerning the Philosophy of *Pancasila*]. Jakarta: Pantjasila University, 1967.

Notohamidjojo, O. *Iman Kristen dan Politik* [The Christian Faith and Politics]. 3rd ed. Jakarta: BPK Gunung Mulia, 1972.

Nugroho, Notosusanto, and Saleh, Ismail. *The Coup Attempt of the "September 30 Movement" in Indonesia*. Jakarta: P. T. Pembimbing Masa-Jakarta, 1968.

Palmier, L. H. *Social Status and Power in Java*. London: University of London, Athlone Press, 1960.

Parker, J. I., ed. *Interpretive Statistical Survey of the World Mission of the Christian Church*. New York: International Missionary Council, 1938.

Parks, R. Keith. *Crosscurrents*. Nashville: Convention Press, 1966.

Pauker, Guy J. *Indonesia in 1966: The Year of Transition*. Santa Monica: Rand Corporation, 1967.

Pauker, Guy J. *Indonesia's Convalescence.* Santa Monica: Rand Corporation, 1967.

_____. *Indonesia: The Age of Reason.* Santa Monica: Rand Corporation, 1968.

_____. *The Rise and Fall of the Communist Party in Indonesia.* Santa Monica: Rand Corporation, February 1969.

_____. *Towards a New Order in Indonesia.* Santa Monica: Rand Corporation, 1967.

Peacock, James L. *Indonesia: An Anthropological Perspective.* Pacific Palisades: Goodyear Publishing Co., 1973.

People of Indonesia, Unite and Fight to Overthrow the Fascist Regime. Peking: Foreign Language Press, 1968.

Perkembangan Sosial-Budaja dalam Pembangunan Nasional [The Growth of Social Culture in National Development]. Jakarta: Lembaga Ilmu Pengetahuan Indonesia, 1970.

Peters, George W. *Indonesia Revival: Focus on Timor.* Grand Rapids: Zondervan Publishing House, 1973.

Polomka, Peter. *Indonesia Since Sukarno.* Middlesex, England: Penguin Books, Harmondsworth, 1971.

Pringgodigdo, A. K. *Sedjarah Pergerakan Rakjat Indonesia* [History of the People's Revolution in Indonesia]. Jakarta: Dian Rakjat, 1970.

Rassars, W. H. Panji. *The Culture Hero: A Structural Study of Religion in Java.* The Hague: M. Nijhoff, 1959.

Ray, J. K. *Transfer of Power in Indonesia, 1942-1949.* Bombay: Manaktlas, 1969.

Roeder, O. G. *Who's Who in Indonesia.* Jakarta: Gunung Agung, 1971.

Salam, Solichin. *Sekitar Wali Sanga* [Concerning the Nine Prophets]. Kudus: Menara, 1972.

Sastroamidjojo, Seno. *Renungan Tentang Pertundjukan Wajang Kulit* [Reflections on Shadow-Play Performances]. Jakarta: Penerbit Kinta, 1964.

Schrieke, B. *Indonesian Sociological Studies.* Vol. 2: *Ruler and Realm in Early Java.* The Hague: W. van Hoeve, 1957.

Selosoemardjan. *The Dynamics of Community Development in Rural Central and West Java.* Ithaca: Southeast Asia Program, Department of Asian Studies, Cornell University, 1963.

_____. *Social Change in Jogjakarta.* Ithaca: Cornell University Press, 1962.

Shaplen, Robert. *Time Out of Hand: Revolution and Reaction in Southeast Asia.* New York: Harper and Row, 1969.

Siddik, Abdullah. *Islamologi* [Islamology]. Jakarta: Tintamas, 1967.

Sidjabat, W. B. *Panggilan Kita di Indonesia Dewasa Ini* [Our Present-Day Call in Indonesia]. Jakarta: Badan Penerbit Kristen, 1964.

_____. *Partisipasi Kristen dalam Nation Building di Indonesia* [Christian Participation in Nation Building in Indonesia]. Jakarta: Badan Penerbit Kristen, 1968.

_____. *Religious Tolerance and the Christian Faith.* Jakarta: Badan Penerbit Kristen, 1965.

The Silent Slaughter. New York: Marzani and Munsell, 1966.

Simatupang, T. B. *Tugas Kristen dalam Revolusi* [The Christian Obligation in the Revolution]. Jakarta: Badan Penerbit Kristen, 1967.

Simon, Sheldon W. *The Broken Triangle: Peking, Djakarta, and the PKI.* Baltimore: John Hopkins Press, 1969.

Sjafa'at. *Pengantar Studi Islam* [A Guide to the Study of Islam]. Jakarta: Bulan Bintang, 1969.

Slamet, Ina E. *Pokok-Pokok Pembangunan Masjarakat Desa: Sebuah Pandangan Antropologi Budaya* [Fundamentals for Developing Village Society: An Anthropological Cultural Perspective]. Jakarta: Bhratara, 1965.

Slametmuljana. *Nasionalisme Sebagai Modal Perdjuangan Bangsa Indonesia* [Nationalism as a Resource for the Struggle of the Indonesian People]. Vol. 1. Jakarta: Balai Pustaka, 1968.

_____. *Runtuhnja Keradjaan Hindu-Djawa dan Timbulnja Negara-Negara Islam di Nusantara* [The Fall of the Javanese Hindu Kingdom and the Rise of Islamic States in the Archipelago]. Jakarta: Bhratara, 1968.

Smith, Ebbie C. *God's Miracles: Indonesian Church Growth.* South Pasadena: William Carey Library, 1970.

Soedjatmoko; Ali, Mohammad; Resnik, G. J.; and Kahin, G. McTurnan. *An Introduction to Indonesian Historiography.* Ithaca: Cornell University Press, 1965.

Soeripto. *Surat Perintah 11 Maret: Muntjulnja Orde Baru, Runtuhnja Orde Lama* [The 11th of March Order: The Emergence of the New Order and the Fall of the Old Order]. Surabaya: Penerbit P. T. GRIP, 1969.

Soeroto. *Indonesia Ditengah-tengah Dunia Dari Abad Keabad* [Indonesia at the Center of the World Throughout the Ages]. 3 vols. Jakarta: Penerbit Djambatan, 1954.

Sosrodihardjo, Soedjito. *Perubahan Struktur Masjarakat di Djawa* [Changes in the Structure of Society in Java]. Yogyakarta: Karya, 1972.

Sosrosudigdo, Sarwedi. *Fungsi dan Arti Kebatinan untuk Pribadi dan Revolusi* [The Function and Meaning of Mysticism for the Individual and the Revolution]. Jakarta: Balai Pustaka, 1965.

Status of Christianity Country Profile: Indonesia. Monrovia, Cal.: Missions Advanced Research and Communication Center, World Vision, 1973.

Suryadipura, R. Paryana. *Alam Pikiran* [The Nature of Thought]. Bandung: Sumur Bandung, 1963.

Tambunan, A. M. *Pembinaan Tata Kehidupan Sosial dan Politik dalam Orde Baru* [The Preservation of Order in the Social and Political Life of the New Order]. Jakarta: Badan Penerbit Kristen, 1968.

Tari, Mel. *Like a Mighty Wind.* Carol Stream, Ill.: Creation House, 1971.

Tasdik. *Motives for Conversion in East Java Since September 1965.* Singapore: Foundation for Theological Education in Southeast Asia, 1970.

Ter Harr, B. *Adat Law in Indonesia.* Jakarta: Bhratara, 1962.

Tippett, Alan R. *God, Man, and Church Growth.* Grand Rapids: William B. Eerdmans Publishing Co., 1973.

Tippett, Alan R. *Verdict Theology in Missionary Theory.* Lincoln,
    Ill.: Lincoln Christian College Press, 1969.

Tjondronegoro, Dharmawan. *Ledakan Fitnah Subversi G-30-S* [The
    Explosion of Slander by the Subversive 30th of September
    Movement]. Jakarta: Matoa, 1965.

Tomosoa, J. J. *Geredja jang Dewasa dan Kesedjahteraan Umat*
    [The Mature Church and the Prosperity of Its People].
    Jakarta: Badan Penerbit Kristen, 1970.

Toward Freedom and the Dignity of Man. Jakarta: Republic of
    Indonesia, Department of Foreign Affairs, 1961.

Ulbricht, H. *Wajang Purwa: Shadows of the Past.* Singapore:
    Oxford University Press, 1970.

United States Army. *United States Army Handbook for Indonesia.*
    Washington: American University, Foreign Area Studies
    Division, Department of the Army, 1964.

Van Akkeren, Philip. *Sri and Christ: A Study of the Indigenous
    Church in East Java.* London: Lutterworth Press, 1970.

Van Bemmelen, R. W. *The Geology of Indonesia.* The Hague:
    Government Printing Office, 1949.

Van der Kroef, Justus Maria. *The Communist Party of Indonesia:
    Its History, Program, and Tactics.* Vancouver: University of
    British Columbia, 1965.

_____. *Indonesia in the Modern World.* Vol. 2. Bandung:
    Masa Baru, 1956.

_____. *Indonesian Social Evolution: Some Psychological
    Considerations.* Amsterdam: C. P. J. van der Peet, 1958.

_____. *Indonesia Since Sukarno.* Singapore: Asia Pacific
    Press, 1971.

Van Niel, Robert. *The Emergence of the Modern Indonesian Elite.*
    The Hague: W. van Hoeve, 1960.

Van Nieuwenhuijze, C. A. O. *Aspects of Islam in Post-Colonial
    Indonesia: Five Essays.* The Hague: W. van Hoeve, 1958.

Verkuyl, J. *Indjil dan Kommunisme di Asia dan Afrika* [The
    Gospel and Communism in Asia and Africa]. Translated from
    Dutch to Indonesian by Trisno Sumardjo. Jakarta: Badan
    Penerbit Kristen, 1966.

Vittachi, Tarzie. *The Fall of Sukarno*. New York: Frederick A. Praeger, 1967.

Vlekke, Bernard H. M. *Nusantara. A History of Indonesia*. W. van Hoeve: 'sGravenhage, 1959.

Warner, Denis. *Reporting South-East Asia*. Sydney: Angus and Robertson, 1966.

Weber, Hans-Ruedi. *Asia and the Ecumenical Movement, 1895-1961*. London: SCM Press, 1966.

Wertheim, W. F. *Indonesian Society in Transition*. The Hague: W. van Hoeve, 1959.

_____, ed. *Selected Studies on Indonesia*. The Hague: W. van Hoeve, 1958.

Widyapranawa, S. H. *Benih yang Tumbuh: Suatu Survey Mengenai Gereja-Gereja Kristen Indonesia Jawa Tengah* [The Seed that Grew: A Survey of the Indonesian Christian Churches in Central Java]. Jakarta: Badan Penerbit Kristen, 1973.

Winstedt, Richard. *The Malays: A Cultural History*. London: Routledge and Kegan Paul, 1961.

Wiriaatmadja, Soekandar M. A. *Pokok-Pokok Sosiologi Pedesaan* [Elements of Rural Sociology]. Jakarta: C. V. Yasaguna, c. 1972.

Zainu'ddin, Alisa. *A Short History of Indonesia*. New York: Praeger Publishers, 1970.

Zwemer, Samuel M. *The Influence of Animism on Islam*. London: Central Board of Missions, 1920.

ARTICLES AND PERIODICALS

"After an Evening with Morning Star: Revolt." *Time* 86 (8 October 1965): 41-42.

Ali, Mukti. "Aliran Kebatinan Bukan Agama" [Mystic Sects Are Not Religions] In *Almanak 1973: Dewi Sri*, pp. 107-11. Edited by Kamadjaja. Yogyakarta: U. P. Indonesia, 1972.

Allison, J. M. "Indonesia: The End of the Beginning?" *Asian Survey* 10 (February 1970): 143-51.

Anderson, Benedict R. O'G. "The Idea of Power in Javanese Culture." In *Culture and Politics in Indonesia*, pp. 1-70. Edited by Claire Holt. Ithaca: Cornell University Press, 1972.

Archer, Raymond L. "Mohammedan Mysticism in Sumatra." *Journal of the Malayan Branch of the Royal Asiatic Society* 15 (1937): 1-126.

"As Indonesia Tries Military Rule." *U.S. News and World Report* 60 (28 March 1966): 46.

"Atlantic Report: Contributing Factors of Coup Failure." *Atlantic Monthly* 217 (January 1966): 12.

Bass, J. R. "PKI and the Attempted Coup." *Journal of Southeast Asian Studies* 1 (March 1970): 96-105.

Benda, H. J. "Decolonization in Indonesia: The Problem of Continuity and Change." *American Historical Review* 70 (July 1965): 1058-73.

"Bible Society Launches Crash Program for Scripture Distribution." *Bible Society Record* 112 (April 1967): 56-57.

Bishop, Jordan, O. P. "Numerical Growth--An Adequate Criterion of Mission?" In *Eye of the Storm*, pp. 121-27. Edited by Donald McGavran. Waco, Texas: Word Books, 1972.

"Bloodbath with Reds on Receiving End." *U.S. News and World Report* 60 (31 January 1966): 34.

Bradshaw, Mac. "A Hand Moving in Indonesia." *East Asia's Millions* 75 (June 1967): 81-83.

Bryan, Gainer. "Indonesia: Turmoil Amid Revival." *Christianity Today* 12 (December 1967): 312-13.

_____. "The South Pacific: Scene of Miracles Today." *Christian Life* 29 (April 1968): 55-56.

"Bung's Bounce: Anti-Red Students Storm Djakarta." *Time* 87 (4 March 1966): 40.

Bunnell, Frederick. "Indonesia's Quasi-Military Regime." *Current History* 52 (January 1967): 22-28.

Butwell, Richard. "Getting Rid of Sukarno: Indonesia's Leaders Have a Surplus of Opponents." *New Republic* 155 (8 October 1966): 12-13.

Clifton, Tony, and Withington, J. W. "Indonesia: Things Look Up." *Newsweek* 78 (12 July 1971): 41-43.

"Communists Behind Every Bush." *Economist* 228 (20 July 1968): 29-30.

"Convenient Confession: Aidit's Reputed Confession." *Newsweek* 67 (21 February 1966): 41.

"Conversions of Moslems over Eighteen Months." *Christianity Today* 12 (7 July 1967): 38.

"Conversion in Indonesia: Evangelical Revival." *Time* 89 (16 June 1967): 56.

"Coup a la Java." *Senior Scholastic* 88 (25 March 1966): 7.

"Coup in Jakarta." *Commonweal* 83 (22 October 1965): 46.

"Counter-counterattack." *Newsweek* 67 (7 March 1966): 46.

Critchfield, Richard. "Indonesia Heads for Violence." *Nation Magazine* 216 (25 June 1973): 809-13.

Crouch, H. "Military Politics under Indonesia's New Order," *Pacific Affairs* 45 (Summer 1972): 206-19.

Cruikshank, R. B. "*Abangan, Santri,* and *Prijaji*: A Critique." *Journal of Southeast Asia Studies* 3 (March 1972): 39-43.

"Crushing Confrontation." *Economist* 219 (30 April 1966): 452.

"Danger and Opportunity: The Challenge to the Indonesian Church." *Bible Society Record* 112 (April 1966): 52-53.

Darmowigoto, Soesilo. "P.I. Setjarah Massal" [Mass Evangelism]. *Warta Geredja* 1 (October 1965): 18-20; 2-3 (November-December 1965): 14-18; 4 (January 1966): 30-33; 6 (March 1966): 4-9.

Davies, J. G. "Church Growth: A Critique." In *Eye of the Storm*, pp. 128-35. Edited by Donald McGavran. Waco, Texas: Word Books, 1972.

"De-communization." *Newsweek* 68 (28 February 1966): 40.

Denoon, David B. H. "Indonesia: Transition to Stability?" *Current History* 61 (December 1971): 332-38.

"Dilemma in Djakarta." *Newsweek* 68 (26 December 1966): 34-35.

Dommen, Arthur J. "The Attempted Coup in Indonesia." *China Quarterly* 25 (January/March 1966): 144-70.

Drewes, G. W. J. "The Struggle between Javanism and Islam as Illustrated by the *Serat Darmangandul.*" *Bijragen tot de Taal-, Land-, en Volkunkunde.* The Hague: 1966, pp. 309-65.

"Eclipse." *Newsweek* 68 (18 July 1966): 38.

"Emergency Time." *Time* 87 (25 March 1966): 25.

"End of the Line for Sukarno: More Power for His Successor." *U.S. News and World Report* 61 (18 July 1966): 20.

Feith, Herbert. "Indonesia--Blot on the New Order." *New Republic*, 13 April 1968, pp. 17-21.

_____. "President Sukarno, the Army and the Communists: The Triangle Changes Shape." *Asian Survey* 4 (August 1964): 969-80.

Fisher, C. A. "Indonesia--A Giant Astir." *Geographical Journal* 138 (June 1972): 154-65.

"Five More Years: Re-election of Suharto." *Time* 101 (2 April 1973): 40.

Foltz, C. S., Jr. "Where Reds Begin to Look Like Losers: Report--Southeast Asia." *U.S. News and World Report* 68 (27 April 1970): 29.

"Gathering in the Paddies: Communist Resistance." *Time* 86 (12 November 1965): 40.

Geertz, Clifford. "Religious Belief and Economic Behaviour in a Central Javanese Town." *Economic Development and Cultural Change* 4, no. 2 (1956): 134-58.

_____. "Ritual and Social Change: A Javanese Example." *American Anthropologist* 49 (1957): 32-54.

_____, and Luethy, Herbert. "Are the Javanese Mad?" *Encounter* 27 (August 1966): 86-90.

Hall, C. W. "Indonesia: Night of Terror, Dawn of Hope:
    September 1965 Coup." *Reader's Digest* 89 (October 1966):
    275-78.

Hanna, Willard A. "The Indonesia Crisis--Mid-1964 Phase."
    AUFS Reports: Southeast Asia Series 12 (August 1964): 1-11.

Hardjono, Anwar. "Masa Depan Hukum Islam di Indonesia" [The
    Future of Islamic Law in Indonesia]. In *Kejakinan dan
    Perdjuangan* [Conviction and Struggle], pp. 368-75. Edited by
    P. D. Latuihamallo, V. Matondang, H. Rosihan Anwar, P. K.
    Ojong, and M. Hoetaoeroek. Jakarta: BPK Gunung Mulia, 1972.

Hidaja, S. "The Mystery in the G.30.S." *Ampera Review*, 2 June
    1968.

Hindley, Donald. "*Aliran* and the Fall of the Older Order."
    Indonesia 9 (April 1970): 46-65.

_____. "Indonesia 1970: The Working of *Pantjasila* Democracy."
    Asian Survey 11 (February 1971): 111-20.

_____. "Indonesia 1971: *Pantjasila* Democracy and the Second
    Parliamentary Elections." *Asian Survey* 12 (January 1972):
    56-68.

_____. "Political Power and the October 1965 Coup in
    Indonesia." *Journal of Southeast Asian Studies* 26 (February
    1967): 237-49.

_____. "Indonesian Politics, 1965-67: The September 30
    Movement and the Fall of Sukarno." *World Today* 24 (August
    1968): 345-56.

"Hey, Slow Down." *Economist* 246 (3 March 1973): 41.

Hoehling, Adolph A., Jr. "Summer in Java: 1967." *Yale Review*,
    (December 1968): 313-20.

Hoekendijk, J. C. "The Call to Evangelism." In *Eye of The
    Storm*, pp. 41-54. Edited by Donald McGavran. Waco, Texas:
    Word Books, 1972.

Hollenweger, Walter J. "Church Growth: A Faulty American
    Strategy." In *Eye of The Storm*, pp. 108-14. Edited by
    Donald McGavran. Waco, Texas: Word Books, 1972.

Hope, F. "Electing Indonesia's Generals." *New Statesman* 81
    (18 June 1971): 834.

Howard, R. C., et al, eds. "Bibliography of Asian Studies,
  1962." *Journal of Asian Studies* 22 (September 1963): 125-35.

_____. "Bibliography of Asian Studies, 1968." *Journal of*
  Asian Studies 28 (September 1969): 156-67.

Howell, Barbara. "Indonesia's Suharto Seeks Vote of Confidence
  in July 3 Parliamentary Election." *Christian Century* 88
  (30 June 1971): 802-3.

"How Many Plots?" *Economist* 218 (5 March 1966): 884.

Hughes, J. "Indonesia for Indonesians: What the Latest Upheaval May Mean." *New Republic* 154 (30 April 1966): 11-12.

"Impatient '66 Generation Driving Hard for Reforms." *Life* 61
  (1 July 1966): 32-33.

"Indonesia after Gestapu." *National Review* 18 (22 February
  1966): 161.

"Indonesia after Sukarno." *Economist* 220 (9 July 1960): 159-61.

"Indonesia: Back from the Brink." *Newsweek* 75 (25 May 1970):
  50-52.

"Indonesian Bible Society." *Indonesian Bible Society Newsletter*
  5 (September 1968).

"Indonesia: The Confused Coup." *Newsweek* 66 (11 October 1965):
  51-54.

"Indonesia's Confrontation with the Future." *Bible Society*
  Record 112 (April 1967): 51.

Indrakusuma, J. "*Pangestu*, Suatu Pandangan Hidup Jawa"
  [*Pangestu*, A Javanese View of Life]. *Archipel* (Paris) 1972,
  pp. 32-45.

"In the Midst of *Mushawarah*." *Time* 86 (5 November 1965): 49.

"Is World's Fifth Largest Nation Turning toward Christ?" *Bible*
  Society Record 112 (April 1967): 55-56.

Jaquet, L. G. M. "From Sukarno to Suharto." *Round Table* 243
  (July 1971): 240-48.

Jaspan, M. A. "Indonesia: Counterrevolution and Rebellion."
  Science and Sociology 30 (Winter 1966): 63-69.

"Java: Lush and Troubled Island." *Life* 68 (26 June 1970): 46-57.

"Javanese Messianic Expectations: Their Origin and Cultural Context." *Comparative Studies in Society and History* 1 (1959): 299-323.

Johns, A. H. "From Buddhism to Islam: An Interpretation of the Javanese Literature of the Transition." *Comparative Studies in Society and History* 9 (October 1966): 40-50.

_____. "Sufism As a Category in Indonesian History." *Journal of Southeast Asian History* 2 (July 1961): 10-23.

Jones, Howard P. "Turnaround in Indonesia." *Reader's Digest* 96 (March 1970): 184-86.

Josey, Alex. "Indonesia: Hope after Massacre." *Nation* 203 (November 1966): 565-70.

Jusuf, M. "Pengalaman Saya Dgn: Super Semar" [My Experience with Super Semar]. *Suara Merdeka* (Jakarta), 17 March 1973, p. 2.

"Just a Pinprick? Sukarno Orders a Halt to Anti-Communist and Anti-Chinese Demonstrations." *Newsweek* 66 (1 November 1965): 53.

"Ketegangan Politik Mendjelang Pemilu" [Political Tensions Approaching the Election]. *Express*, 22 February 1971, pp. 5-6.

"Killing Starts Again." *Economist* 229 (31 August 1968): 36.

"King of Kings: New Policy Emerging." *Newsweek* 67 (2 May 1966): 59.

King, Seth S. "Great Purge Indonesia: Slaughter of Indonesian Communist Party." *New York Times Magazine*, 8 May 1966, p. 25.

Kirk, Donald. "The Anti-Communist Crusade of Indonesia's Moslems." *Reporter* 34 (27 January 1966): 41-44.

_____. "Bali Exorcises an Evil Spirit." *Reporter* 35 (December 1966): 42-43.

_____. "Indonesia's Fragmented Revolution." *New Leader* 49 (March 1966): 9-11.

Kirk, Donald. "Indonesia's New Policy: Chaos Versus Charisma."
  New Leader 49 (June 1966): 11-13.

_____. "Indonesia's Revolutionary Justice." *New Leader* 49
  (November 1966): 3-5.

_____. "Suharto Is the Name, Not Sukarno." *New York Times
  Magazine*, (24 July 1966): 18-19.

_____. "Sukarno's Holdouts in Central Java: Nationalist-
  Moslem Conflict." *Reporter* 35 (8 September 1966): 39-41.

Koentjaraningrat. "Javanese Data on the Unresolved Problems of
  the Kindred." *Ethnology* 7 (January 1968): 53-58.

Kraft, Charles H. "Toward a Christian Ethnotheology." In
  God, Man, and Church Growth, pp. 109-26. Edited by Alan R.
  Tippett. Grand Rapids: William B. Eerdmans Publishing Co.,
  1973.

Kwast, Lloyd. "Christianity and Culture: Biblical Bedrock."
  In *Crucial Issues in Missions Tomorrow*, pp. 159-71. Edited
  by Donald McGavran. Chicago: Moody Press, 1972.

"Langkah Mukti Kepedesaan" [Mukti's Step Toward Rural Areas].
  Tempo, 6 November 1971.

Lev, Daniel S. "Indonesia 1965: The Year of the Coup." *Asian
  Survey* 6 (February 1966): 103-10.

_____. "Political Parties in Indonesia." *Journal of South-
  East Asian History* 8 (March 1967): 52-67.

_____. "Political Role of the Army in Indonesia." *Pacific
  Affairs* 36 (Winter 1963-64): 349-64.

Liddle, R. W. "Evolution from Above: National Leadership and
  Local Development in Indonesia." *Journal of Asian Studies*
  32 (February 1973): 287-309.

"Losing Face: Post-Coup Conditions." *Newsweek*, 25 October
  1965, p. 53.

Lubar, Robert. "Indonesia's Pot-holed Road Back." *Fortune*
  77 (1 June 1968): 104-13, 130-37.

Luethy, Herbert. "The Indonesian Mystery." *The New York
  Review of Books*, 26 May 1966.

McElrath, William N. "Has the Movement Gone Worldwide?" *Home Missions*, June-July 1971, p. 69.

MacFarquhar, R. "Indonesia's New Order." *New Statesman* 73 (31 March 1967): 426-27.

MacLeish, Kenneth. "Java: Eden in Transition." *National Geographic* 1939 (January 1971): 1-43.

McLennan, B. N. "Politics and Change in Indonesia." *International Journal of Comparative Sociology* 7 (March 1966): 138-52.

Mackie, J. A. C. "Indonesia: A Background to Confrontation." *World Today* 20 (April 1964): 139-47.

Makarim, Nono Anwar. "Student Activism in Indonesia." In *Kejakinan dan Perdjuangan* [Conviction and Struggle], pp. 274-81. Edited by P. D. Latuihamallo, V. Matondang, H. Rosihan, P. K. Ojong, M. Hoetaoeroek. Jakarta: BPK Gunung Mulia, 1972.

Martin, R. P. "Indonesia: Hope Where Once There Was None." *U.S. News and World Report* 60 (6 June 1966): 70-72.

Mellor, B. "Political Killings in Indonesia." *New Statesman* 72 (5 August 1966): 189.

Merick, W. S. "Indonesia: New Hope for 120 Million People." *U.S. News and World Report* 70 (2 May 1971): 80-81.

Milone, P. D. "Indische Culture and Its Relationship to Urban Life." *Comparative Studies in Sociology and History* 9 (July 1967): 407-26.

Mortimer, Rex. "Class, Social Cleavage, and Indonesian Communism." *Indonesia* 8 (October 1969): 1-14.

_____. "Indonesia: Emigre Post-Mortems on the PKI." *Australian Outlook*, December 1968.

Moser, D. "Haunted Face of a Red Defeat: Vengeance Against Communists." *Life* 61 (1 July 1966): 24-33.

Mulder, J. A. Niels. "*Aliran Kebatinan* as an Expression of the Javanese Worldview." *Journal of Southeast Asian Studies* 1 (September 1970): 105-14.

Neve, Hebert. "Christian Presence: One of Its Critics." In
    Eye of The Storm, pp. 166-70. Edited by Donald McGavran.
    Waco, Texas: Word Books, 1972.

Nortier, C. W. "A 'Younger Church' Grows into Maturity: The
    Role of the Laity in the Life and Mission of Christ's Church
    in East Java, Indonesia." *Laity* 4 (November 1957).

Oates, W. A. "Afdeling B: An Indonesian Case Study." *Journal
    of Southeast Asian History* 9 (March 1968): 107-16.

"One Cheer for Suharto's Democracy." *Economist* 240 (10 July
    1971): 18.

"One Million Dead?--and How They Died." *Economist* 220 (20
    August 1966): 727-28.

Paget, Roger K. "Indonesian Politics: The New Order Emerges."
    Bulletin of the Atomic Scientists 24 (February 1968): 30-34.

"Partai-Partai: Profil Disimpang Djalan" [The Parties: Profile
    at the Crossroads]. *Tempo*, 12 July 1971, p. 7.

Pauker, E. T. "Has the Sukarno Regime Weakened the PKI?"
    Asian Survey 4 (September 1964): 1058-70.

_____. "Political Consequences of Rural Development Programs
    in Indonesia." *Pacific Affairs* 4 (Fall 1968): 386-402.

_____. "Suharto's Indonesia." *Round Table* 57 (October 1967):
    386-90.

Peacock, J. L. "Ritual, Entertainment, and Modernization: A
    Javanese Case" (with reply by R. R. Jay). *Comparative
    Studies in Sociology and History* 10 (April 1968): 328-36.

"Pernjataan dan Seruan Dewan Geredja-Geredja di Indonesia"
    [Declaration and Call of the Indonesian Council of Churches].
    Warta Gereja (Salatiga, GKJ Church) 1 (November-December
    1965): 5-7.

Plowman, E. E. "Demythologizing the Indonesian Revival."
    Christianity Today, 2 March 1973.

Pluvier, J. M. "Recent Dutch Contributions to Modern Indonesian
    History." *Journal of Southeast Asian History* 8 (September
    1967): 201-25.

"Pride and Fall." *Nation* 202 (28 March 1966): 346.

Purukan, P. "Indonesian Phenomenon: Interdenominational Evangelistic Crusade." *Christianity Today* 14 (21 November 1969): 40.

"Question of Unanimity: Sukarno Heroes' Day Speech." *Newsweek* 66 (22 November 1965): 54.

Ra'anan, Uri. "The Coup That Failed: A Background Analysis." *Problems of Communism* 5 (March-April 1966): 37-43.

Range, W. "Sukarnoism: An Interpretation." *Orbis* 10 (Summer 1966): 488-506.

Ransom, David. "The Berkeley Mafia and the Indonesia Massacre." *Ramparts*, (October 1970): 27-29, 40-49.

"Reference for Privacy." *Time* 87 (21 January 1966): 25B.

Reid, Anthony. "Nineteenth Century Pan-Islam in Indonesia and Malaysia." *Journal of Asian Studies* 24 (February 1967): 267-83.

Rey, Lucian. "Dossier of the Indonesia Drama." *New Left Review*, 23 December 1965.

Roeder, O. G. "Death of a Rebel." *Far Eastern Economic Review*, 23 December 1965.

Samson, Allan A. "Army and Islam in Indonesia." *Pacific Affairs* 44 (Winter 1971-72): 545-65.

_____. "Indonesia 1972: The Solidification of Military Control." *Asian Survey* 13 (February 1973): 127-39.

Sanders, S. W. "Indonesia: The Reds Are on the Run but . . . " *U.S. News and World Report* 59 (1 November 1965): 63-64.

_____. "Red Paper Tiger: Failure in Indonesia: Interview." *U.S. News and World Report* 59 (22 November 1965): 82.

Simatupang, T. B. "The Situation and Challenge of the Christian Mission in Indonesia Today." *South East Asia Journal of Theology* 10 (April 1969): 10-27.

"Situation Normal: Arrests and Appointments." *Newsweek* 67 (18 March 1966): 48-49.

"Small Price to Pay." *Newsweek* 69 (23 January 1967): 42.

"Smoldering Struggle." *Newsweek* 66 (8 November 1965): 56.

Soedarmo, R. "Confessing the Faith in Indonesia Today." *South East Asia Journal of Theology* 8 (July-October 1966): 155-59.

Sterba, J. B. "Report from the Majority of the World." *New York Times Magazine*, (5 September 1971): 12-13, 22-26.

Sukarno. "Address to the Joint Session of the United States Congress, 17 May 1956." Reprinted in *Toward Freedom and the Dignity of Man*, pp. 25-35. Jakarta: Republic of Indonesia, Department of Foreign Affairs, 1961.

_____. "The Birth of Pantja Sila, 1 June 1945." Reprinted in *Toward Freedom and the Dignity of Man*, pp. 3-21. Jakarta: Republic of Indonesia, Department of Foreign Affairs, 1961.

"Sukarno Gives Way." *Economist* 219 (2 April 1966): 31.

"Sukarno Struts as Chen Yi Snoozes: During Anniversary Parade." *Life* 59 (3 September 1965): 36-36A.

Sundhaussen, U. "Military in Research on Indonesian Politics." *Journal of Asian Studies* 31 (February 1972): 355-65.

Sutter, John O. "Two Faces of *Konfrontasi*: 'Crush Malaysia' and the *Gestapu*." *Asian Survey* 6 (October 1966): 523-46.

Sutton, Horace. "Indonesia's Night of Terror." *Saturday Review*, 4 February 1967.

Tasdik. "New Congregations in Indonesia." *South East Asia Journal of Theology* 10 (April 1969): 1-9.

Tasrif, S. "McCarthyism Alarm Sounds in Indonesia." *Atlas* 17 (June 1969): 52-54.

Taubinger, L. M. "Indonesia: The Plot That Failed." *National Review* 18 (22 February 1966): 160.

"Terrible Toll: Post Coup Death Figures." *Newsweek* 67 (31 January 1966): 50.

Thomson, Alan C. "The Churches of Java in the Aftermath of the Thirtieth of September Movement." *South East Asia Journal of Theology* 11 (March 1970): 1-18.

"30 September, 7 Tahun Kemudian" [Seven Years After the 30th of September Movement]. *Tempo*, 2 September 1972.

"Time on Whose Side?" *Economist* 219 (14 May 1966): 692.

"Tubuh Islam Jang Purba" [The Ancient Body of Islam]. *Tempo*, 23 October 1971, pp. 38-39.

"Turmoil Rules in Indonesia: Sukarno's Battle with Army Leaders." *Business Week*, 19 March 1966, p. 44.

"Uproar of Peace: End of Indonesia's *Konfrontasi* with Malaysia." *Time* 87 (10 June 1966): 39-40.

van der Kroef, J. M. "'Gestapu' in Indonesia." *Orbis* 10 (Summer 1966): 458-87.

_____. "Indonesian Nationalism Reconsidered." *Pacific Affairs* 45 (Spring 1972): 42-59.

_____. "Indonesia's First National Election: A Sociological Analysis." *American Journal of Economics and Sociology* 16 (April 1957): 237-49, and 16 (July 1957): 497-520.

_____. "Indonesia: The Mystique of Permanent Revolution." *South Atlantic Quarterly* 64 (Winter 1965): 1-14.

_____. "Interpretations of the 1965 Indonesian Coup: A Review of the Literature." *Pacific Affairs* 43 (Winter 1970-71): 557-77.

_____. "Javanese Messianic Expectations: Their Origin and Cultural Context." *Comparative Studies in Society and History* 1 (1959): 299-323.

_____. "New Political Patterns in Indonesia." *World Today* 25 (March 1969): 219-30.

_____. "Origins of the 1965 Coup in Indonesia: Probabilities and Alternatives." *Journal of South East Asian Studies* 3 (September 1972): 277-98.

_____. "Peking, Djakarta, and the Malaysia Problem." *Contemporary Review* 205 (July 1964): 348-51.

_____. "Sociology of Confrontation." *Southwestern Social Science Quarterly* 45 (December 1964): 220-38.

_____. "Sukarno's Fall." *Orbis* 11 (Summer 1967): 491-531.

van Dusen, H. P. "Indonesia Today." *Christian Century* 82 (5 May 1965): 584-88; (12 May 1965): 616-17.

"Vengeance with a Smile." *Time* 88 (15 July 1966): 22-26.

"View from Jakarta: Public Reaction to the Indonesian Crisis."
Nation 202 (14 February 1966): 171.

Walkin, Jacob. "Muslim-Communist Confrontation in East Java,
1964-1965." *Orbis* 13 (Fall 1969): 822-47.

"Wanted: A Magician: After the Coup." *Time* 86 (15 October
1965): 37-38.

Ward, Kenneth. "Some Comments on Islamic Reactions to Recent
Developments in Indonesia." *Review of Indonesian and
Malayan Affairs*, (April-June 1968): 37-46.

Warner, D. "Indonesia: Generals Who Got Away." *Reporter* 33
(21 October 1965): 39-40.

_____. "Indonesia's Communists: Down But Not Out." *Reporter*
33 (18 November 1965): 23-26.

_____. "Indonesia's Unfinished Revolution." *Reporter* 35
(July 1966): 28-29.

Wartopo, Ali. "Golkar: Mandat Telah Diberikan" [Golkar: A
Mandate Has Been Given]. *Expres*, (19 July 1971): 5-10.

Weinstein, A. "Blood in Paradise." *Atlas* 11 (April 1966):
210-14.

"We're Not a Party, We're Functional." *Economist* 239 (26 June
1971): 45-46.

Wertheim, W. F. "Indonesia Before and After the Untung Coup."
Pacific Affairs 39 (Spring-Summer 1966): 115-27.

_____. "Peasants, Peddlers, and Princes in Indonesia."
Pacific Affairs 37 (Fall 1964): 307-11.

"We Too Can Persecute." *Economist* 228 (31 August 1968): 36.

"What Is Sukarno up to in Southeast Asia?" *Senior Scholastic*
86 (25 February 1965): 8-11.

"What the Guru Said: What Suharto Does." *Economist* 219 (16
April 1966): 232.

Willner, Ann Ruth. "Communist Phoenix and the Indonesian
Garuda." *World Politics* 19 (April 1967): 500-520.

_____. "Social Change in Javanese Town-Village Life."
Economic Development and Cultural Change 6 (April 1958):
229-42.

Winter, Ralph D. "Quality or Quantity." In *Crucial Issues in Missions Tomorrow*, pp. 175-87. Edited by Donald McGavran. Chicago: Moody Press, 1972.

Woodman, D. "End of Sukarno." *New Statesmen* 73 (13 January 1967): 32.

"World Around Us." *Christian Century* 84 (5 April 1967): 449-50.

UNPUBLISHED MATERIALS

Archer, Raymond L. "Muhammadan Mysticism in Sumatra." Ph.D. dissertation, Hartford Seminary Foundation, 1932.

Bakker, J. W. M. "Indonesia 1970: A General Survey of Society." Yogyakarta, 1969. (Mimeographed for private circulation.)

"Buku Programa Pekan Alkitab 1973" [Program Booklet for Bible Week 1973]. Jakarta: Lembaga Alkitab Indonesia, 1973.

Cooley, Frank. "The Church in Indonesia, 1945-1973." (Typewritten.)

_____. "Memperkenalkan Gereja Kristen Jawa Tengah Utara" [Introducing the North Central Java Christian Church]. February 1974. (Typewritten report.)

_____. Notes of interview with the Moderator and Clerk of the Synod of the *Gereja Kristen Jawa Tengah Utara*. 10 October 1971. (Typewritten.)

_____. Research notes of interviews held with GKJW leaders at the synodal office. Malang, 18 November 1972 and 23 April 1973. (Typewritten.)

_____. "Suatu Laporan Tentang Gereja Kristen Jawa Tengah Utara" [A Report on the North Central Java Christian Church]. February 1974. (Typewritten.)

Darmowigoto, Soesilo. "Pemashuran Indjil Keradjaan Allah" [Spreading of the Kingdom of God]. Salatiga, Synod of the Javanese Christian Churches, n.d. (Mimeographed.)

Dimjati, Jahja. "Peranan Sarekat Islam Dalam Menanamkan Kesadaran Nasional di Indonesia" [The Role of *Sarekat Islam* in Planting National Consciousness in Indonesia]. Yogyakarta, Report of Second National History Seminar, 26-29 August 1970.

Fagg, Donald. "Authority and Social Structure: A Study of Javanese Bureaucracy." Ph.D. dissertation, Harvard University, 1958.

Garthe, Iugo. Cuntel. Interview, 15 April 1973.

Gereja Kristen Jawa Tengah Utara, Cuntel. Interviews with selected members, 13 March to 16 April 1973.

Gondosubroto, Purwoto. "Provisional Report on Research in Villages in Banjumas Residency." Unpublished manuscript, University of Indonesia, 1959.

Hadiwijono, Harun. Sekolah Theologia Tinggi Duta Wacana, Yogyakarta. Interview, 6 June 1973.

Hutagalung, S. M. "The Problem of Religious Freedom in Indonesia, 1800 to the Present." Ph.D. dissertation, Yale University, 1958.

"Ichtisar Statistik Tentang Geredja Katholik di Indonesia: 1949-1967" [A Statistical Summary of the Catholic Church in Indonesia]. First report. Lembaga Penelitian dan Pembangunan Sosial. Jakarta: n.d.

Jay, Robert Ravenell. "*Santri* and *Abangan*: Religious Schism in Rural Central Java." Ph.D. dissertation, Harvard University, 1957.

Joyodiharjo. Home of Rector Akademi Kristen Wiyata Wacana, Pati. Interview, 13 April 1973.

Karjoredjo, J. Sardi. "Perkembangan Jumaat G.K.J." [Growth of the Javanese Christian Church]. Den Haag, January 1973. (Mimeographed.)

Kumaat, Martati. "Laporan Self-Study Gereja Injili Tanah Jawa" [Self-Study Report of the Javanese Evangelical Church]. (Mimeographed.)

Kuntowidjojo. "Angkatan Oemat Islam 1945-1950: Beberapa Tjatatan Tentang Pergerakan Sosial" [Islamic Forces 1945-1950: Several Notes Concerning Social Movements]. Yogyakarta, Second National History Seminar, 26-29 August 1970.

"Minutes, . . . Annual Session, Indonesian Baptist Mission." Bandung, 1952-1971. (Mimeographed.)

Mostoko, Ismanoe. "Report of Badan Pekabaran Injil Sinode Gereja Kristen Jawi Wetan" [Report of the Evangelism Board of the East Java Christian Church]. In "Pedoman Pelaksanaan Pilot Projek Djumaat Missioner" [Manual for the Pilot Project of a Missionary Church]. 19 October 1969, pp. 1-2. (Mimeographed.)

Nance, John Irvin. "A History of the Indonesian Baptist Mission: 1950-1960." M.A. thesis, Baylor University, 1969.

Nicholson, Clara K. "The Introduction of Islam into Sumatra and Java: A Study in Cultural Change." Ph.D. dissertation, Syracuse University, 1965.

Notoatmodjo, Modestus Widojoko. "*Gotong Royong* in Indonesian Administration: A Concept of Human Affairs." Ph.D. dissertation, Indiana University, 1962.

Paulus, Sujoko. Seminari Theologia Baptis di Indonesia, Semarang. Interview, 13 March 1973.

"Pedoman Pelaksanaan Pilot Projek Djumaat Missioner" [Manual for the Pilot Project of a Missionary Church]. Badan Pekabaran Indjil Sinode GKDW, 1969. (Mimeographed.)

Peters, George W. "Indonesia: An Evaluative Study of East and Central Java." Dallas Theological Seminary, 1974. (Typewritten.)

Quiko, Eduard. "The Role of Foreign Minister Subandrio in Indonesian Politics: An Analysis of Selected Indonesian Foreign Policies, 1957-1965." Ph.D. dissertation, Southern Illinois University, 1970.

Reinhardt, Jon McEwen. "Nationalism and Confrontation in the Southeast Asian Islands: The Sources of Indonesian Foreign Policy." Ph.D. dissertation, Tulane University, 1967.

Siagian, Toengoel Papaloan. "The *Operasi Karya*." Paper on the involvement of the Indonesian Army in rural development.

Silverman, Jerry Mark. "Indonesian Marxism-Leninism: The Development and Consequences of Communist Policentrism 1919-1966." Ph.D. dissertation, Claremont Graduate School, 1967.

Sjadzali, Munawir. "Indonesia's Muslim Parties and Their Political Concepts." M.A. thesis, Georgetown University, 1959.

Sloan, Stephen. "A Case Study of the Indonesian Coup of 1965."
    Ph.D. dissertation, New York University, 1967.

Smith, Ebbie C. "What Did the Questionnaires Say?" 1971.
    (Mimeographed.)

Soegiri, Iman. "Study dan Penelitian Gereja-Gereja Kristen Jawa
    Tengah" [Study and Research of the Central Java Christian
    Churches]. c. 1970. (Mimeographed.)

Sosrodihardjo, S. A. "A Sectarian Group in Java, with Reference
    to a Midland Village: A Study in the Sociology of Religion."
    M.A. thesis, London School of Economics, 1959.

Subandrio, Hurustiati. "Javanese Peasant Life: Villages in
    East Java." Academic Postgraduate Diploma in Anthropology
    dissertation, University of London, 1951.

Sukarno. "Transcript of President Sukarno's Interview with
    C.B.S. News Correspondents" on "Face the Nation." San
    Francisco: Consulate of Indonesia, 31 January 1965.

Sukrisno. Office of Evangelism, Gereja Kristen Jawi Wetan,
    Surabaya. Interview, 16 May 1973.

Sumanto, I. "Sadjarah Geredja Karangdjoso: Hidup Sadrach dan
    Kegiatan2nya" [The History of the Karangjoso Church: The
    Life of Sadrach and His Activities]. Jakarta, GKJ Files,
    Department of Study and Research, Indonesian Council of
    Churches, 1971.

Sumarjono. His home in Semarang. Interview, 15 April 1973.

Tan, Tiat-han. "The Attitude of Dutch Protestant Missions
    toward Indonesian Nationalism, 1945-1949." Ph.D. disserta-
    tion, Princeton University, 1967.

Tasdik. His home in Yogyakarta. Interview, 6 June 1973.

Tarapa, Julianus E. "Pertemuan Sukabumi" [The Sukabumi Meeting].
    Mimeographed pamphlet, 1 June 1971.

Weatherbee, Donald E. "Aspects of Ancient Javanese Politics."
    Ph.D. dissertation, John Hopkins University, 1968.

Wasi'an, Abdullah. "Benteng Islam" [Fortress of Islam].
    Surabaya, December 1967. (Mimeographed.)

Willis, Avery, Jr. "Base Design of the Indonesian Baptist
   Theological Seminary." June 1975. (Mimeographed.)

_____. "Spiritual Breakthrough in Indonesia." Holland,
   Michigan: Portable Recording Ministries, 1971. (Two tapes.)

_____. "Survey Usaha Baptis: Konsep I" [Survey of Baptist
   Work: First Draft]. 1 November 1970. (Mimeographed.)

Win, Gandasari Abdullah. "Political Socialization in
   Indonesia." Ph.D. dissertation, Claremont Graduate School,
   1968.

Wiriadinata, Eddy. "Survey Usaha Baptis: Konsep II" [Survey of
   Baptist Work: Second Draft]. 16 June 1973. (Mimeographed.)

Avery T. Willis, Jr. has been a missionary in Indonesia since
1964. His present position is president of the Indonesian Baptist Theological Seminary.

A native of Arkansas, Dr. Willis is a graduate of Oklahoma
Baptist University and of Southwestern Baptist Theological Seminary, where he received his Th.D. degree in 1974 with a major
in missions and minors in philosophy and preaching. He pastored
churches in Oklahoma and Texas for ten years before being appointed by the Foreign Mission Board of the Southern Baptist
Convention.

As a missionary, Dr. Willis has had unusual opportunities to
observe church growth in Indonesia, both through personal involvement and through research into the activities of others.
He was the first Baptist missionary in Bogor, West Java, and
later the first to serve in Jember, East Java. He was transferred to the seminary in 1970 as professor of practical theology, then became acting president in 1972 and president in 1973.
He has been largely instrumental in shifting from a single campus approach to an expanded program including extension centers
in many areas. During the 1970's, total Baptist seminary en-
rollment in Indonesia has increased from 125 students to more
than 400.

Dr. Willis has held numerous positions of responsibility,
both among his fellow missionaries and in cooperative efforts
with Christians of Indonesia. In 1968 he co-chaired the first

nationwide consultation of Indonesian Baptists, and later served on a joint missionary-national continuation committee that grew out of it. He was also chairman of a Baptist self-study done in cooperation with a survey of all Indonesian Christianity, sponsored by the Indonesian Council of Churches and directed by Dr. Frank L. Cooley.

Dr. Willis has written a programmed instruction textbook in the Indonesian language for theological education by extension, on the subject of church growth. He has co-authored other similar TEE books in Indonesian on Colossians and on the Holy Spirit. Articles written by him in English have appeared in *Theological Education Today*, *The Asia Theologian*, *Asia Perspective*, and *The Commission*. Dr. Willis has also produced films for use in both Indonesia and America, including *Edge of the Light*, a film on missions distributed by the Radio-Television Commission of the Southern Baptist Convention.

Both while serving in Indonesia and while furloughing in America, Dr. Willis is frequently in demand as a conference speaker and revival preacher. With his wife, the former Shirley Morris, he makes his home on the central campus of the Indonesian Baptist Theological Seminary in Semarang, Central Java. Two of the Willises' five children are now attending college in the U.S.

BOOKS BY THE
WILLIAM CAREY LIBRARY

GENERAL

American Missions in Bicentennial Perspective edited by R. Pierce Beaver, $8.95 paper, 448 pp.

The Birth of Missions in America by Charles L. Chaney, $7.95 paper, 352 pp.

Education of Missionaries' Children: The Neglected Dimension of World Mission by D. Bruce Lockerbie, $1.95 paper, 76 pp.

Evangelicals Face the Future edited by Donald E. Hoke, $6.95 paper, 184 pp.

The Holdeman People: The Church in Christ, Mennonite, 1859-1969 by Clarence Hiebert, $17.95 cloth, 688 pp.

On the Move with the Master: A Daily Devotional Guide on World Mission by Duain W. Vierow, $4.95 paper, 176 pp.

The Radical Nature of Christianity: Church Growth Eyes Look at the Supernatural Mission of the Christian and the Church by Waldo J. Werning (Mandate Press), $5.85 paper, 224 pp.

Social Action vs. Evangelism: An Essay on the Contemporary Crisis by William J. Richardson, $1.95x paper, 64 pp.

STRATEGY OF MISSION

Church Growth and Christian Mission by Donald A. McGavran, $4.95x paper, 256 pp.

Church Growth and Group Conversion by Donald A. McGavran et al., $2.45 paper, 128 pp.

Committed Communities: Fresh Streams for World Missions by Charles J. Mellis, $3.95 paper, 160 pp.

The Conciliar-Evangelical Debate: The Crucial Documents, 1964-1976 edited by Donald McGavran, $8.95 paper, 400 pp.

Crucial Dimensions in World Evangelization edited by Arthur F. Glasser et al., $7.95x paper, 480 pp.

Evangelical Missions Tomorrow edited by Wade T. Coggins and Edwin L. Frizen, Jr., $5.95 paper, 208 pp.

Everything You Need to Grow a Messianic Synagogue by Phillip E. Goble, $2.45 paper, 176 pp.

Here's How: Health Education by Extension by Ronald and Edith Seaton, $3.45 paper, 144 pp.

The Indigenous Church and the Missionary by Melvin L. Hodges, $2.95 paper, 108 pp.

A Manual for Church Growth Surveys by Ebbie C. Smith, $3.95 paper, 144 pp.

Mission: A Practical Approach to Church-Sponsored Mission Work by Daniel C. Hardin, $4.95x paper, 264 pp.

Readings in Third World Missions: A Collection of Essential Documents edited by Marlin L. Nelson, $6.95x paper, 304 pp.

AREA AND CASE STUDIES

Aspects of Pacific Ethnohistory by Alan R. Tippett, $3.95 paper, 216 pp.

A Century of Growth: The Kachin Baptist Church of Burma by Herman Tegenfeldt, $9.95 cloth, 540 pp.

Christian Mission to Muslims - The Record: Anglican and Reformed Approaches in India and the Near East, 1800-1938 by Lyle L. Vander Werff, $8.95 paper, 384 pp.

Church Growth in Burundi by Donald Hohensee, $4.95 paper, 160 pp.

Church Growth in Japan by Tetsunao Yamamori, $4.95 paper, 184 pp.

Church Planting in Uganda: A Comparative Study by Gailyn Van Rheenen, $4.95 paper, 192 pp.

Circle of Harmony: A Case Study in Popular Japanese Buddhism by Kenneth J. Dale, $4.95 paper, 238 pp.

The Deep-Sea Canoe: The Story of Third World Missionaries in the South Pacific by Alan R. Tippett, $3.45x paper, 144 pp.

Frontier Peoples of Central Nigeria and a Strategy for Outreach by Gerald O. Swank, $5.95 paper, 192 pp.

The Growth Crisis in the American Church: A Presbyterian Case Study by Foster H. Shannon, $4.95 paper, 176 pp.

The How and Why of Third World Missions: An Asian Case Study by Marlin L. Nelson, $6.95 paper, 256 pp.

I Will Build My Church: Ten Case Studies of Church Growth in Taiwan edited by Allen J. Swanson, $4.95 paper, 177 pp.

Indonesian Revival: Why Two Million Came to Christ by Avery T. Willis, Jr., $5.95 paper, 288 pp.

Industrialization: Brazil's Catalyst for Church Growth by C.W. Gates, $1.95 paper, 96 pp.

The Navajos Are Coming to Jesus by Thomas Dolaghan and David Scates, $5.95 paper, 192 pp.

New Move Forward in Europe: Growth Patterns of German-Speaking Baptists by William L. Wagner, $8.95 paper, 368 pp.

People Movements in the Punjab by Margaret and Frederick Stock, $8.95 paper, 388 pp.

Profile for Victory: New Proposals for Missions in Zambia by Max Ward Randall, $3.95 cloth, 224 pp.

The Protestant Movement in Bolivia by C. Peter Wagner, $3.95 paper, 264 pp.

Protestants in Modern Spain: The Struggle for Religious Pluralism by Dale G. Vought, $3.45 paper, 168 pp.

The Religious Dimension in Hispanic Los Angeles by Clifton L. Holland, $9.95 paper, 550 pp.

The Role of the Faith Mission: A Brazilian Case Study by Fred Edwards, $3.45 paper, 176 pp.

La Serpiente y la Paloma (La Iglesia Apostolica de la Fe en Jesuchristo de Mexico) by Manual J. Gaxiola, $2.95 paper, 194 pp.

Solomon Islands Christianity: A Study in Growth and Obstruction by Alan R. Tippett, $5.95x paper, 432 pp.

Taiwan: Mainline Versus Independent Church Growth by Allen J. Swanson, $3.95 paper, 300 pp.

Tonga Christianity by Stanford Shewmaker, $3.45 paper, 164 pp.

Toward Continuous Mission: Strategizing for the Evangelization of Bolivia by W. Douglas Smith, $4.95 paper, 208 pp.

Treasure Island: Church Growth Among Taiwan's Urban Minnan Chinese by Robert J. Bolton, $6.95 paper, 416 pp.

Understanding Latin Americans by Eugene A. Nida, $3.95 paper, 176 pp.

A Yankee Reformer in Chile: The Life and Works of David Trumbull by Irven Paul, $3.95 paper, 172 pp.

APPLIED ANTHROPOLOGY

Becoming Bilingual: A Guide to Language Learning by Donald Larson and William A. Smalley, $5.95x paper, 426 pp.

Christopaganism or Indigenous Christianity? edited by Tetsunao Yamamori and Charles R. Taber, $5.95 paper, 242 pp.

The Church and Cultures: Applied Anthropology for the Religious Worker by Louis J. Luzbetak, $5.95x paper, 448 pp.

Culture and Human Values: Christian Intervention in Anthropological Perspective (writings of Jacob Loewen) edited by William A. Smalley, $5.95x paper, 466 pp.

Customs and Cultures: Anthropology for Christian Missions by Eugene A. Nida, $3.95 paper, 322 pp.

Manual of Articulatory Phonetics by William A. Smalley, $5.95x paper, 522 pp.

Message and Mission: The Communication of the Christian Faith by Eugene A. Nida, $3.95x paper, 254 pp.

Readings in Missionary Anthropology edited by William A. Smalley, $5.95x paper, 384 pp.

Tips on Taping: Language Recording in the Social Sciences by Wayne and Lonna Dickerson, $4.95x paper, 208 pp.

THEOLOGICAL EDUCATION BY EXTENSION

Principios del Crecimiento de la Iglesia by Wayne C. Weld and Donald A. McGavran, $3.95 paper, 448 pp.

The World Directory of Theological Education by Extension by Wayne C. Weld, $5.95x paper, 416 pp., *1976 Supplement only*, $1.95x, 64 pp.

Writing for Theological Education by Extension by Lois McKinney, $1.45x paper, 64 pp.

REFERENCE

An American Directory of Schools and Colleges Offering Missionary Courses edited by Glenn Schwartz, $5.95x paper, 266 pp.

Bibliography for Cross-Cultural Workers, edited by Alan R. Tippett, $4.95 paper, 256 pp.

Church Growth Bulletin, Second Consolidated Volume (Sept. 1969-July 1975) edited by Donald McGavran, $7.95x paper, 512 pp.

Evangelical Missions Quarterly Vols. 7-9, $8.95x cloth, 330 pp.

The Means of World Evangelization: Missiological Education at the Fuller School of World Mission edited by Alvin Martin, $9.95 paper, 544 pp.

Protestantism in Latin America: A Bibliographical Guide edited by John H. Sinclair, $8.95x paper, 448 pp.

The World Directory of Mission-Related Educational Institutions edited by Ted Ward and Raymond Buker, Sr., $19.95x cloth, 906 pp.

(05940

POPULARIZING MISSION

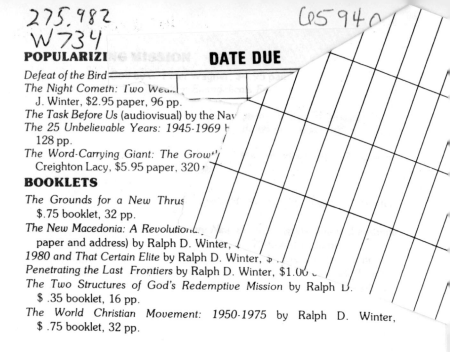

Defeat of the Bird
The Night Cometh: Two Wea...
    J. Winter, $2.95 paper, 96 pp.
The Task Before Us (audiovisual) by the Nav
The 25 Unbelievable Years: 1945-1969 ⊢
    128 pp.
The Word-Carrying Giant: The Grow''
    Creighton Lacy, $5.95 paper, 320 ⁊

BOOKLETS

The Grounds for a New Thrus
    $.75 booklet, 32 pp.
The New Macedonia: A Revolution...
    paper and address) by Ralph D. Winter, ↓
1980 and That Certain Elite by Ralph D. Winter, ᴅ ./
Penetrating the Last Frontiers by Ralph D. Winter, $1.00 ↙
The Two Structures of God's Redemptive Mission by Ralph D.
    $ .35 booklet, 16 pp.
The World Christian Movement: 1950-1975 by Ralph D. Winter,
    $ .75 booklet, 32 pp.

HOW TO ORDER

Send orders directly to William Carey Library, 1705 N. Sierra Bonita
Avenue, Pasadena, California 91104 (USA). Please allow four to six weeks
for delivery in the U.S.

William Carey Library